Aloha-
[illegible]
1990

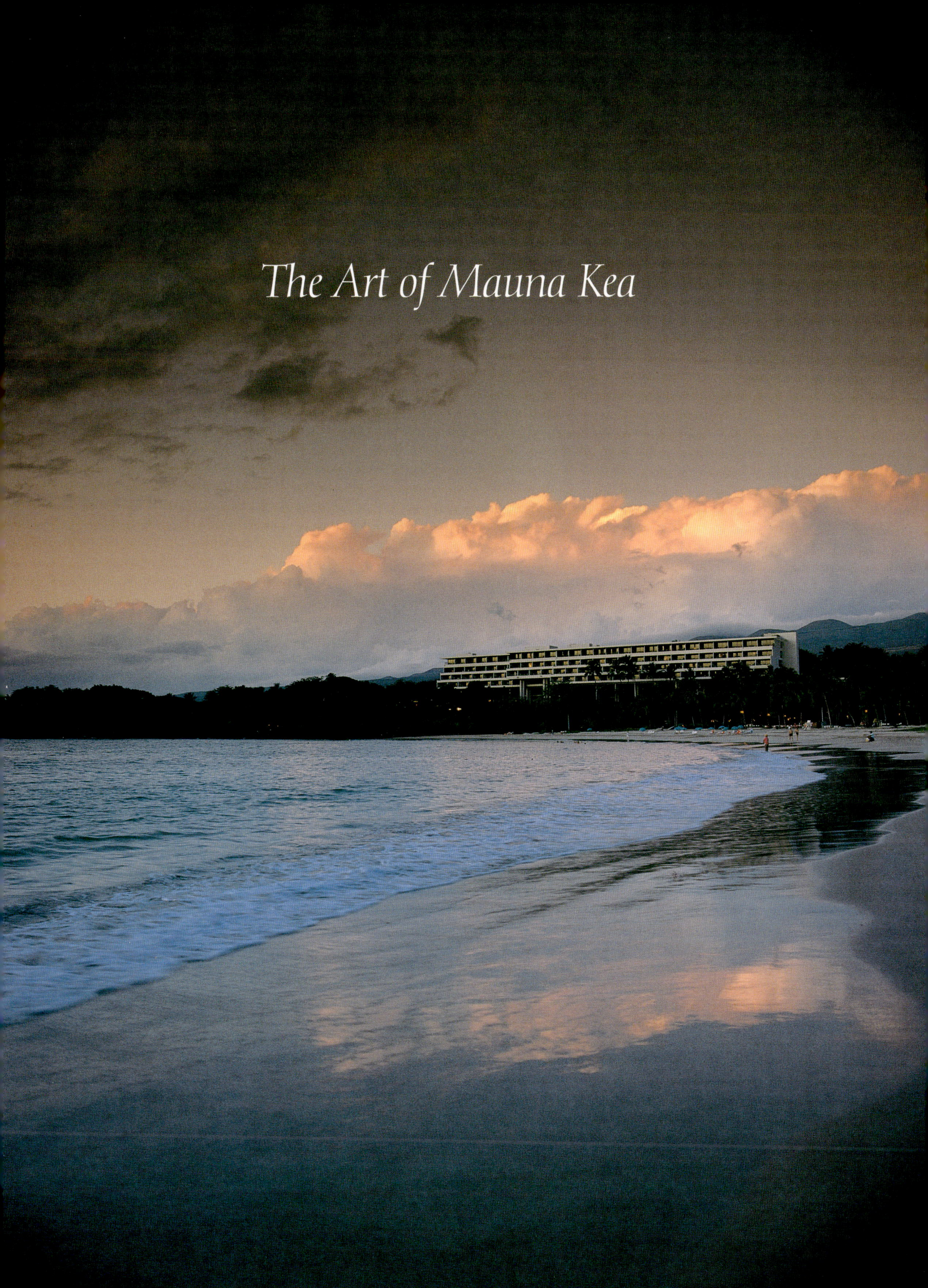

The Art of Mauna Kea

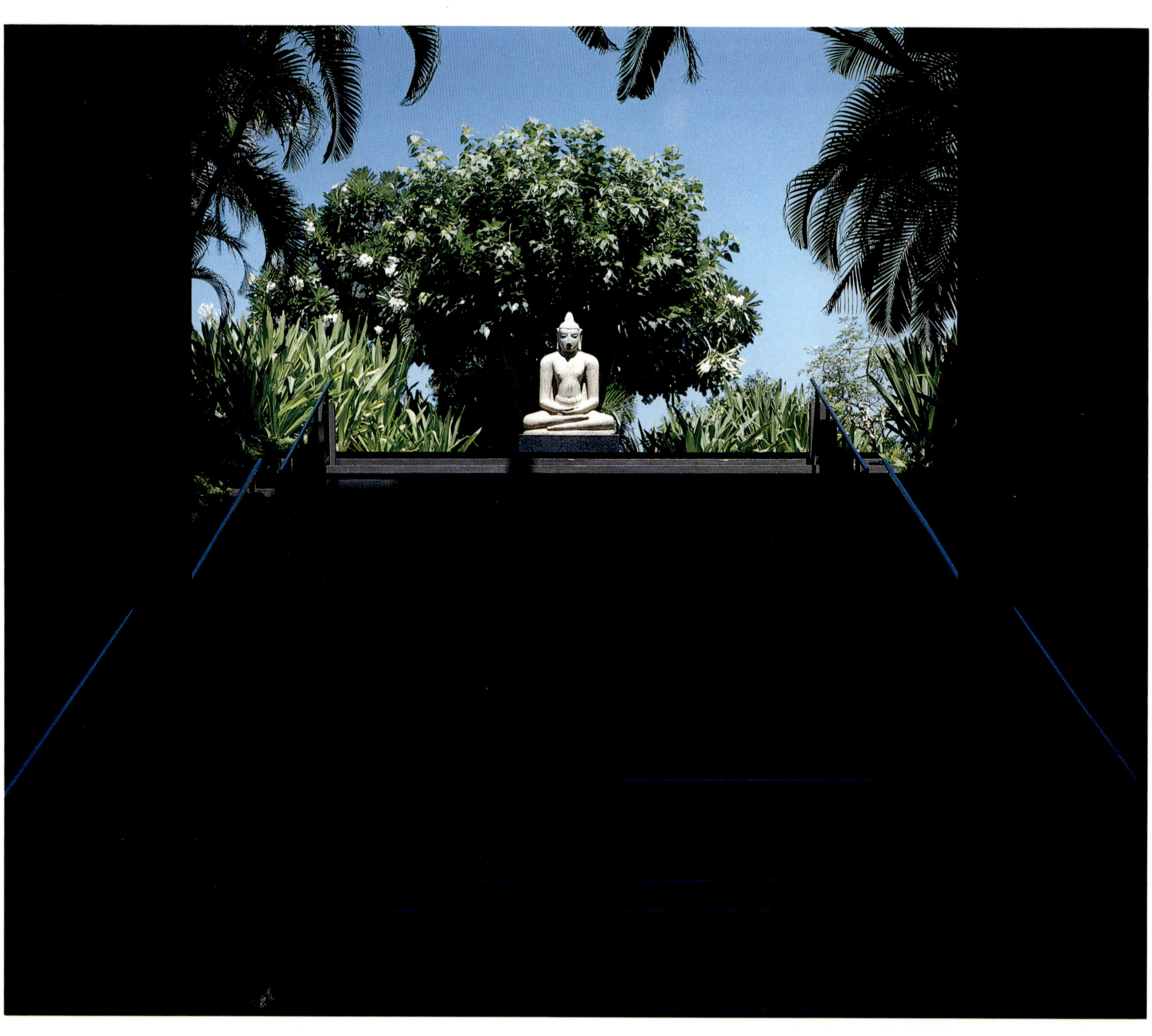

The Art of Mauna Kea

Asian and Oceanic Art at Mauna Kea Beach Hotel

DON AANAVI

East–West Center • Honolulu

FRONTISPIECE ILLUSTRATION:
Installed at the head of the staircase to the North Garden is the Mauna Kea's oldest art work, a seventh century seated Buddha sculpture from India

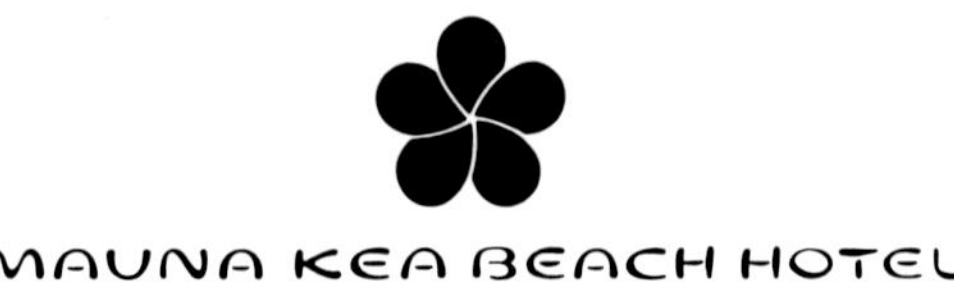

PRINTED IN JAPAN
LIBRARY OF CONGRESS CATALOG CARD NUMBER 89–046477
ISBN 0–86638–122–8

For more information on the Mauna Kea Beach Hotel's art collection, or to order additional copies of this book, write:
Mauna Kea Beach Hotel
One Mauna Kea Beach Drive
Kohala Coast, Hawai'i, 96743–9706

PUBLISHED BY:
EAST–WEST CENTER
1777 EAST–WEST ROAD
HONOLULU, HAWAI'I 96848

DESIGNED BY BARBARA POPE

*

Am I?
Am I not?
What am I?
How am I?
Whence came this existing being?
Whither is it to go?

Visuddhi-Magha, Buddhist scriptures

*

Ahuwale ka nane hūnā

The hidden answer to the riddle is seen.

ʻŌlelo Noʻeau, Hawaiian Proverbs and Poetical Sayings

*

He made from one the whole human
race to dwell on the entire surface
of the earth, and he fixed the
ordered seasons and the boundaries
of their regions, so that people
might seek God, even perhaps grope
for him and find him, though indeed
he is not far from any one of us.

ACTS 17:26–27

THE EAST-WEST CENTER *is a public, nonprofit educational institution established in Hawaii in 1960 by the United States Congress with a mandate "to promote better relations and understanding among the nations of Asia, the Pacific and the United States through cooperative study, training and research."*

Some two thousand research fellows, graduate students and professionals in business and government each year work with the Center's international staff on major Asia–Pacific issues relating to population, economic and trade policies, resources and development, the environment, culture and communication, and international relations. Since 1960, more than twenty-five thousand men and women from the region have participated in the Center's cooperative programs.

Principal funding for the Center comes from the United States Congress. Support also comes from more than twenty Asian and Pacific governments, as well as private agencies and corporations. The Center has an international board of governors.

CONTENTS

FOREWORD

Laurance S. Rockefeller 10

Victor Hao Li 11

PREFACE 12

THE MAUNA KEA COLLECTION 15

ASIAN ARTS 33

India 35

Southeast Asia 48

China and Japan 76

OCEANIC ARTS 108

Melanesia 112

Polynesia 140

LIST OF WORKS IN THE COLLECTION 166

GLOSSARY 173

SELECTED BIBLIOGRAPHY 177

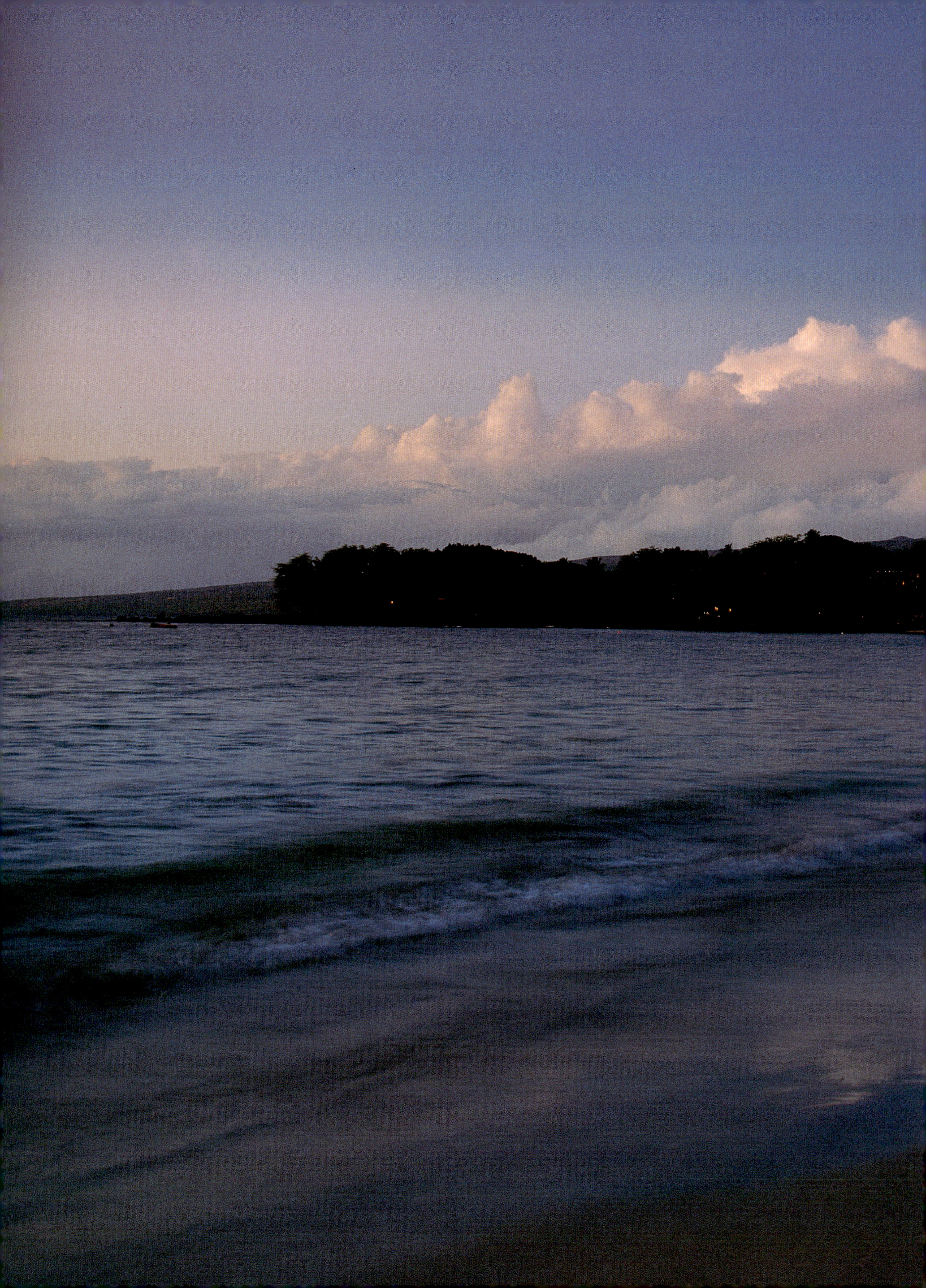

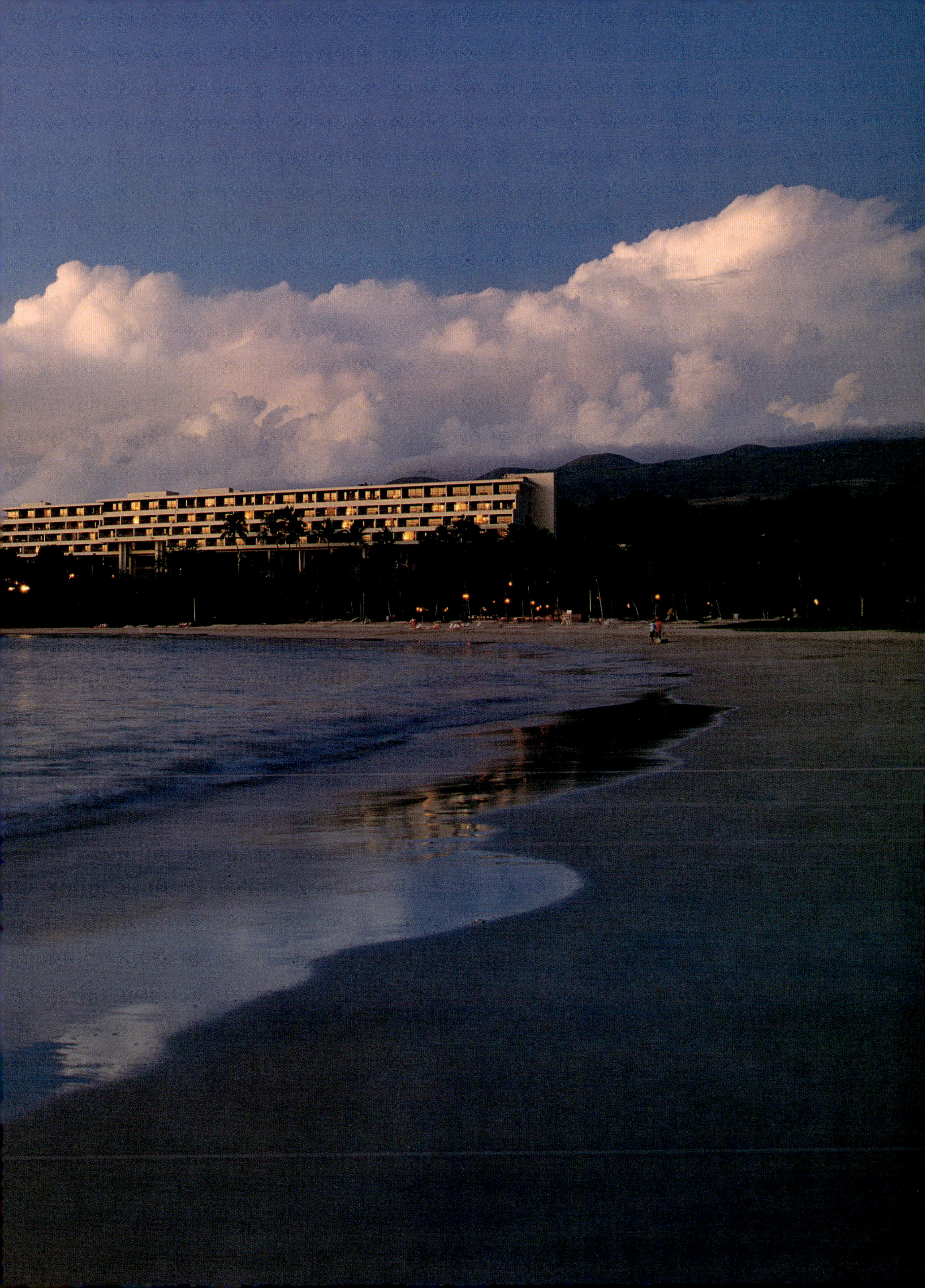

Foreword

MAUNA KEA BEACH HOTEL was the last—and in many ways the most rewarding—of our several successful nature-oriented resorts. In our quest to create the most attractive resorts with the best possible facilities and services, we always tried to place our projects where they would be surrounded by natural beauty. Nature can be the most constructive of influences, and that is why we designed each of our projects to work in harmony with the environment. In my view this is why our resorts were perceived as being unique, and why they were so remarkably well accepted.

Working closely with nature was much in my mind when planning the Mauna Kea, but because of its location in Hawai'i—between East and West—I sensed an opportunity that should be considered. I have always felt that there is much the ancient East can teach the West and saw the Mauna Kea as providing us with a unique opportunity to bring an awareness of the spirit and wisdom of the East to our resort. We decided to incorporate Asian and Pacific arts into the design of the Mauna Kea in such a way that the art could become, just as the elements of nature would become, a constant influence.

We assembled a team of knowledgeable experts to help us locate ancient and contemporary art for effective placement in the hotel and outside areas. In this way, our visitors could encounter the works often and easily, get to know and appreciate them, and even, in some cases, study them. Our hope was that these encounters would succeed in conveying to our visitors an awareness of, and an appreciation for, the traditions of the East.

All of this took place more than a quarter of a century ago. The exciting and significant Asian and Pacific arts arrived and were carefully placed in and around the resort. By any measure, they quickly became far more than decorations; they are an enduring source of inspiration.

We are fortunate that Professor Aanavi, in his studies and teaching, chose to focus on the arts of the Mauna Kea. His work has led to the book that you now have, and a beautiful and brilliant one it is. I am particularly attracted to his observation on page 34: *Most of the arts in this collection communicate ideas intuitively; visual arts are able to communicate significant expression without words.*

This would appear to be evidence that our attempts to foster an awareness of the East through its arts have been successful. The arts of Mauna Kea have become the active influence we sought to establish.

LAURANCE S. ROCKEFELLER

A PHYSICAL as well as cultural distance separates the United States and the Asia-Pacific region. The physical separation is rapidly shrinking because of technological advances in telecommunications and travel, and because geopolitical and socioeconomic changes of the last decade or more have made the various regions of the world highly interdependent. But striking differences in beliefs, values, and traditions remain. One of the major tasks facing the Asia-Pacific region today is to increase global understanding of the region's diverse cultures and people so that the physical and cultural distances do not divide societies and individuals, but rather enrich the human condition.

Hawai'i plays a unique role as a meeting place between East and West. Its multiethnic population and Pacific location make it a natural bridge over the cultural barriers of the region. Laurance S. Rockefeller recognized this and his creative vision for Mauna Kea Beach Hotel in 1965 encompassed a collection of art that would celebrate and reveal the cultures of Asia and the Pacific. Religious, secular, ancient, and modern traditions are represented in the Mauna Kea's collection of more than one thousand pieces from the cultures of India, Southeast Asia, China, Japan, Melanesia, and Polynesia.

As an institution dedicated to promoting cooperation and mutual understanding between East and West, the East-West Center has long emphasized culture and communications. Since its establishment by the U.S. Congress in 1960, the Center has included among its programs the study of culture through the arts. Publication of this book significantly furthers our educational objectives for intercultural understanding. We appreciate the assistance of Yoshiaki Tsutsumi, owner of Seibu Railway Group and Mauna Kea Beach Hotel, and Laurance S. Rockefeller in making this project possible.

The Mauna Kea Beach Hotel art collection gives us an opportunity to glimpse the richness and diversity of the artistic traditions of Asia and Oceania. The pieces in the collection evoke a direct response and appreciation for cultural values, beauty, and artistic ideals. It is the East-West Center's hope that this compilation of the history and significance of the collection will afford readers an unusual opportunity to experience the voices of many cultures through art and to come away with a heightened appreciation and understanding of Asia and the Pacific.

VICTOR HAO LI
President
East-West Center

Preface

WHEN I ARRIVED on the island of Hawai'i in 1974 to teach at the University of Hawaii at Hilo, I had many enthusiastic students, but the island lacked a museum broad enough in scope to provide examples of the arts I discussed in courses in art history, religious studies, and Japanese studies. Mauna Kea Beach Hotel held such a collection, I discovered, and through General Manager Adi Kohler, arrangements were made so that my students and I could study the works of art in the splendid environment of the resort. Eventually, many hotel guests joined us on these excursions, and I was asked to give regular weekly tours exclusively for visitors to the resort. This book is the outcome of lectures on the collection presented to students, colleagues, and guests at the hotel.

I am thankful to Mr. Kohler for his initial hospitality and for ensuring continuation of this arrangement with the University during the Mauna Kea's recent transition to ownership by Seibu Railway Group. I am also grateful to the Honorable George R. Ariyoshi, former governor of Hawai'i and president of Mauna Kea Beach Hotel, and to William F. Mielcke, vice-president of Mauna Kea Beach Hotel, for their support of educational opportunities for my students, as well as for their commitment to this publication.

This book is designed to offer a context for viewing the collection. As author, I accept responsibility for its contents. In keeping with the lecture format, it contains no footnotes, and the bibliography lists only those works on which I have most depended. I am grateful to the University of Hawaii at Hilo for granting me a sabbatical in 1987 during which I completed my research on the collection. I also wish to thank Irene Uyeda Matsuura of the University's Humanities Division for her continuing practical assistance and encouragement in preparing the text.

This book is also an expression of collegiality and friendship that reaches back a quarter of a century: in 1964, the East-West Center gave me a fellowship to begin graduate studies in Asian and Pacific arts and culture. I am honored that the Center should now be my publisher, and I greatly appreciate its confidence. I give special thanks to my friend Mary L. Ho, vice-president of the East-West Center Foundation, for her support of this publication. Jacqueline A. D'Orazio offered expert assistance and guidance in production as the Center's publications and graphics manager.

There are many people without whose participation I cannot imagine having written this book. Davis Allen and Phyllis Brownlee provided invaluable information about the acquisition of the works of art. Charles Bassett and Marc Goldstein of Skidmore, Owings and Merrill were generous in sharing insights into the architectural concepts used in planning the resort. Photographer David Franzen brought extraordinary talent and creativity to the task of capturing and interpreting the beauty and meaning of these works of art. I deeply appreciate the editorial assistance of Dorothy M. Foster. I thank Barbara Pope for her visual sensibility in producing a handsome book design. Patti Cook has contributed in innumerable ways. Solveig K. Nordwall of Kobe, Japan, kindly assisted in Japanese translations. My most personal thanks are to my son, Michael Aanavi, who has been as much a counselor to me as I have tried to be to him.

I have saved the most important individuals for last. Yoshiaki Tsutsumi, the owner of Seibu Railway Group, has provided tangible support for what otherwise might have remained an academic dream. Through Mr. Tsutsumi's commitment and appreciation of fine art, Seibu will continue to maintain the integrity of the Mauna Kea and, especially, its art collection.

Finally, I would like to express my deepest gratitude to Laurance S. Rockefeller, whose insights into the collection have helped me enormously in articulating its diversities. From the beginning he was enthusiastic about having students and resort guests learn from these predominantly devotional works of art. It is he who most inspired me with his strong spiritual beliefs and conviction that the interactions between East and West can enhance our human community.

I dedicate this book to all visionaries who reject nothing that is true in others and who grasp our common destiny.

DON AANAVI
Nīnole, Hawai'i

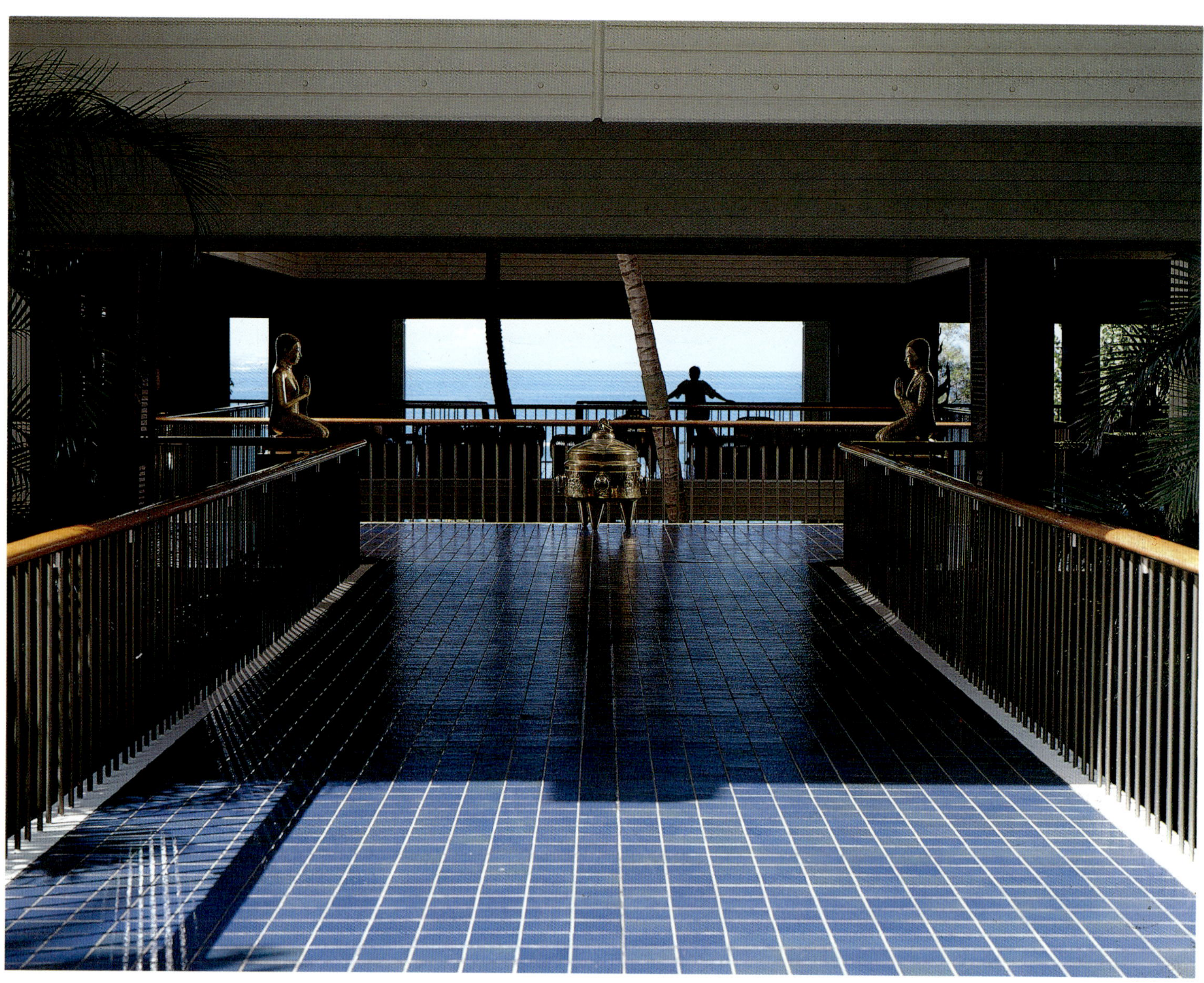

The Mauna Kea's entryway reflects the resort's overall aesthetic. The hotel's original architectural firm, Skidmore, Owings and Merrill, helped pioneer the Modernist approach to form and has created some of the most innovative structures in America; Charles Bassett led the design team.

The Mauna Kea Collection

THIS BOOK describes a splendid collection of art in an unusually beautiful setting. Rarely does one find such a large collection of significant art works in a resort hotel. The history of how this unique collection came into being is revealed in the history of the hotel itself, as the two were conceived together.

Mauna Kea Beach Hotel, in its elegance and design, bears the imprint of Laurance S. Rockefeller, its original developer and owner. The building of the Mauna Kea on ancient lava flows in a dry wilderness on the island of Hawai'i was an awesome undertaking. The hotel, which was the first tourism development on the Big Island's Kohala Coast, grew out of the state's efforts to expand the visitor industry beyond O'ahu to the "neighbor islands" of Kaua'i, Maui, and Hawai'i.

Soon after Hawai'i became the country's fiftieth state in 1959, Governor William Quinn, along with George Mason, head of the state's Office of Economic Development, invited Laurance Rockefeller to visit Hawai'i and tour the neighbor islands, hoping that he would consider creating a resort that would attract visitors to sites beyond already well-known Waikīkī Beach on the island of O'ahu.

The spectacular natural beauty of the Big Island's Kohala Coast appealed to Rockefeller's aesthetic sense. In particular, he was taken with a remote and perfectly formed white-sand beach at Kauna'oa Bay surrounded by barren lava flows. Building at this site in the Kawaihae region offered both Rockefeller and the state a creative challenge, as there were no highways, jet airports, or sources of fresh water nearby.

Mounting economic distress in the area provided a special incentive. The decline of sugar plantations on the island already had left many unemployed, and the Kohala sugar mill—the major local employer—had recently announced it would soon shut down, exacerbating the area's economic and social woes. In 1962, newly elected Governor John Burns committed state support for development of the Kohala Coast by funding construction of the necessary massive infrastructure. In 1965, Mauna Kea Beach Hotel was completed. Today, tourism thrives on the neighbor islands and the Mauna Kea remains one of the largest private employers on the island of Hawai'i.

Committed to responsible and responsive land development, Rockefeller designed the Mauna Kea to preserve the beauty of the land and to ensure its usefulness for years to come. Long recognized as a primary conservationist, he was appointed chairman of the first White House Conference on Natural Beauty in May 1965, a few months before the resort opened to the public. For Rockefeller, such activities continued the family commitment to the national park system and conservation, and the family concept of philan-

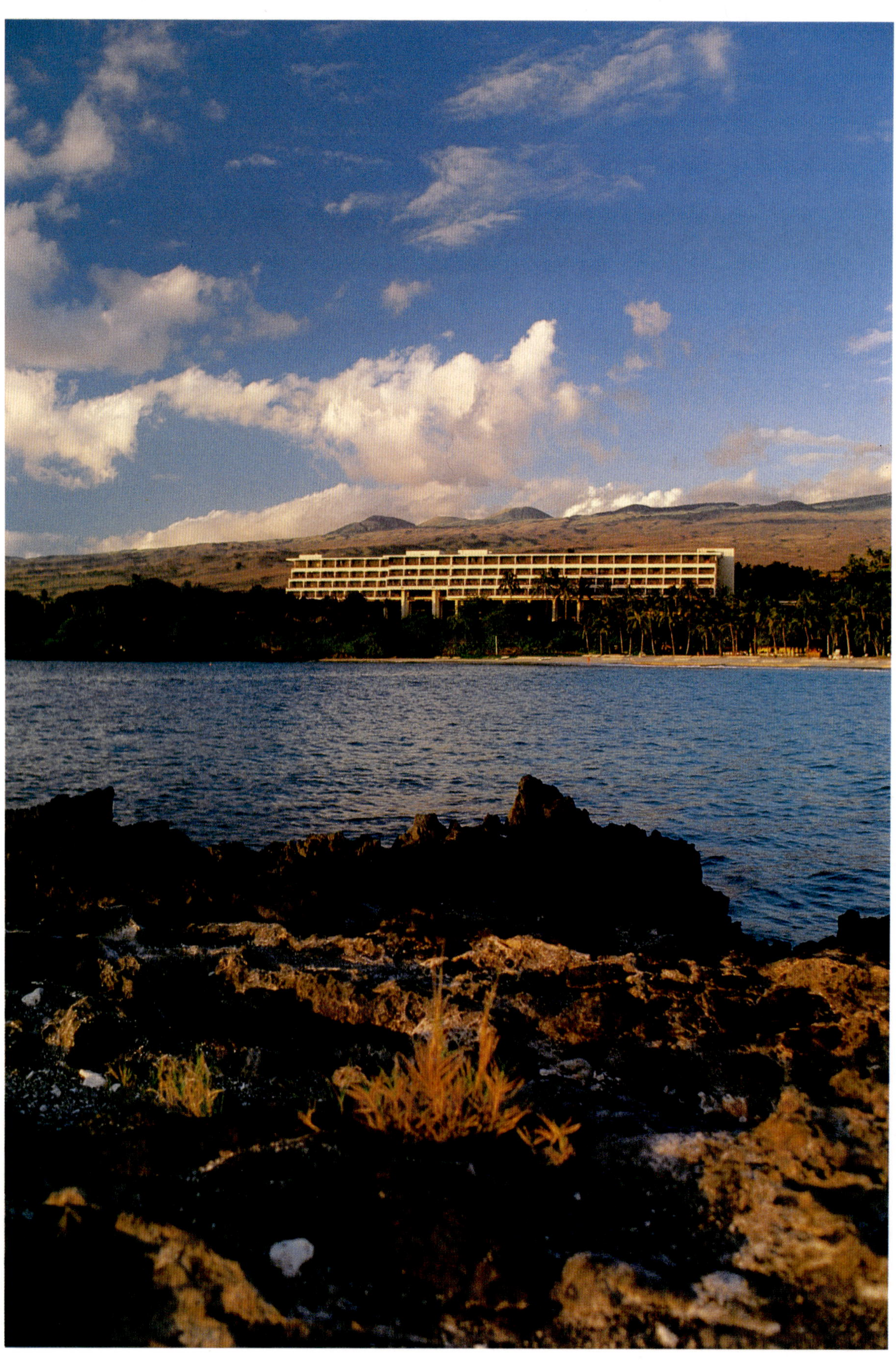

thropic responsibility: to function as caretaker rather than possessor, whether of landholdings or collections of art, and to share those resources with the public.

Just as the Mauna Kea affirms Rockefeller's views on the use of natural resources, it also exemplifies his belief that the best way to understand the goals and ideals of a culture is through its arts. Rockefeller defined the character of the resort by incorporating into both its public and private spaces a selection of art works from many Asian and Oceanic cultures. He hoped the collection would promote cultural understanding among the peoples of the West, Asia, and Oceania. The collection contains works from India, Southeast Asia, China, Japan, Melanesia, and Polynesia, mirroring the mingling of Asian and Pacific peoples and traditions that makes Hawai'i so unique.

The Mauna Kea's holdings constitute one of the most extensive collections of Asian and Oceanic arts assembled by one individual since mid-century. Acquired for the most part in their countries of origin, the pieces were selected to inspire, intrigue, and inform the novice as well as the connoisseur. In form and function they range from religious to secular, metropolitan to provincial, primitive to urbane. Many of the works demonstrate historic interactions between civilizations of Asia and the Pacific Basin.

The collection also reveals Rockefeller's appreciation for the spirituality evident in all cultures. Many of the items he acquired for the hotel are explicitly religious. They represent, through the talents of inspired artists in each culture, the universal human longing that unites all people.

Rockefeller planned and developed the art collection as an integral feature of the resort environment, intentionally selecting some works for outdoor display, choosing others for exhibition in particular lounges, corridors, or more intimate alcoves and niches. All the works were gathered, and their installation needs defined, during the evolutionary process of the hotel's design and construction.

The hotel's innovative architectural scheme was produced by Skidmore, Owings and Merrill, a national architectural firm recognized for creating some of the most impressive American structures in this century; Charles Bassett was in charge of design. Rockefeller selected Skidmore, Owings and Merrill for the excellence of their designers' talents and their proven ability to demonstrate concern for the environment in their creations. Their late-Modernist design for the Lever House, for example, on a prime urban site in New York in the early 1950s, was a landmark in American corporate architecture and highly influential in its subordination of potential real estate profits to beauty and open space. Similarly, Rockefeller sought and obtained a design for the Mauna Kea consistent with his sense of public responsibility for protecting the environment of Kauna'oa Bay.

Bassett's design fused the many anticipated functions of the Mauna Kea with the resort's diverse scenery, producing a structure that interacts with and complements the environment. The plan emphasizes a free flow of interior spaces into outdoor areas, and juxtaposes wild and formal gardens. While certain aspects of the Mauna Kea's form and

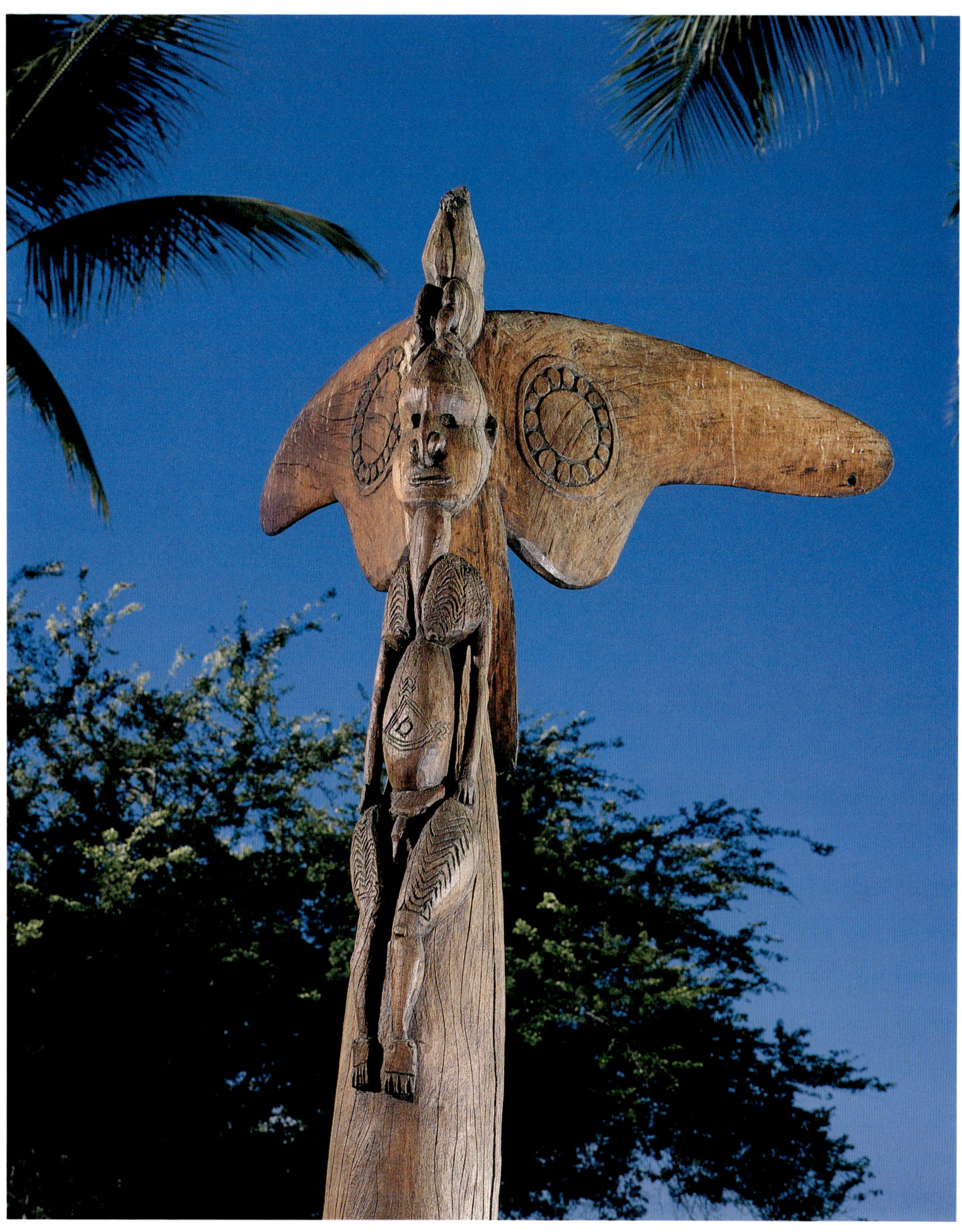

This New Guinea figural sculpture (originally a ritual-house roof finial) combines a bird form, a protective image, with an ancestral figure to create a symbol of clan prestige and aggressive prowess.

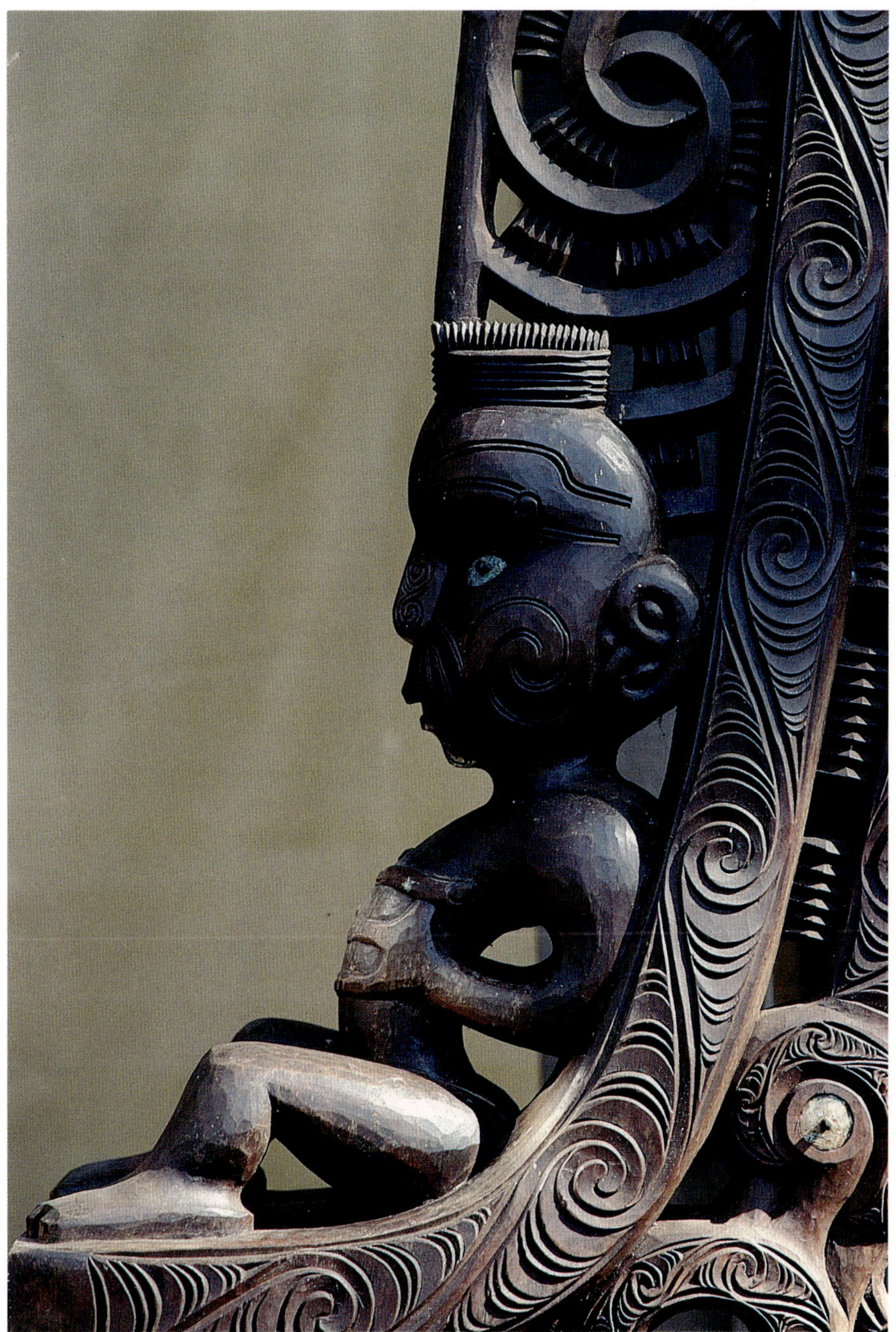

Seated at the base of this elaborately decorated Maori canoe stern is a traditional protective figure whose carved face shows customary tattoo patterns. The inlay of iridescent shell is a common feature of Maori maritime arts.

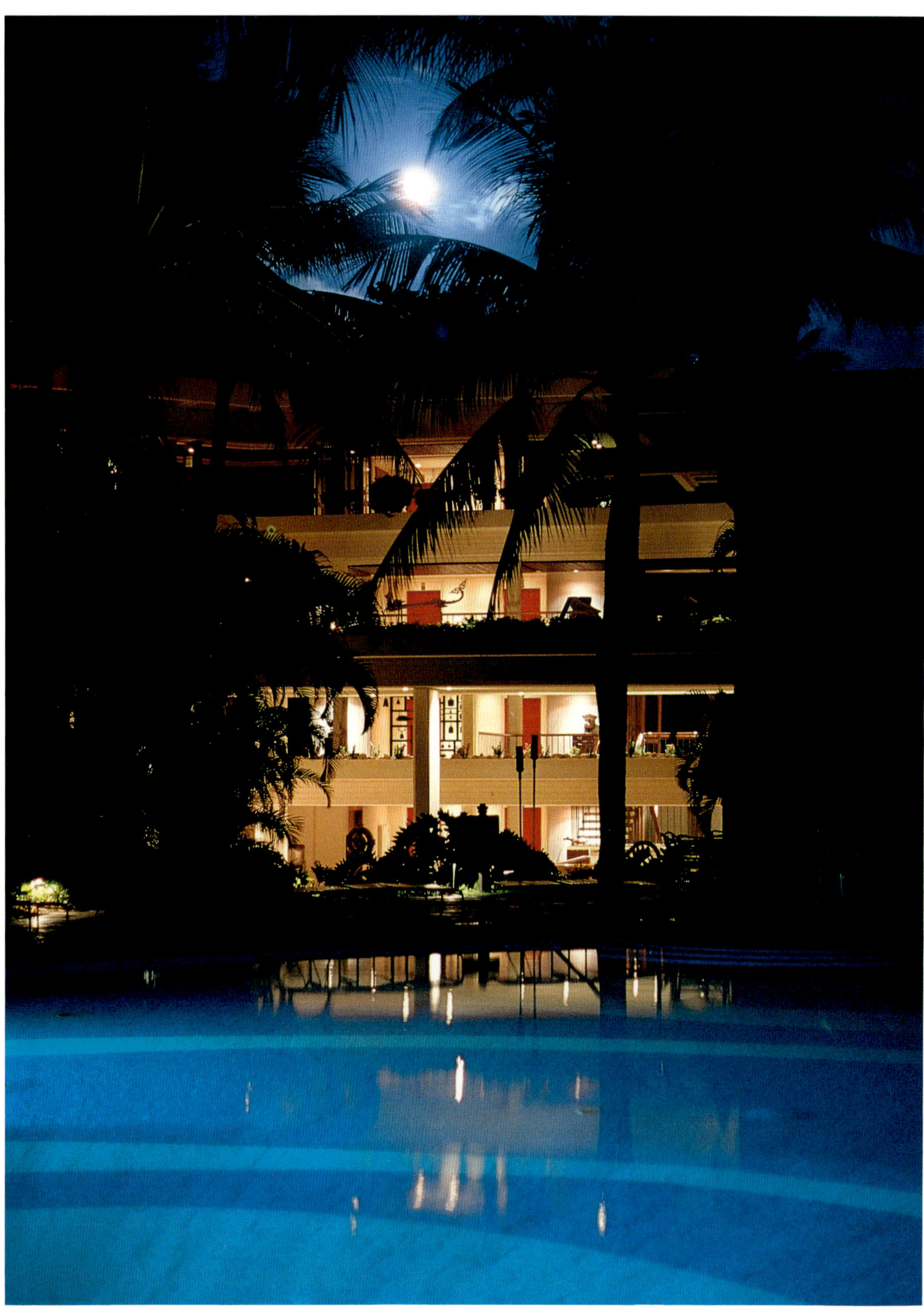

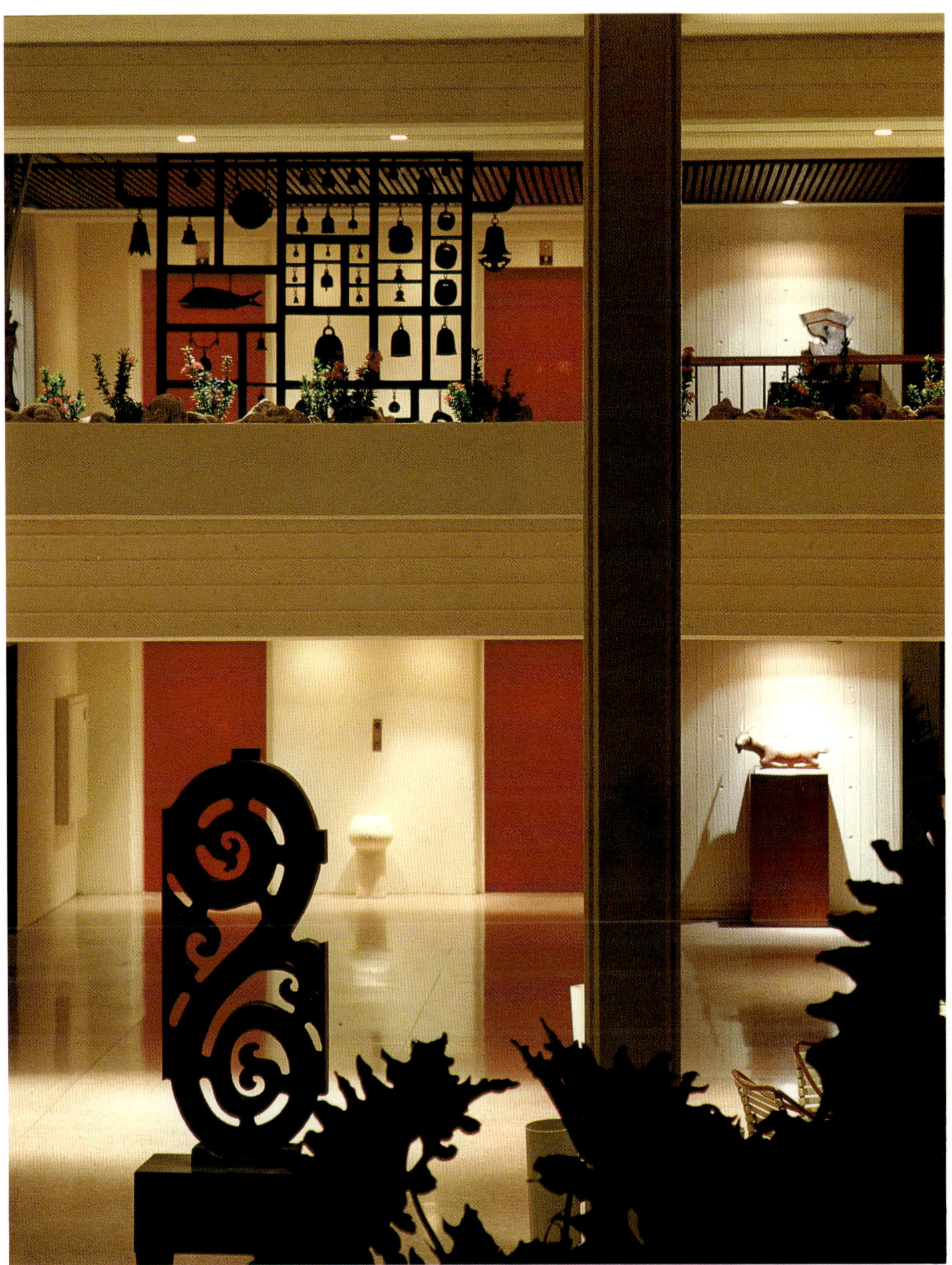

Breezeways throughout the Mauna Kea's main building and Beachfront Wing exhibit a variety of art works. In this view, an abstract, curvilinear sculpture by contemporary Hawaiian artist Sam Ka'ai is seen on the lower level and a display of Asian musical sculptures, the Pacifica Collection, is silhouetted above.

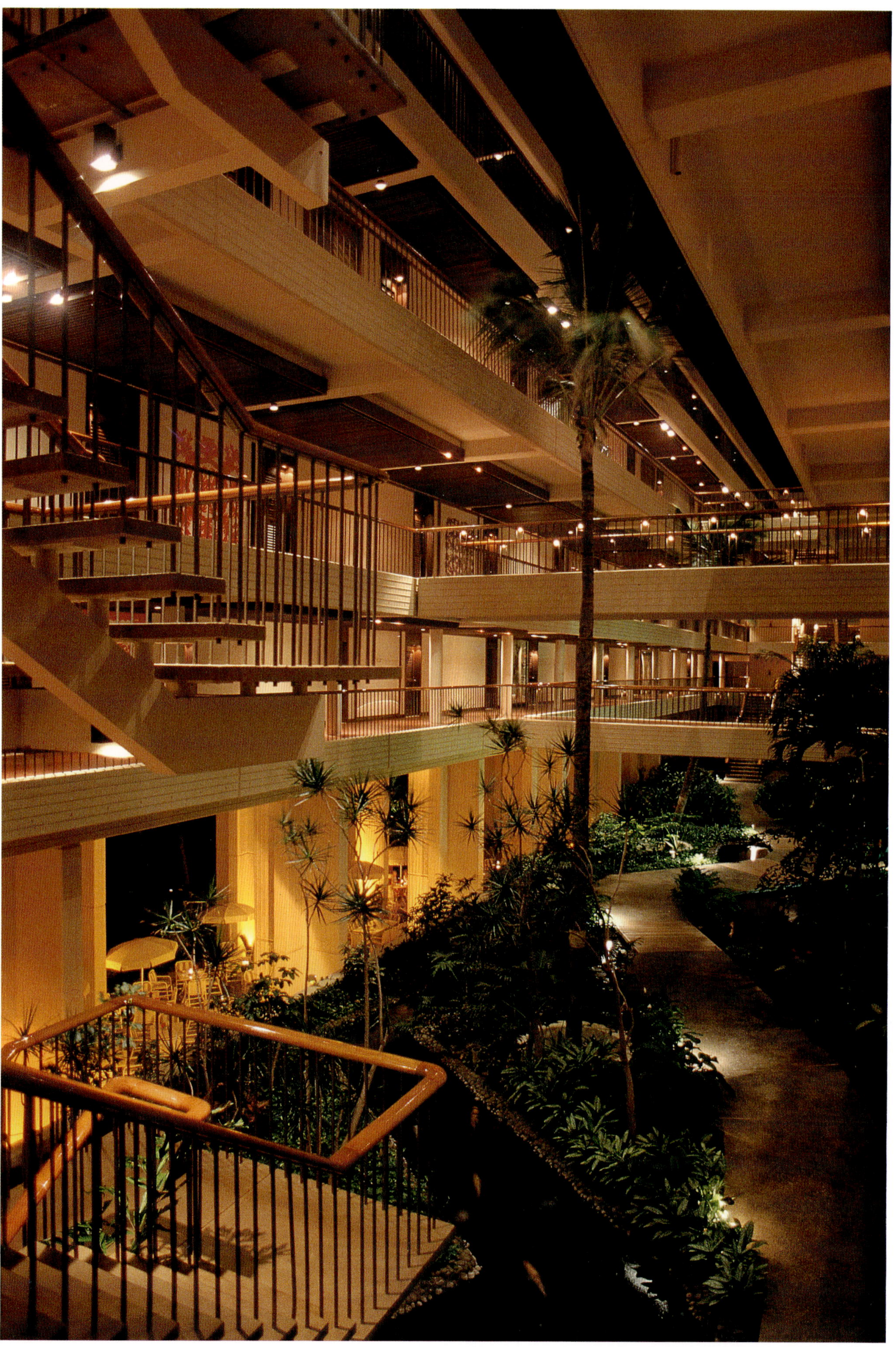

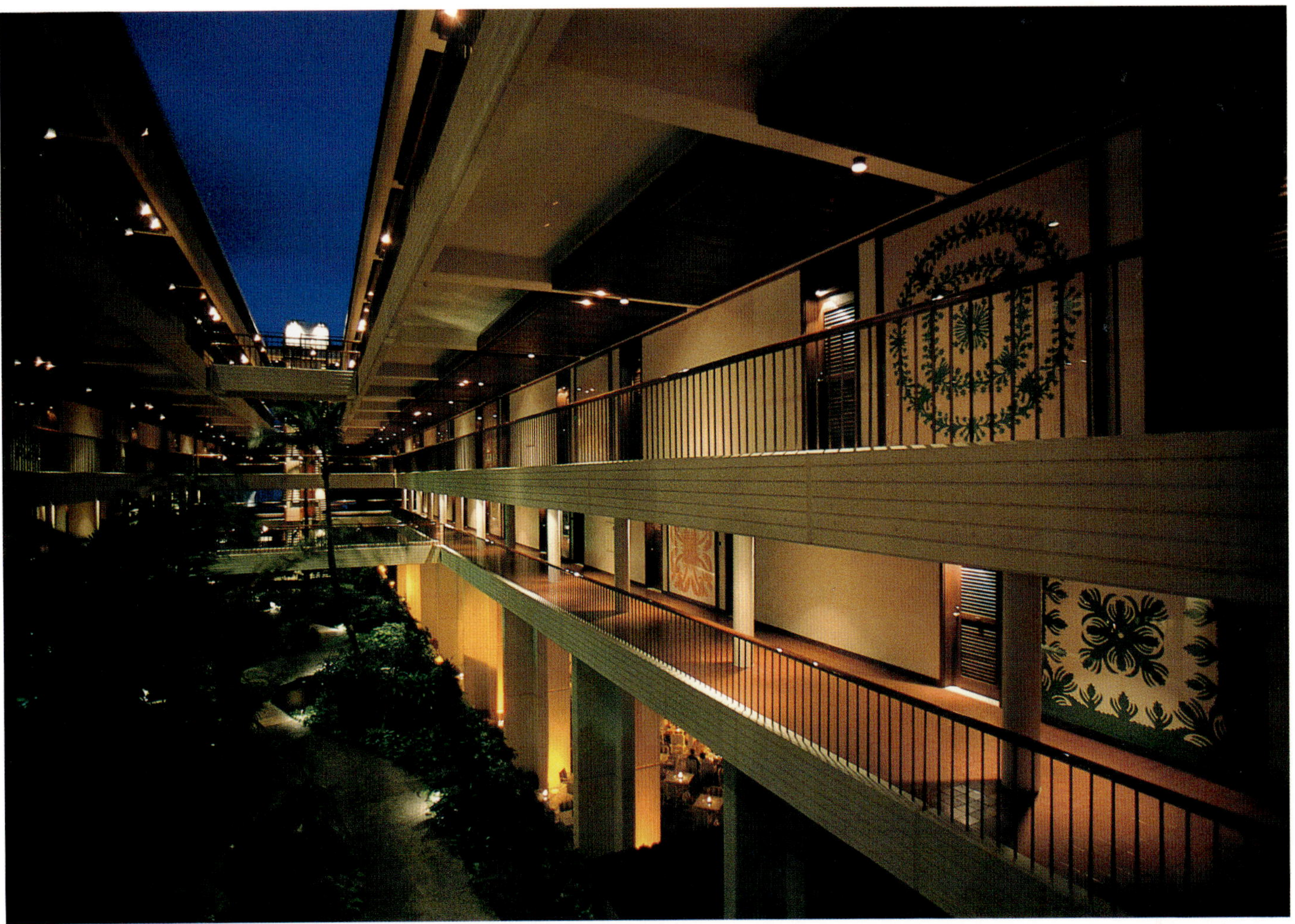

Laurance Rockefeller drew upon the talents of architects, interior designers, landscapers, archaeologists, historians, painters, sculptors, tapa makers, and quilt makers in achieving his goal to define the character of the hotel through the arts. Thirty Hawaiian quilts, the largest standing display of this medium in Hawai'i, are installed on the fifth and sixth floors of the main building, as shown here.

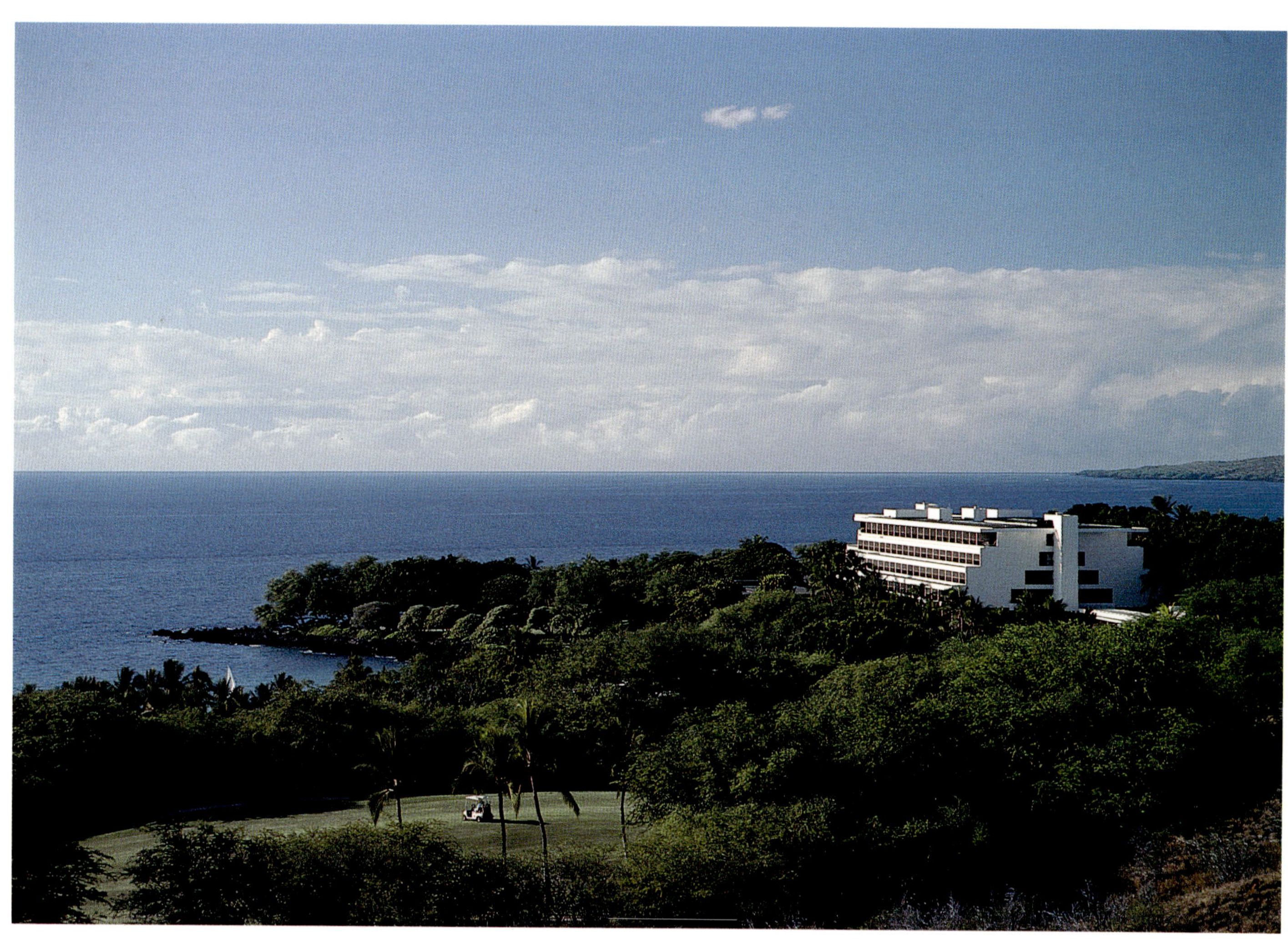

On leaving Māmalahoa Highway and passing an unimposing gatehouse, visitors to the Mauna Kea travel a landscaped drive that affords glimpses of the resort's golf course and the ocean beyond.

structure, such as the temple style of the dining pavilions, spring from Japanese architectural inspiration, its monumental lava-rock walls and other shapes are derived from indigenous Hawaiian traditions. The two mingle in a successful synthesis with many Modernist architectural elements. For all this variety, a sense of traditional and classic balance pervades, achieved through an equilibrium of the functional and the purely aesthetic.

The resort is built in a series of stepped levels that extend toward mountains and ocean. This scheme is not immediately obvious because the interplay of light and shadow on exterior surfaces and lush vegetation mitigate any suggestion of imposing form. Inside, the lobby's sea-blue tile floor harmonizes with the glint of ocean immediately in view. The basic structural elements, sand-colored concrete pillars and walls, are configured in an open network that reveals many vistas. The main building's architectural focal point is a six-story atrium that also links indoor and outdoor spaces, so that even in the center of the building, gardens and sky are both within view. Cantilevered lounges gather around the atrium in a free-flowing architectural style perhaps attributable to Japanese sources. These lounges flow into corridors that join mountain-view and ocean-view wings, where sweeping views of either mountains or ocean maintain the constancy of relationship with the outdoors. Inside, simple textures, natural colors, and teak ceiling panels reinforce the impression created by the structure, tying together all the parts of the hotel.

The most unifying feature of the atmosphere, however, is the art collection. This book describes only a relatively small number of the hotel's more than one thousand art objects, focusing on works displayed in public areas. Just as Rockefeller intended to offer stimulating examples of regional arts rather than an exhaustive survey, the following pages will introduce a selection of the hotel's most noteworthy artistic treasures—an invitation to appreciate more thoroughly the creative works and the diversity of the peoples of Asia and Oceania.

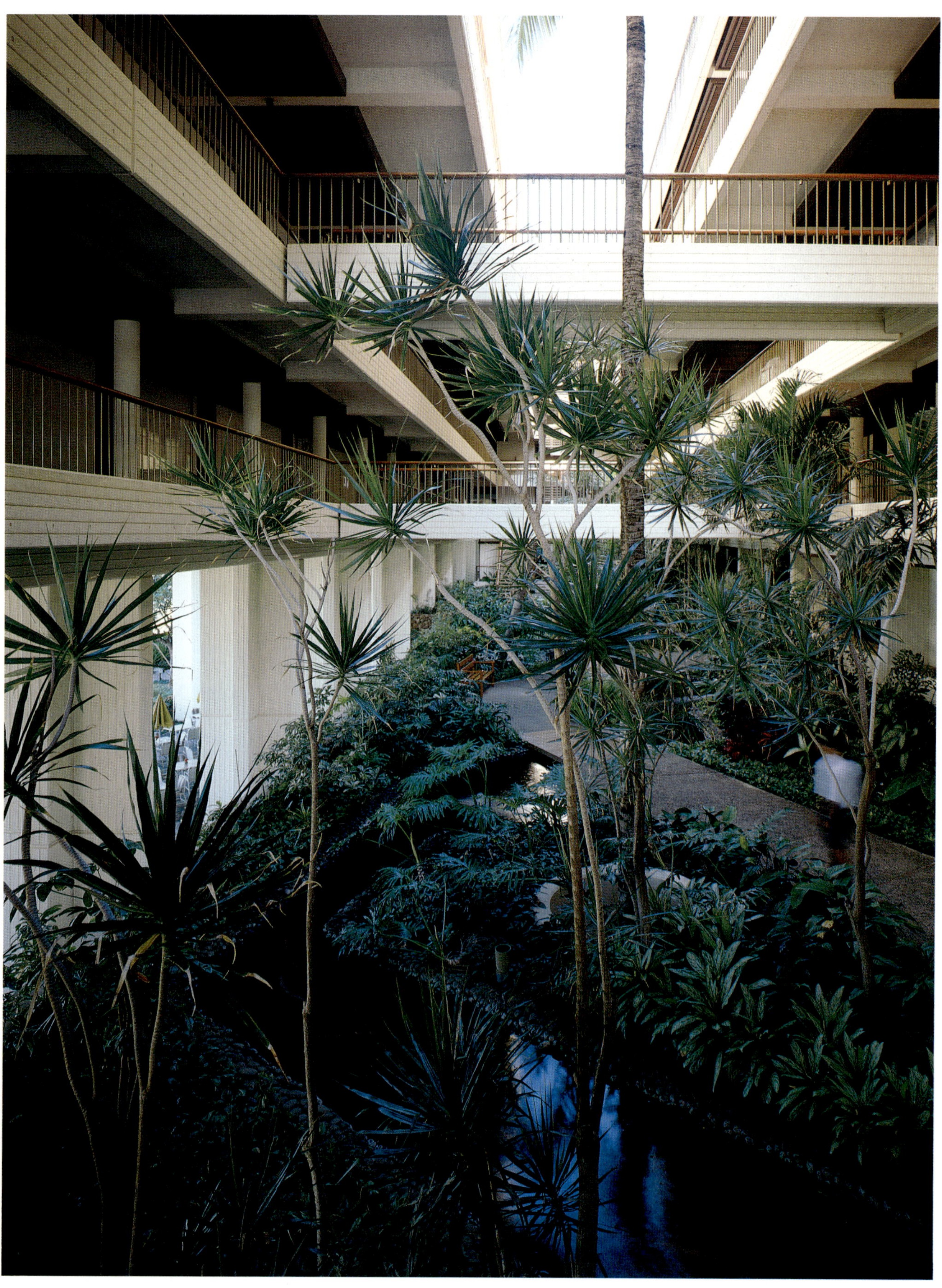

The mountain-view and ocean-view wings of the resort's main building are linked by dramatically cantilevered walkways and bridges. Gardens and *koi*-filled ponds are asymmetrically arranged in a Japanese manner around the walkway below, one of the most frequently traveled paths in the resort.

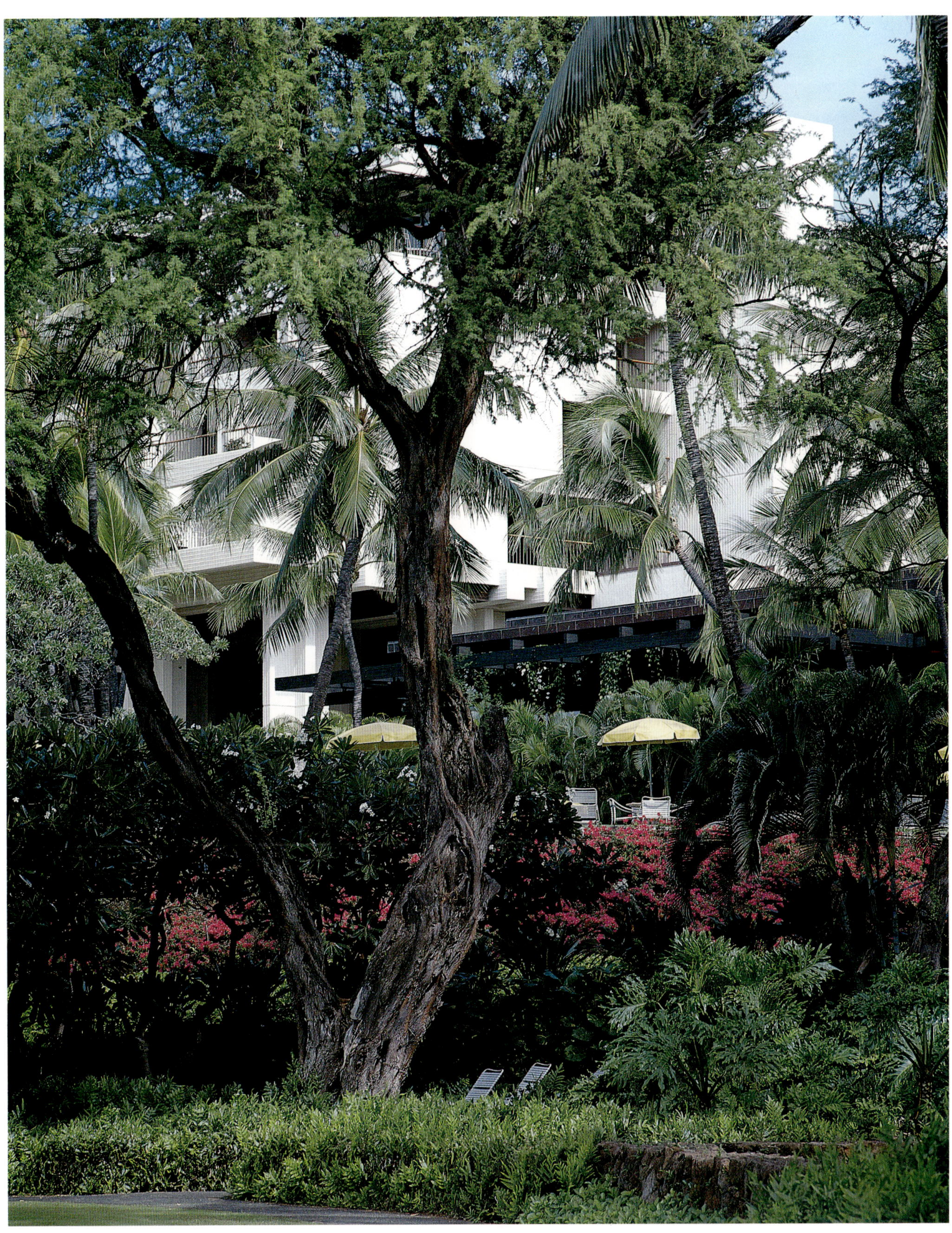

The lush surroundings of the Mauna Kea belie the initial difficulties of creating a modern resort in the lava-bound Kawaihae region of the island of Hawai'i. Today, twenty-four groundskeepers maintain the flowering plants and trees and two nurseries. Because rainfall typically amounts to less than ten inches per year, the gardens are nourished by five million gallons of water per month.

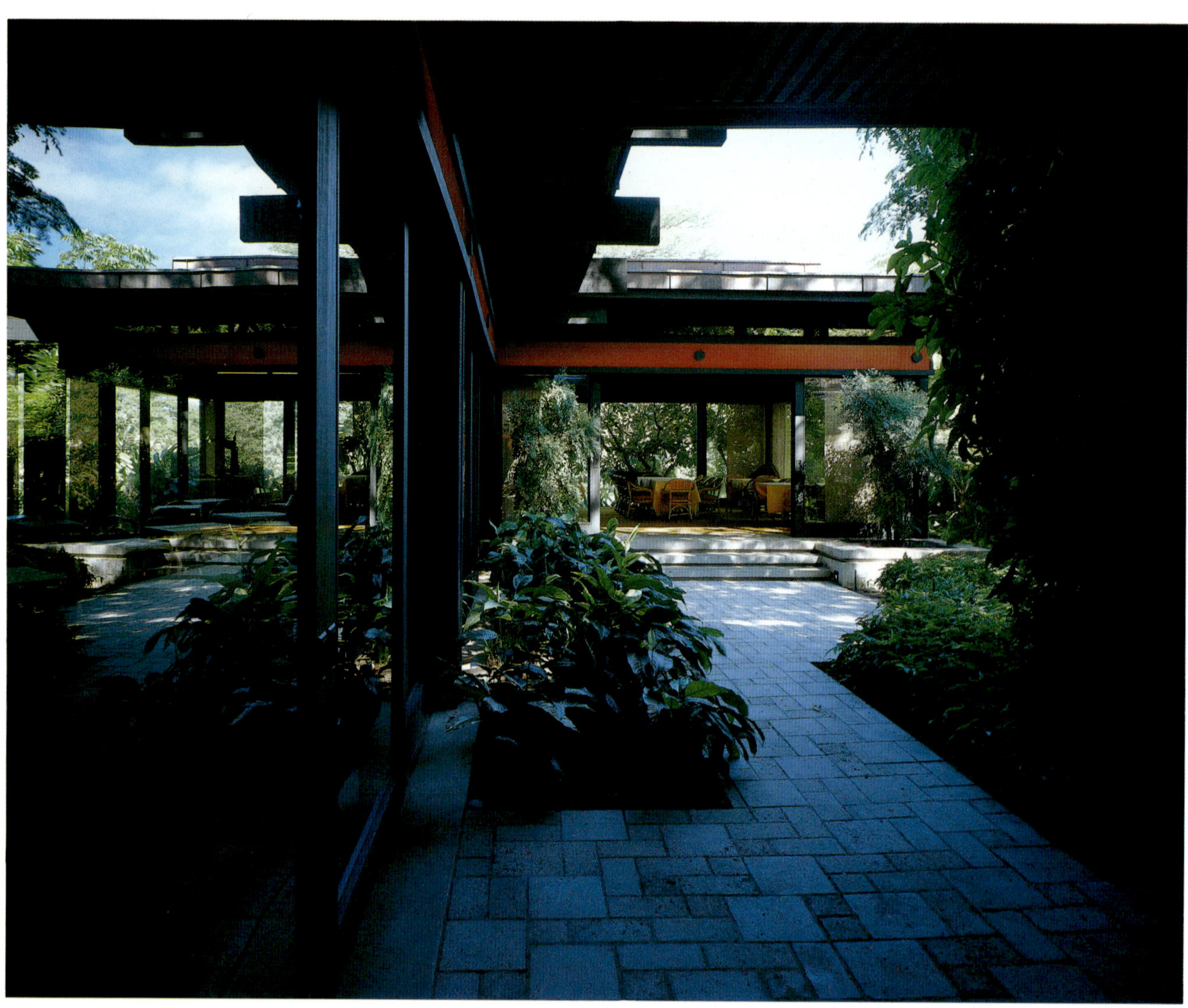

East Asian Buddhist temple architecture inspired the form of the Pavilion restaurant, an association emphasized by the structure's vermillion cornice, seen here across the terraced entry. The Mauna Kea's dining facilities offer a variety of cuisines and formal and informal modes of repast.

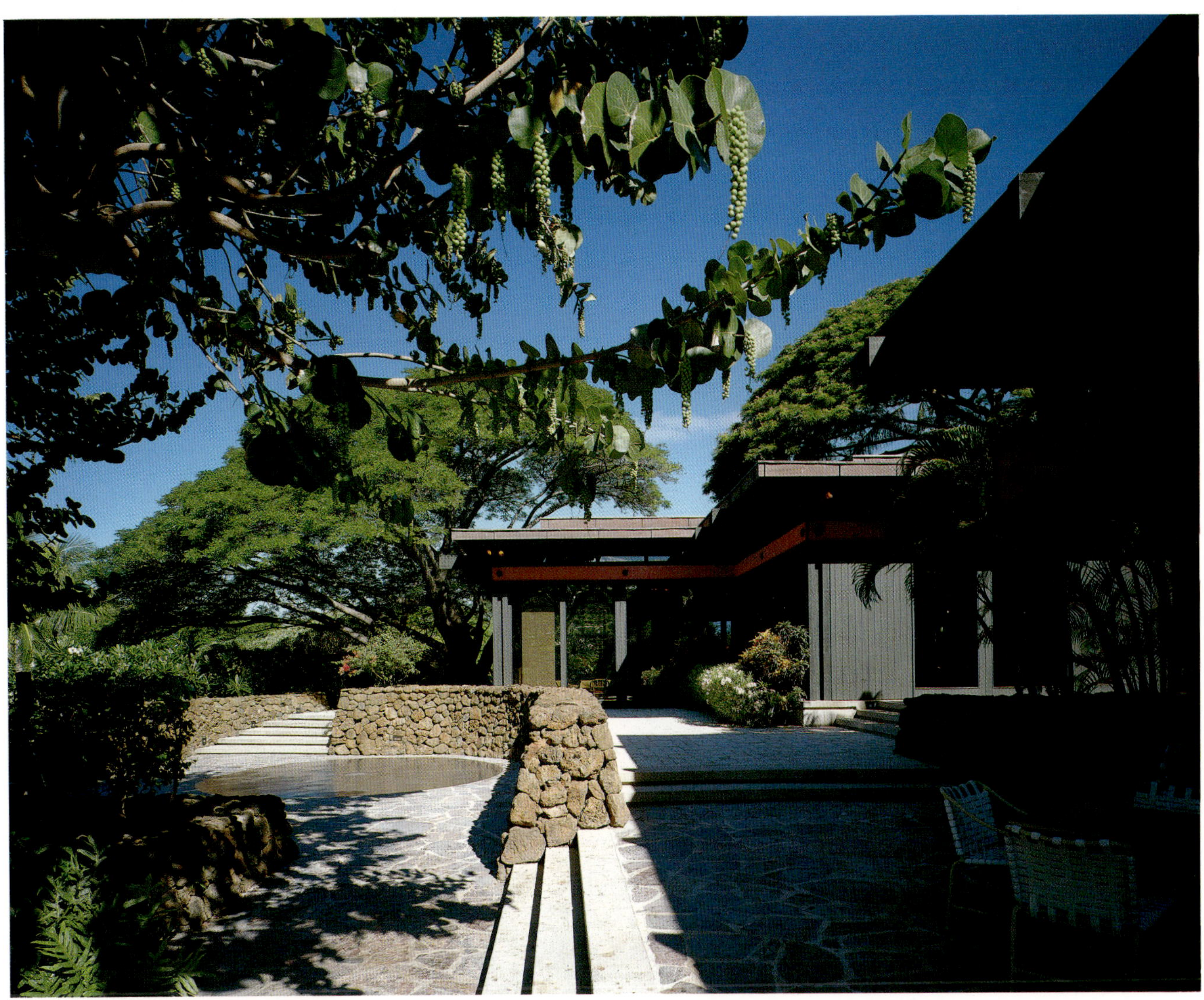

The multiple, gently stepped levels of the resort are obvious in this view of the beach-side approach to the Garden restaurant. Walls of lava rock, such as the low one seen here, define and accentuate paths and stairways throughout the grounds.

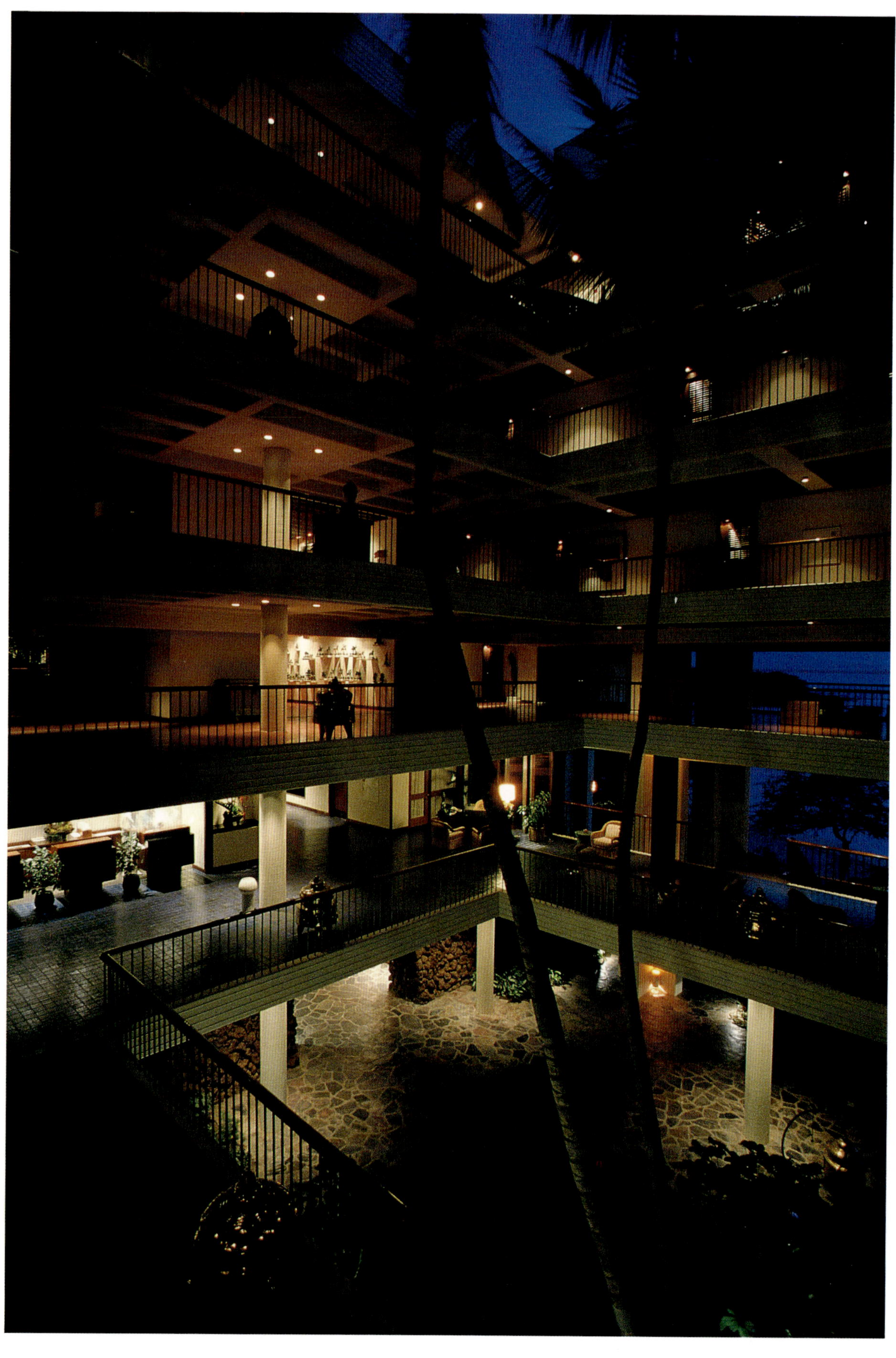

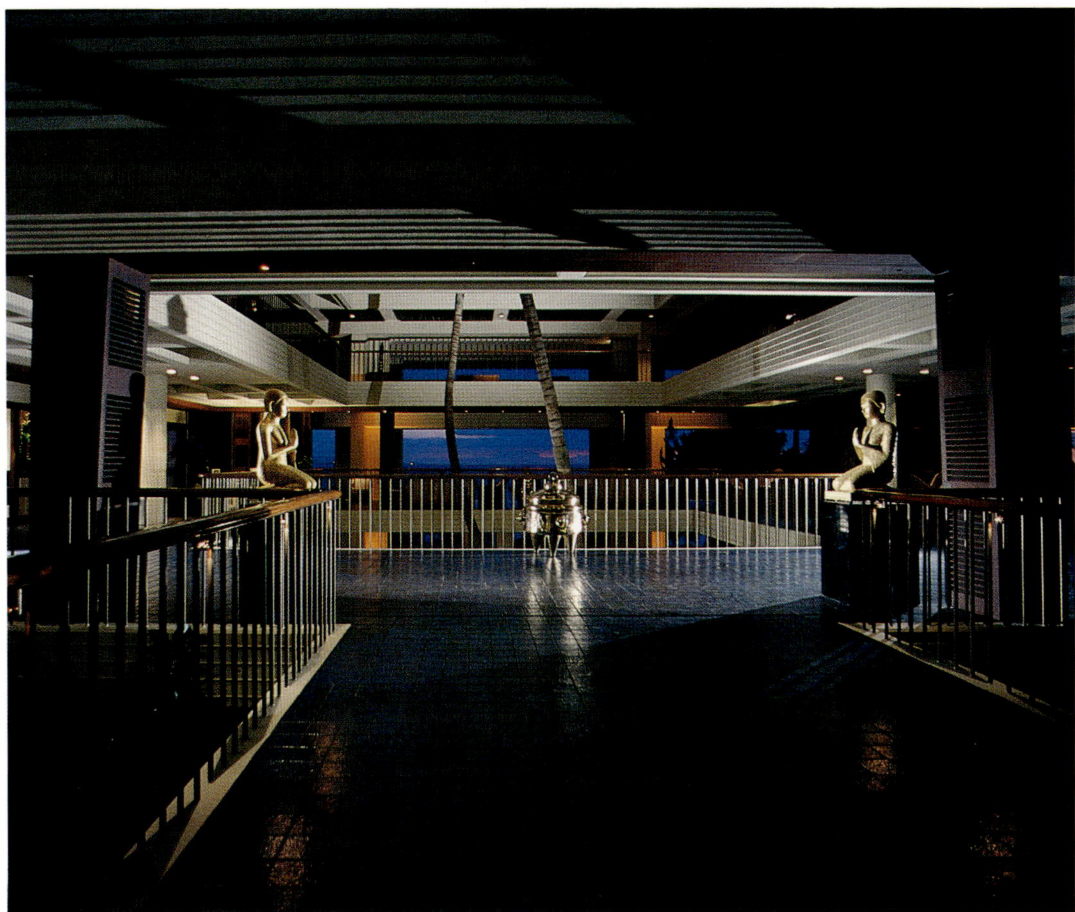

Skidmore, Owings and Merrill conceived Mauna Kea Beach Hotel as interrelated wings around a skylit atrium. Recently, the Skidmore, Owings and Merrill foundation selected as its national headquarters a Chicago residence executed by the noted American architect Frank Lloyd Wright. Like the Mauna Kea, the Wright residence gains appeal through use of a tall atrium and Japanese design elements.

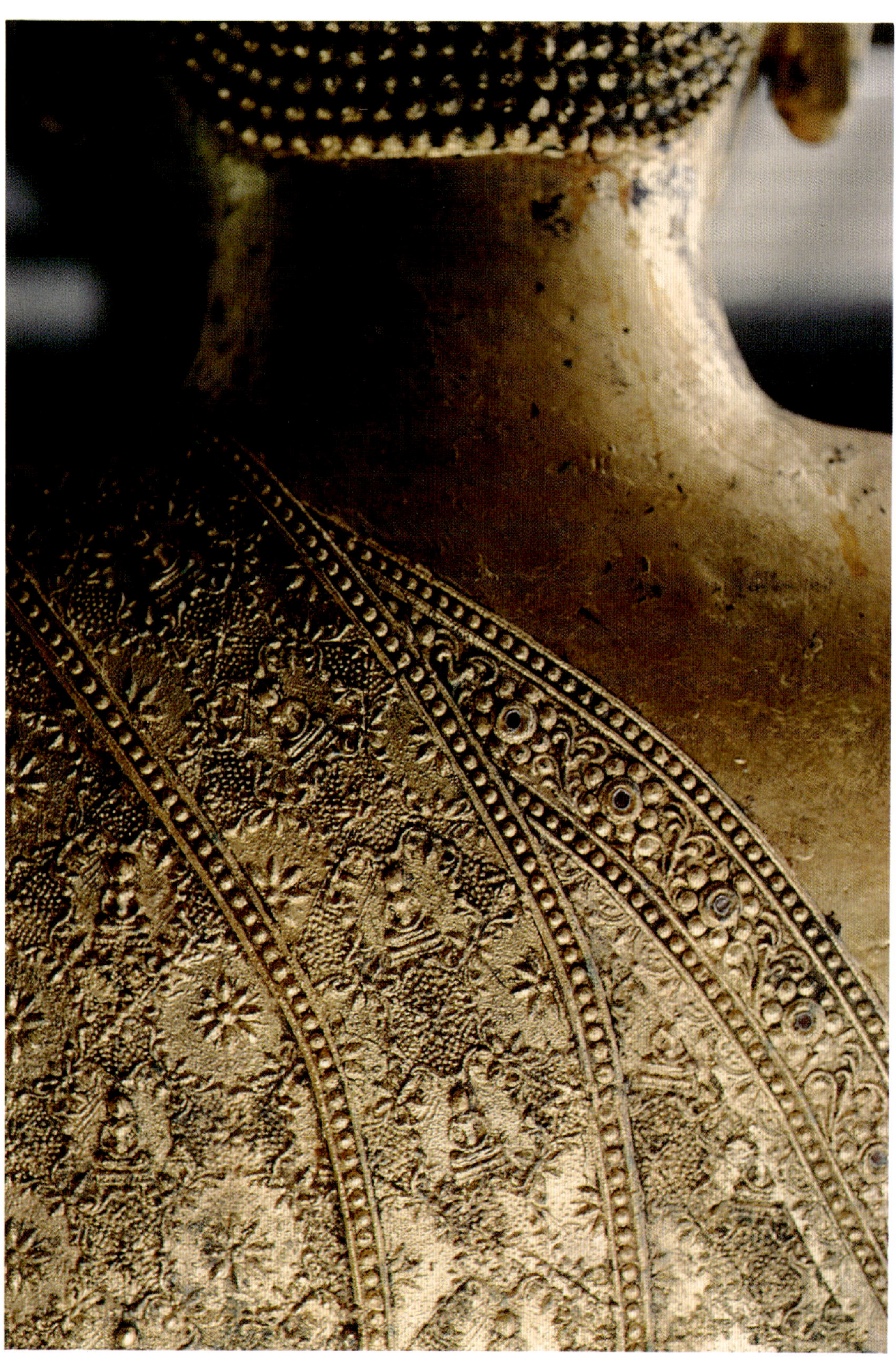

This detail photograph of the garment of one of the Thai Buddhist disciple sculptures in the resort's lobby shows a particularly intricate metalwork design: a diaper pattern in which floral motifs alternate with representations of the Buddha seated in meditation. Each of the Buddhas measures about one-half inch in height.

Asian Arts

THE ASIAN works of art Laurance Rockefeller collected for the Mauna Kea are predominantly Buddhist in subject, style, or cultural association. Rockefeller believed the process of cultural interchange in the visual arts of Asia is illustrated best through the arts of Buddhism, whose aesthetics were constantly transformed by indigenous cultures. It was his intent to introduce the arts of Asia through the unity of faith exemplified in devotional objects and, further, to select art works that might provide insights into the relatedness and diversity of Asian cultures.

Buddhism was the first proselytizing religion in Asia to offer salvation to all mankind, and the first Indian system of beliefs to spread to central, southeastern, and far eastern Asia. The Mauna Kea's Asian arts reflect this phenomenon: selections from the collection are presented in this book in a geographic and chronological sequence that approximates the expansion of Buddhist culture in Asia, moving from India to Southeast Asia, China, and Japan.

As world religions, Buddhism and Christianity are profoundly distinct in practice and belief, yet they share a number of similarities: both can be experienced through central, orthodox traditions or through sectarian beliefs; both expanded through missionary activity, have been affected by indigenous cultures, and were founded on the ideals of personal sacrifice and saintly behavior.

Just as Jesus came not to abolish the laws and the prophets but to fulfill them, the historic Buddha similarly built upon existing Indian religious—Brahmanic—traditions that had roots over a millennium before his birth in the sixth century B.C. and that eventually evolved into the system of beliefs known as Hinduism. These traditions entailed belief in the transmigration of the soul through a cycle of births, deaths, and rebirths (reincarnation) determined by *karmic* reward and punishment that brought one closer to or further from the divine godhead. The Buddha was a paragon for personal and social discipline, and his teachings demonstrated the futility of selfish and wicked actions. The goal most desired was *bodhi,* enlightenment, through which one might attain *nirvana* and thus be released from the otherwise continuing cycle of births, deaths, and rebirths.

Siddhartha Gautama, the man who became the Buddha, was a prince by birth and therefore, in the Brahmanic scheme of things, well along on the path to spiritual fulfillment. He became a model for some Asian rulers who identified with his teachings. Buddhism benefited tremendously from the royal patronage it received as a result of these associations and perhaps would not otherwise have become a world religion extending beyond geographic, ethnic, and linguistic boundaries. Indian Emperor Ashoka (third century B.C.) was particularly noteworthy in this regard, for once he proclaimed his belief in Buddhism, he spent the rest of his life advocating the Buddhist ideal of peace throughout his vast empire and beyond.

The Buddhist arts in the Mauna Kea's collection are highly diverse and yet unified in spirit, for despite distinctions in style and subject, they cleave to a broad set of visual conventions handed down since the earliest images of the Buddha were created. The primary function of most Buddhist art was to support religious practice, and rather than giving vent to artistic innovation, the artists who created Buddhist images sought to perpetuate elaborate symbolism and artistic formulas that had been perfected long before. These works of art commemorated the sacred and encouraged believers to feel as well as to think about their religion. Most of the arts in this collection communicate ideas intuitively; visual arts are able to communicate significant expression without words.

INDIA

INDIA displays great diversity in geography, ethnicity, and religion, yet it has produced one of the few cultures in the world where linguistic and religious practices are clearly continuous with those of thousands of years ago. These traditions spring primarily from spiritual belief, and they are evident in the Indian art works at the Mauna Kea.

The roots of Indian religion are ancient fertility cults, often referred to as Dravidian or pre-Aryan beliefs. The Aryan peoples who conquered the Indus Valley in the second millennium B.C. brought with them the priestly Brahmanical religion, founded on belief in a world soul.

Although the Buddha was born in the sixth century B.C., the earliest known Buddhist arts in India were created in the third century B.C. under the patronage of Emperor Ashoka. Some of these early works were narrative and figurative, but the Buddha himself was only depicted symbolically, never in human form. During this time, the school of Buddhism known as Theravada (Teaching of the Elders) prevailed. This school emphasized the doctrines and moral codes of Buddhism rather than worship of the Buddha as superhuman. To the present day, Theravada continues to venerate the historic Buddha, Siddhartha Gautama, and is the form of Buddhism practiced in much of Southeast Asia.

The sudden appearance of anthropomorphic images of the Buddha may have been the result of foreign influence in northern India from the first through the early fourth centuries A.D. This region was then ruled by the Kushan, a people who migrated from their homeland in central Asia to invade India. During the Kushan period, Mahayana (The Greater Vehicle) Buddhism developed, a deistic school that emphasized worship of Buddhas and Bodhisattvas. Mahayana beliefs characterize many of the Buddhist cultures of East Asia, and it was Mahayana patronage that inspired the first images of the Buddha as a deified being.

During the Kushan dynasty, many Western ideas entered India, especially in the northwestern province of Gandhara, known also as Bactria and corresponding to present-day Afghanistan. This region was conquered by Alexander the Great in 327 B.C., and it was during this period, and in this region, that Hellenistic arts of the Mediterranean began to influence Buddhist imagery. In the subsequent Gupta dynasty (fourth to sixth centuries A.D.), Greco-Roman and indigenous Indian artistic styles fused to form the classical Indian Buddhist style that came to influence much of the Asian world. Iconic images were based on strict canons of proportion that transcended physical truths, which were considered ephemeral. Indian artists evolved a measurement-based system to determine how to form and shape parts of the body for Buddha images such that the size of each part of

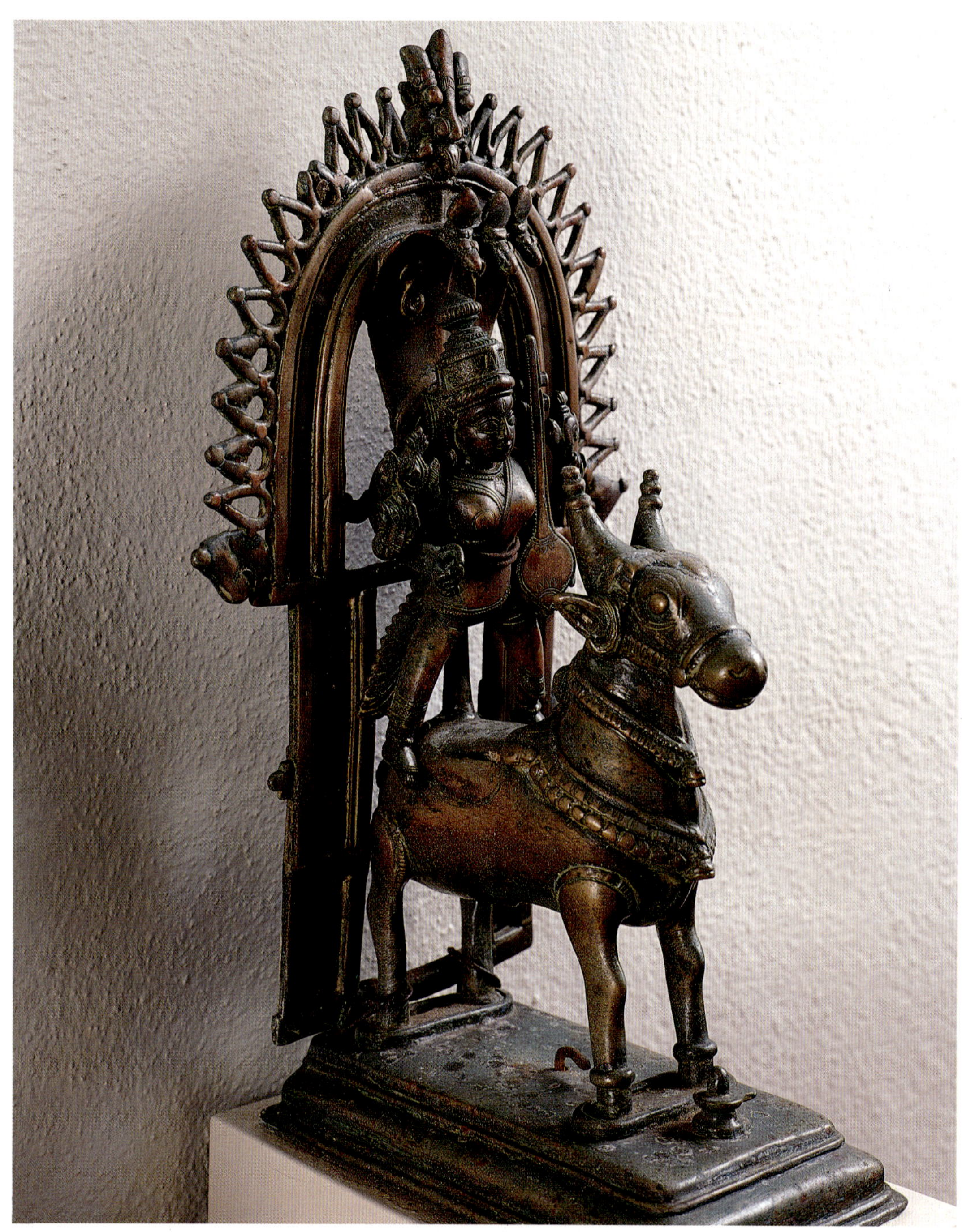

This Indian votive offering features the goddess Parvati riding a bull, the emblem of her husband, Shiva, the Hindu god of fertility and regeneration.

the work (nose, fingers, feet, etc.) was standardized in relation to the others. The unit of measure that determined these proportions was usually based on finger and palm measurements of the individual commissioning the art work. The donor's measurements were multiplied by auspicious numbers to arrive at the final dimensions for the sculpture. Although those who commissioned great works of art were honored in India, the makers of these works were not similarly acknowledged. Buddhist craftspeople were expected to possess great faith, spirituality, and concentration, but society considered them skilled workers rather than artists. In the Christian Middle Ages in Europe, as well, the creators of important religious art works were anonymous.

Through the fifth century A.D., Buddhism thrived and became the dominant faith throughout most of India through official, royal patronage. It expanded beyond the borders of India because of this patronage and missionary practice. Portable works of art created to propagate Buddhism incidentally facilitated the dissemination of Indian artistic style and iconography throughout India as well as to various Southeast Asian cultures. During the millennium in which Buddhism evolved in India, however, the Hindu culture from which it originally derived also continued to develop and flourish. In the sixth century, Buddhist dominance was challenged by the proliferation of Hindu states. The vast pantheon of Hinduism incorporated the Buddha but reduced him in stature, honoring him as only one of many deities. The arts of Hinduism transformed Buddhist aesthetic conventions and canons of proportion, as demonstrated by the eighteenth and nineteenth century bronze votive sculptures in the collection.

Seated Buddha

India, 7th century, granite, height 63 inches.

THE OLDEST and most important work in the Mauna Kea's collection of Asian art is an Indian sculpture of the historic Buddha. From Nagapattinam in southern India, the sculpture was created during the Pallava dynasty, whose arts significantly influenced those of Sri Lanka and Southeast Asia as a result of sea contact. Nagapattinam was an important port, the site of many Buddhist monasteries and shrines, and a significant destination as well as departure point for Buddhist pilgrims when this sculpture was created. Not long after, however, Buddhism disappeared almost entirely from India, and most of the Buddhist holy places that survived were eventually destroyed during Islamic conquests. The Mauna Kea's sculpture is thus not only a superb example of Pallava achievement in the arts but also represents the culmination of Buddhist creativity in South India. A related work from the same site is in the collection of the Chicago Art Institute.

The granite sculpture portrays the prince prophesied to become either a universal king or a Buddha, an enlightened one. Eventually, through renunciation of his high status, luxurious possessions, and family (including his wife and infant son), this prince of the Shakya clan began to pursue his ultimate goal, an answer to the age-old problems of sickness, old age, and death. For seven years he practiced ascetic and penitential austerities, all of which he found ultimately useless. Finally, he took up meditation under a pipal tree (*Ficus religiosa*), vowing not to arise until he had resolved his questions. After a series of miraculous events, quite similar to the trials and temptations of Christ during his forty days in the wilderness, the young prince achieved enlightenment and thus became the Buddha, also known as Shakyamuni, the sage of the Shakya clan. Ever since, the pipal has been known as the *bodhi* (enlightenment) tree, and the sculpture is fittingly displayed under a *bodhi* tree in the resort's North Garden.

The Buddha's first sermon presented the central doctrine of the faith in the form of four noble truths: to live as a being in this world is to suffer; the cause of suffering is desire, or selfish craving; the way to end suffering is to cease selfish craving; the method by which this can be accomplished is the eight-fold path of correct behavior and attitude that will end the pain of life by eliminating the endless succession of births, deaths, and rebirths. The eight-fold path entails a comprehensive code of right thought, right speech, and right action. The four noble truths evolved into cosmological symbolism that determined the form of Indian relic shrines, *stupas*, that were devotionally circumambulated. The *stupas* were architecturally oriented to the four cardinal directions, to affirm worshippers' faith in the four noble truths and to convey the truths' universality.

This first sermon is referred to metaphorically as the Wheel of the Law sermon—a doctrine that set into motion all other truths and laws. As with other Indian metaphors,

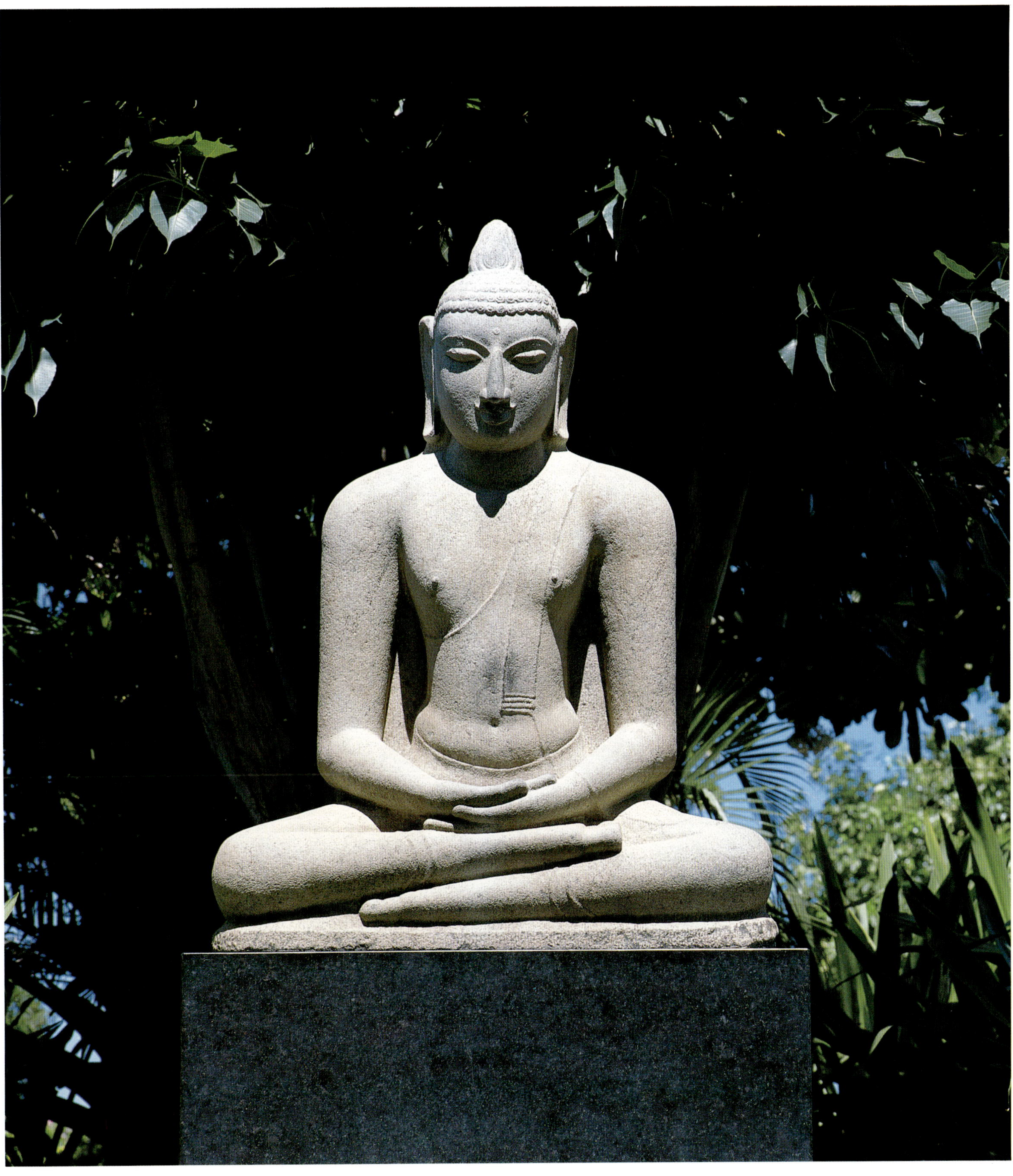

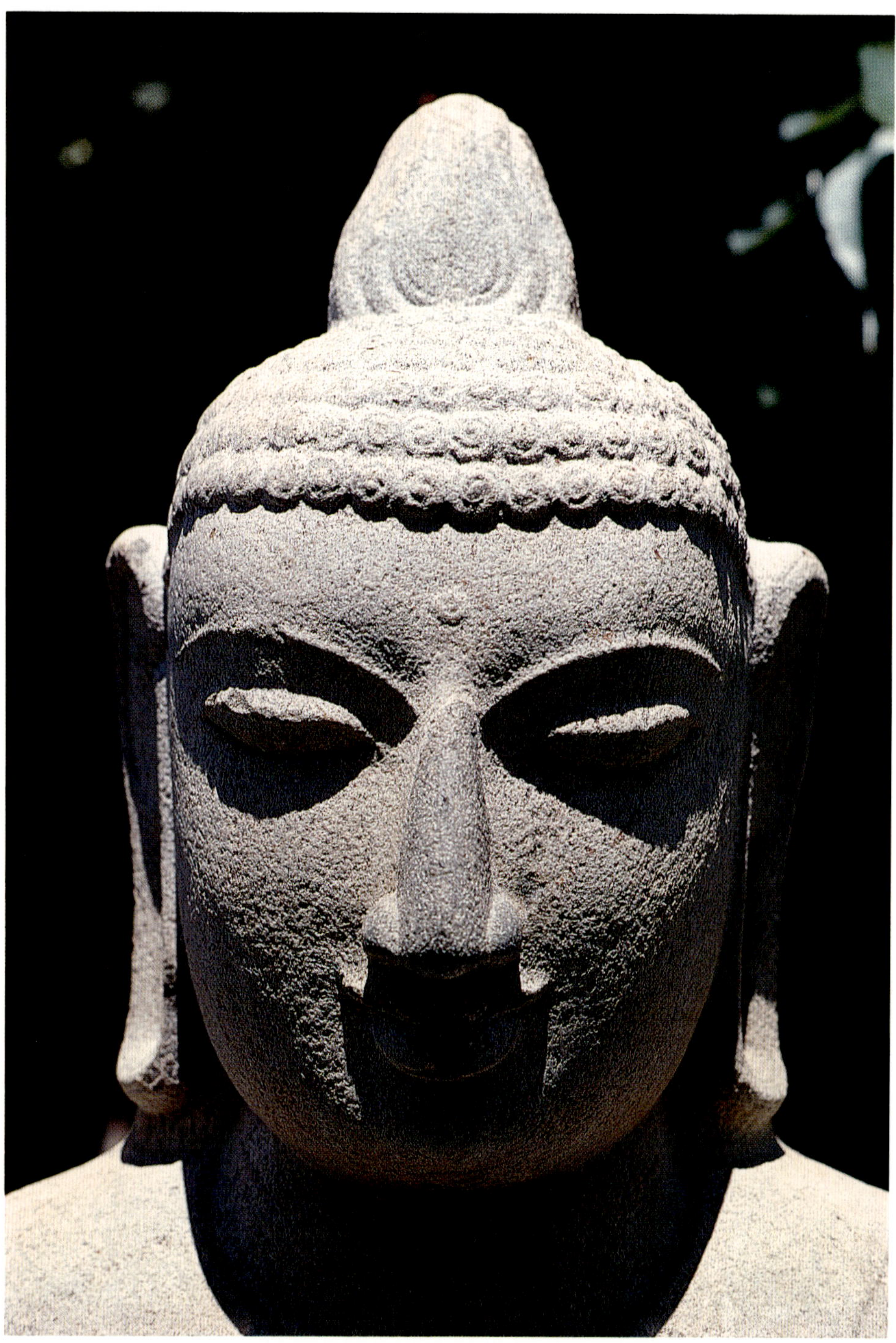

Representations of the head of the Buddha include body marks symbolic of the superhuman powers attributed to him. Such symbols are intended to convey an aura of divine radiance, but are not necessarily meant to portray the Buddha as a divinity. The facial features of this sculpture relate to a spiritualized, perfect form, rather than to the transient beauty of a human model.

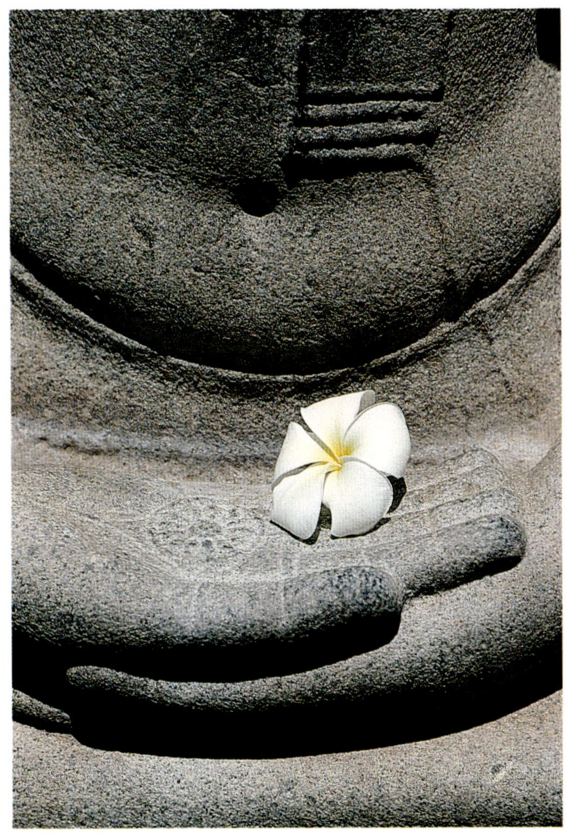

This detail photograph shows the Buddhist "Wheel of the Law" inscribed in the Buddha's right palm. Buddhism is practiced throughout the Hawaiian Islands. On Bodhi Day, the annual celebration of Siddhartha Gautama's enlightenment, Buddhist members of the Mauna Kea staff ritually bathe and decorate the sculpture. Throughout the year, visitors to the resort often honor the Buddha with flowers.

this metaphor was literally interpreted in art work, and a low-relief depiction of a small wheel, its spokes emphasized, is carved in this sculpture on the upturned palm of the Buddha's hand. Though not a feature of all sculptures of the Buddha, the wheel is often present, carved or painted somewhere on the body. It was often positioned behind his head, a placement perhaps influenced by Persian arts and sun symbolism found in ancient Iran. In this location, the wheel resembles a halo but is different in meaning and predates the appearance of halos in Christian arts.

Some scriptures attribute superhuman powers to the Buddha, and these powers came to be conveyed through a series of body marks, *lakshana,* here and on all such sculptures. Three *lakshana* on this figure's head are traditional. At the peak of the cranium is the *ushnisha,* a projection on the skull that was understood metaphorically to convey the Buddha's extraordinary wisdom, as if he bore an auxiliary brain. On the forehead is the *urna,* a mark indicating a "third eye," suggesting the Buddha's supreme powers of perception. The elongated earlobes signify the Buddha's royal birth and life as a prince, for heavy earrings typically worn by the upper class distended the lobes. The absence of earrings is intended as a reminder of Shakyamuni's sacrifice in renunciation of royal life.

The Buddha's hands form the *dhyani mudra,* or meditative gesture, indicating that this sculpture depicts Shakyamuni at the moment of his Great Enlightenment. The Buddha is seated in *padmasana*, the traditional yogic meditation posture. Here the left foot is placed under the right leg, an arrangement associated with images from South India, the Deccan region, and Sri Lanka; elsewhere, the left foot is tucked up onto the right thigh.

Each part of the Buddha's body, as well as his clothing, refers symbolically to a phenomenon of this world, to show the extension of Buddhahood into the lives of humans. The eyes, for instance, are shaped as lotus blossom petals. The lotus is an auspicious flower, since the plant grows in marshes and stagnant ponds but produces beautiful white blossoms, a fit symbol of enlightenment. Buddhists equated the world with swampy environs and the Buddha himself with the lotus blossom, rising up from earthly preoccupations to become enlightened.

The sculpted Shakyamuni wears the traditional monastic garment, the *sanghati*, draped to leave the right shoulder bare. The body strains the diaphanous *sanghati* as if filled with *prana*, "life-breath," a spiritual presence indicated by the gentle swelling of the belly. To this day, Buddhist meditation is linked with awareness of the breath, and the carved swelling here was intended to convey Shakyamuni's extraordinary discipline.

The body's simple contours lend the sculpture a monumental character, while details of the garment, pose, and gesture create a believable image of supreme tranquility; the facial features successfully portray a contemplative mood through raised brows and heavy eyelids. Decorative elements, such as the linear patterns on the *sanghati* (immediately above the navel) and the snail-shell hair curls, help animate the form.

The expressive strength of the sculpture is intensified by the granulitic stone, a material characteristic of similar works created during the Pallava dynasty. In several places, such as between earlobes and shoulders and between elbows and thighs, the stone has not been chiseled smooth or carved away. This untransformed granite may be an artistic metaphor for the Buddha's unyielding strength to reinforce the story of his enlightenment, for he adamantly persisted at meditation despite the temptations of Mara, the evil god of illusion.

The sculpture is an excellent example of Pallava interpretation of the graceful Gupta style. The classical Gupta style arose in northern India in the fourth through sixth centuries and was refined during the Pallava period in southern India, producing an ideal of balance and harmony between decorative linear patterns and sensuous, swelling forms. These same qualities were emulated centuries later in other Asian cultures influenced by the Indian classical style. The Buddha's contemplative, spiritual expression is also seen in the Khmer sandstone sculptures at the Mauna Kea (page 50), the Thai stucco head of a Buddha (page 56), and the bronze Thai disciples, whose bodies are revealed through clinging, intricately patterned drapery that accentuates their rounded forms (page 60).

Votive Sculpture Collection

India, 18th and 19th centuries, bronze and brass, heights 8½ to 23 inches.

THE LARGE GROUP of eighteenth and nineteenth century bronze and brass votive sculptures, or "temple toys," at the Mauna Kea were created in India's northern states and reflect the popular devotions of Hindu believers. Unlike the Buddha sculpture from Nagapattinam, which is an example of sophisticated metropolitan taste, these votive sculptures represent provincial traditions. They also convey artistic and religious links between antiquity and the present. Objects associated with children—toys and playthings such as rattles, miniature animals pulling carts, game boards, and the like—have been important in Indian family life from the ancient Indus Valley culture in the second millennium B.C. into the much later years of Buddhist and, eventually, Hindu culture. Sometimes these objects were made as toys for children, but they were also created as offerings to Hindu deities. Always, they manifest the Indian villagers' everyday concerns about birth, marriage, procreation, and death.

Temple offerings were frequently commissioned out of concern for a child's well-being and fear of the evil spirits that could assault him or her. In working-class homes, simple shrines preserved the mythic tales of Hindu gods through images made of materials such as paper, fiber, or terra cotta. In wealthier households, bronze and sometimes brass—relatively extravagant materials—were used, as seen in the Mauna Kea collection. These expensive materials exemplified the donor's adoration of the patron deity and were presented to temples in the name of a child. Studies indicate that artisans who created these

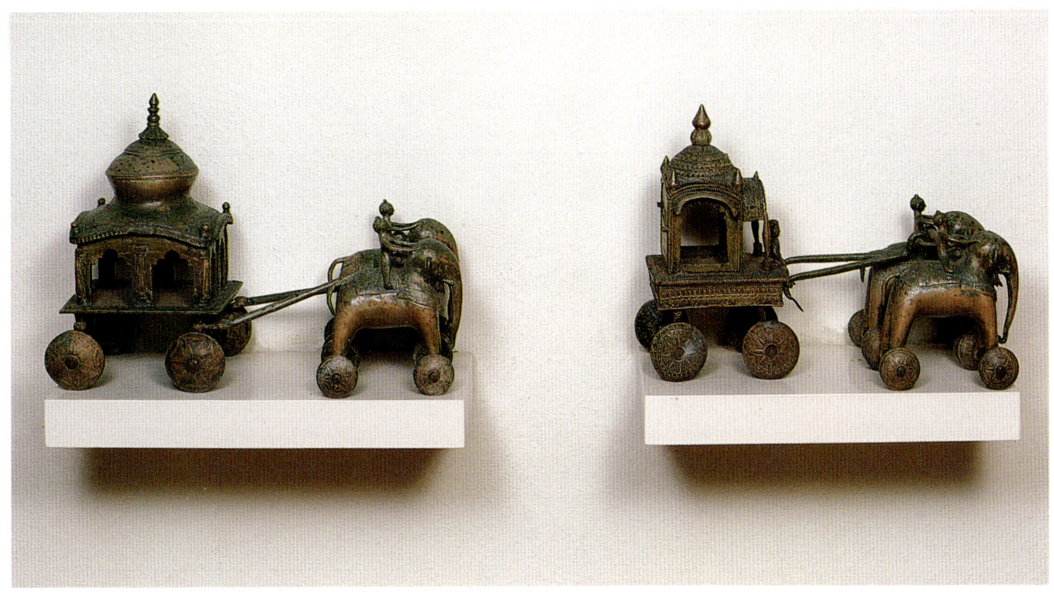

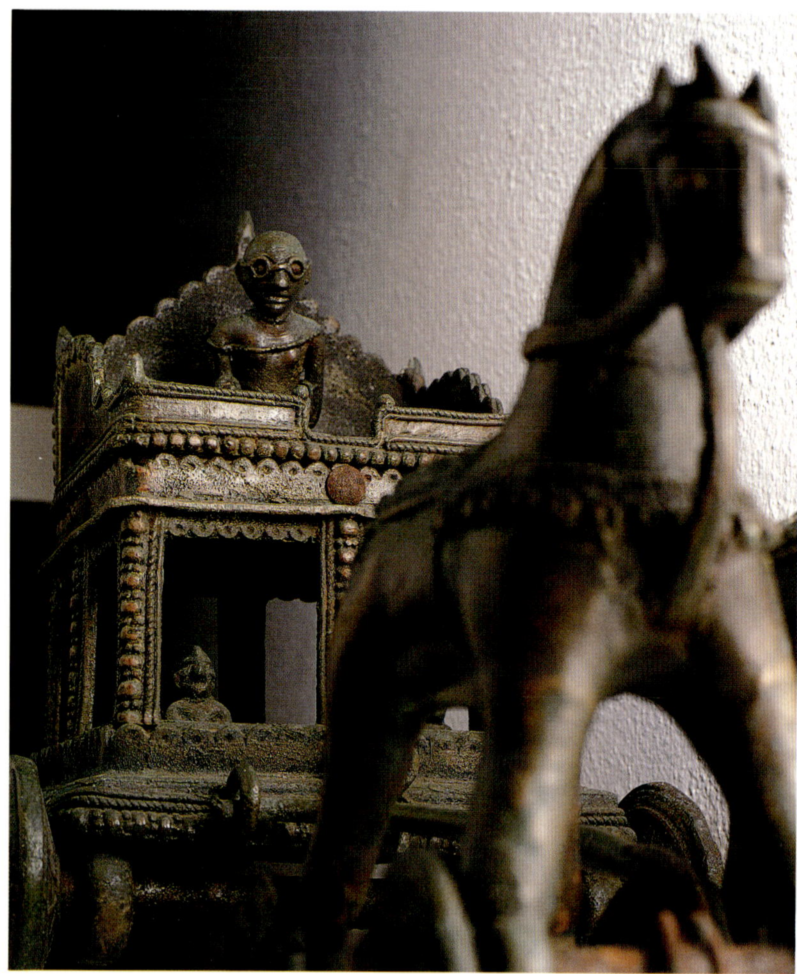

The charioteer of this nineteenth century bronze temple offering wears large spectacles, a fashionable accessory of the time in many Asian countries. Eyeglasses were introduced to India in the early sixteenth century by St. Francis Xavier, "Apostle to the Indies," a Spanish Jesuit who brought them as gifts; the saint's body is enshrined at a church in Goa, India.

works were sometimes given a family possession, such as a father's prized tool or a mother's heirloom brass anklets, to melt down and recast. The presence of treasured family property in the offering intensified the personal nature of the supplication.

The craftsmen who created secular objects usually created religious ones as well. Toys could be "enlivened" for religious use through acts of empowerment, just as the most sacred of temple images were ritually placed into *puja*, or worship, before they were considered fit dwelling places for the gods.

The Mauna Kea's sculptures include representations of Parvati (Shiva's consort) and Lakshmi (goddess of wealth and prosperity). The bull, Shiva's emblem, is a frequent subject in this group, as is the elephant, associated since ancient times with clouds, rain, and agricultural fertility. Many of the animals pull ornate chariots and carts, vehicles probably intended as provisional abodes for spirits and deities. In contemporary village life, carts very similar to these miniature sculptures still sometimes function as rolling temples and shrines. They are occasionally transported to holy places to provide an opportunity for the residing deity to communicate with other spirits and gods.

The artistic conventions of these votive offerings are also traditional. Female figures are narrow-shouldered, full-breasted, and large-hipped—descendants of ancient fertility goddesses. The male figures are likewise reminders of fertility deities, with narrow hips, full bellies, broad shoulders, and deep chests. Some of these deities are surrounded by body nimbuses on which can be seen *nagini*, embodiments of auspicious serpent spirits.

One figure in the Mauna Kea votive sculpture collection stands out by breaking the traditional decorum. This charioteer with goggle-like spectacles suggests that at least one rural artisan and patron took delight in emulating the high fashions of the nineteenth century. While it is possible that the person represented actually required eyeglasses, it is more likely that the glasses were included in the sculpture for prestige, a borrowed sign of status in the world of British colonialism.

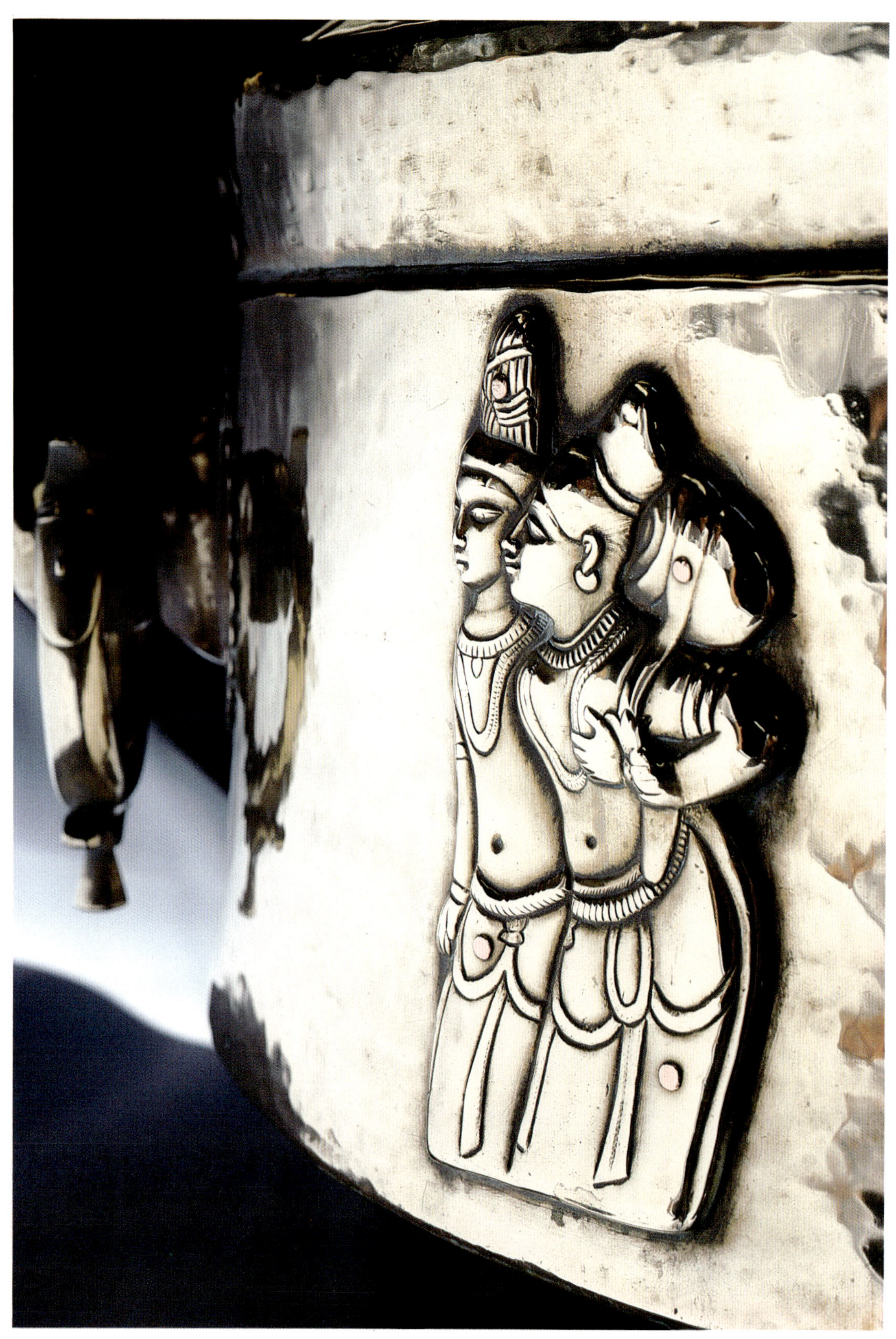

Storage Vessels (*Chamlas*)

India, 19th century, brass, heights 37 to 44 inches.

BRASS, a traditional metal in India, has been used for at least a millennium in household as well as ceremonial vessels. The tripod storage chests, *chamlas*, displayed at the resort are from northern India. Designed for security and portability, all have hinged locks and ring-shaped handles that make them easy for household servants to carry. In addition to the gleam achieved through polishing—fundamental to their aesthetic appeal—such vessels frequently were decorated by engraving and embossing through a chasing technique. A repoussé technique was also used, by which a design was created in relief on the thin metal by beating upward from the underside as the vessel was turned on a lathe; irregularities were filed down by hand.

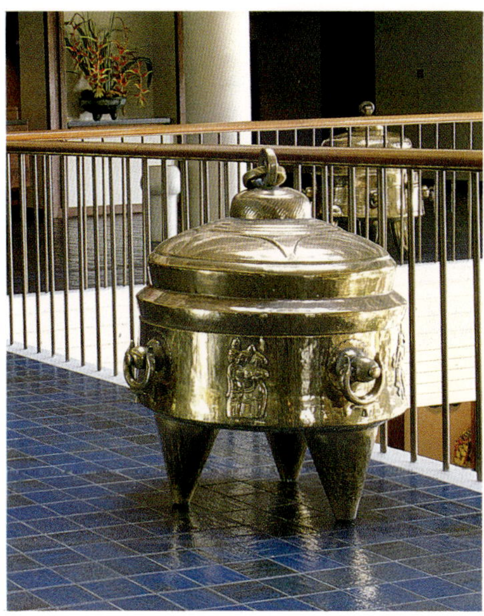

Most *chamlas* in the collection have relatively simple geometric designs. A few, however, are more ornate and complex and show figural motifs. On one a young woman stands rigid, hands folded below her emphasized breasts, balancing on her head a series of vessels as if to personify domestic stability. On another a young man and woman of lithe and sensuous build dance suggestively as the woman holds one of her hands to her breasts.

Chamlas often functioned as a public sign of luxury and wealth, whatever their size and nature of decoration. In both village and urban life, they were typically purchased to serve as "hope chests" in anticipation of a daughter's wedding. A generous dowry is still a focal point of wedding ceremonies in India: weddings are celebrations of wealth that exists, as well as wealth to come.

SOUTHEAST ASIA

SOUTHEAST ASIA includes the countries of Cambodia, Burma, Thailand, Laos, and Vietnam. The history of this region is one of large migrations of peoples, with attendant conflict and cooperation, producing a multiplicity of ethnicities and cross-cultural patterns in art and religion. The influence of Indian culture on the region began over two thousand years ago through peaceful mercantile and proselytizing activities. From the fourth and fifth centuries on, Indian culture was evident in Cambodia, Burma, and Thailand, the countries from which many art works at the Mauna Kea originated. Chinese and Islamic civilizations as well have had an impact on the region.

Initially, traders from India were attracted to Southeast Asia by the lucrative commerce in spices. They settled in major ports on trade routes, intermarried, and became respected members of local chieftains' families. These Indian colonies were important bases for the proselytizing efforts of Buddhist monks and Hindu Brahmins who introduced Southeast Asians to Indian religion, science, technology, and art. The local rulers were quick to grasp the advantages of acquiring Indian culture: literary skills, once mastered by the rulers, proved instrumental in extending their region of control. The cultures of Southeast Asia formed through these Indian contacts were notably different from those of their Buddhist and Hindu sources, just as in the Middle Ages the peoples of northern Europe produced a Christian culture remarkably unlike that of its Mediterranean source.

Cambodia is the kingdom of the Khmer people. The capital and center of Cambodian art from the ninth to fifteenth centuries was Angkor (a Khmer name derived from the Sanskrit word for city or town), where a series of extraordinary temples, sanctuaries, and palaces were built. This city of temples was built over many miles of swamp land and was served by a sophisticated system of dams, irrigation canals, and drainage culverts. Until its abandonment as the capital in 1431, ostensibly for a more defensible site, Angkor was also a central collection and storage site for the agricultural products of the kingdom.

Religion and politics were intimately bound together in the Khmer culture. Khmer rulers derived their power from Buddhist, Hindu, and indigenous beliefs. From the eighth century on, the kings of the Khmer people stressed either Buddhist or Hindu religious practices, depending on their particular religio-political views. The king was referred to as a *devaraja*, a "god-king," inasmuch as he and his subjects believed him to be a manifestation of divine energy. Palaces and temples enshrined numerous symbolic portraits of the *devaraja* to convey his religious and political sovereignty. These multiple portraits, and other forms of Cambodian art, were characterized by stylistically similar facial features that convey the artistic ideal of the Khmer.

In their travels to Burma, Indian missionaries and pilgrims often carried with them small relic containers made of gold, silver, or bronze, and equally extravagant gilt metal images for worship and ritual. Such portable works of art from India have been excavated in Burma, some dating from as early as the sixth century. Thereafter, the metalwork skills of Burmese artists grew more refined and eventually brought distinction to the arts of the country. By the eighteenth century, Burmese foundries were producing monumental works for Buddhist shrines, including one of the largest bells ever cast, a giant weighing eighty tons. These large works required casting multiple pieces that were later welded together, a technique not common to Indian or other Southeast Asian cultures. Size, technique, and refined detail gave Burmese metalworks a certain status and desirability in foreign lands.

Most of the Burmese works created for export, like most metalwork created in India and other parts of Southeast Asia, were cast using the lost-wax (*cire perdue*) method. In this method, wax was used to craft a double-walled clay mold, into which molten metal was poured and allowed to harden. The metal form was released by breaking the clay and then smoothed and finished by hand. This technique was used in producing the bronze drums that represent Burmese culture in the Mauna Kea collection.

The Thai people originally migrated from southern and southwestern China to Siam (now Thailand), where they came under Khmer rule. In the thirteenth century they renounced their Khmer overlords and extended their independent kingdom, taking over much of Siam. Their culture shows influences of Chinese and Indian theology, symbolism, and technology, and also adoption of materials and techniques from many Southeast Asian cultures. Like the Khmer, the Thai admired the classical Indian Gupta style; in adapting and developing it, they achieved a distinctly eclectic Thai artistic style.

The resort collection presents many types of Thai art. Some works are folk arts, showing provincial styles and a rural emphasis on magic as well as spirituality. Other works exemplify aristocratic and metropolitan tastes, in the styles of important cultural periods such as Sukhodaya, Ayudhya, and Bangkok; all indicate the importance of Buddhist practice in the arts of Thai society. The Buddhist arts largely represent the Theravada school of Buddhism, which emphasizes the doctrines of the historic Buddha rather than worship of him. In this school, individuals performed acts of merit to work out their salvation, and believers who sponsored the creation of a Buddhist image hoped for an especially generous spiritual recompense.

Khmer Heads of Deified Ancestors

Cambodia, *circa* 1300, sandstone, height 21 inches; 15th century, sandstone, height 24 inches.

THE MAUNA KEA'S two Cambodian sandstone portrait heads show how Indian religious views imported into the country were affected by Khmer ancestral worship and deification of royalty. The royal portrait images created in India were true to human form and did not suggest the presence of superhuman powers, unlike the Khmer portraits.

Many Khmer kings built huge sandstone temples that included a tall central spire. Colossal portraits of the *devaraja* were carved on the four sides of the central spire, providing a feature unique in the history of Southeast Asian architecture. Smaller portraits of the *devaraja* adorned walls of subsidiary towers, and yet more portraits—of deified kings, priests, and officials, all repeating the features and expression of the god-king—were displayed in small, vaulted galleries inside the towers. The thirteenth century portrait in the Mauna Kea collection most likely depicts a royal ancestor as a palace official; the fifteenth century portrait is also thought to represent a venerated royal ancestor.

The Mauna Kea's portrait sculptures show a number of similarities because court artists typically sought to continue the artistic conventions of their predecessors; thus their works portrayed an idealized concept of a *devaraja* rather than the characteristic features of an individual. Both portrait heads wear ornate, jeweled headdresses and bear gentle expressions. These portraits are also faithful to the ethnic features idealized by the Khmer: almond-shaped, somewhat sloping eyes, high cheekbones, broad noses, and full-lipped mouths forming enigmatic smiles.

The thirteenth century portrait, despite some noticeable damage, is more successful in depicting the elusive ideal of blissful enlightenment. Its abstract and geometricized headdress contrasts with and intensifies the sensuous planes of the face and the subtlety of expression. The fifteenth century piece is not as gentle and peaceful in expression; for example, carved lines clearly bound the eyes and the edges of the lips. This sculpture dates from the last moment of Khmer national strength: during the fifteenth century, Angkor was destroyed by invading Siamese forces; thereafter, Khmer artistic style was appropriated by Thai artists, who in time further modified and transformed it.

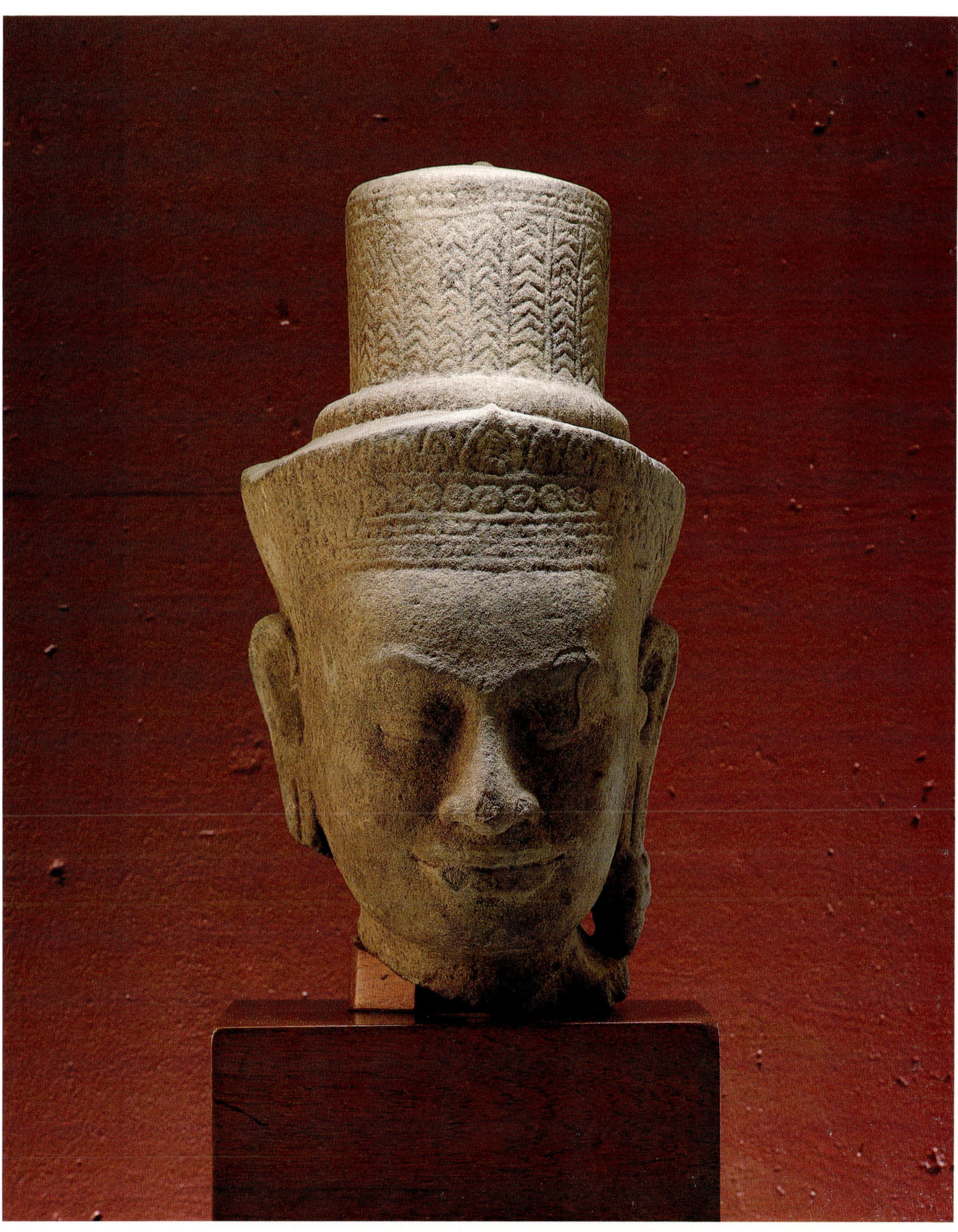

The contrast between the ornate, flared diadem and the rounded features of the face in this thirteenth century portrait sculpture helps to create an aura of intense energy and power.

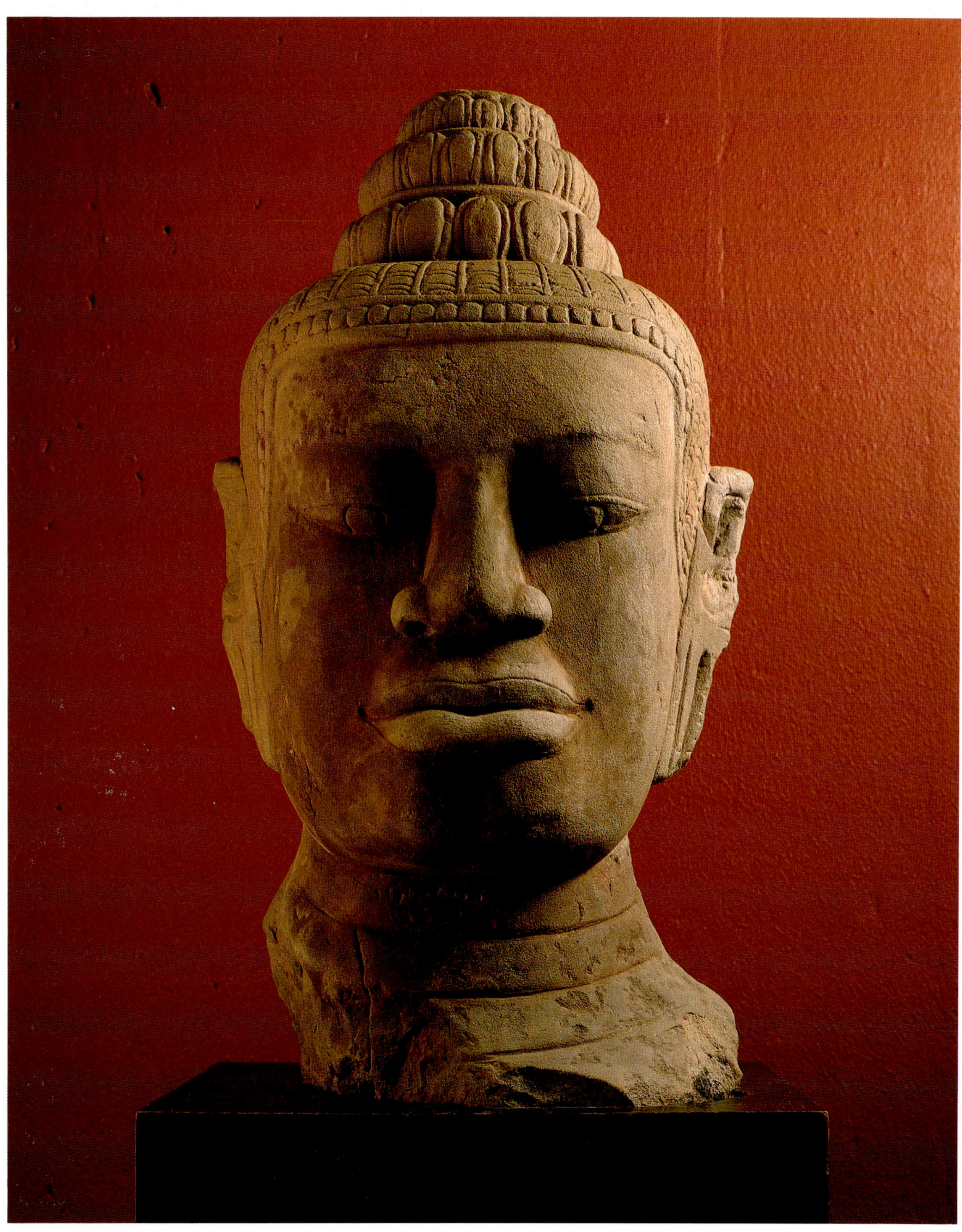

The creators of this fifteenth century sandstone portrait head first incised the facial features and then carved the head into a shape that retains the block-like form of the original stone. Khmer men were frequently honored posthumously with the names of deities and were often represented in the form of the temple's patron deity.

Bronze Drums

Burma, 18th century, bronze, heights 16½ to 21½ inches.

Seventeen bronze drums are displayed throughout interior lounges at the resort. Researchers have at times defined their provenance as Thailand, Laos, or Burma, a confusion resulting from the fact that these pieces were created for export and therefore are frequently found outside their country of origin. Sometimes referred to in art history literature as "frog drums" because of their decorative motif, these bronzes are examples of some of the most interesting export art ever created in Southeast Asia.

The latest research convincingly describes these drums as having been created in the eastern regions of Burma by craftsmen using the *cire perdue* casting technique. They were primarily manufactured from the eighteenth century on, for export to various clans of the Karen hill tribes dwelling in the mountainous regions of Burma and the northernmost regions of Thailand and Laos. The Karen tribes, whose population today exceeds two million, are thought to have migrated to Southeast Asia from southern China. During the eighteenth century these hill tribes maintained overtly animist beliefs and practices, reflected in the iconography of these drums, and seem not to have been affected by the Buddhist faith of surrounding peoples. Asian and Western scholars believe the hill peoples used bronze drums for ritual communication with forest and ancestral spirits. As the

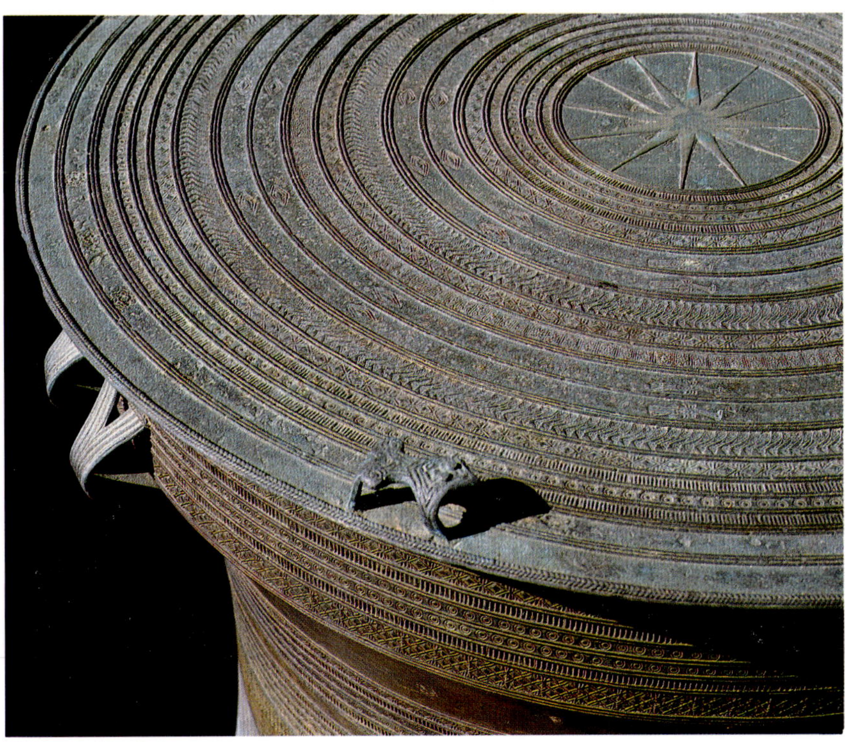

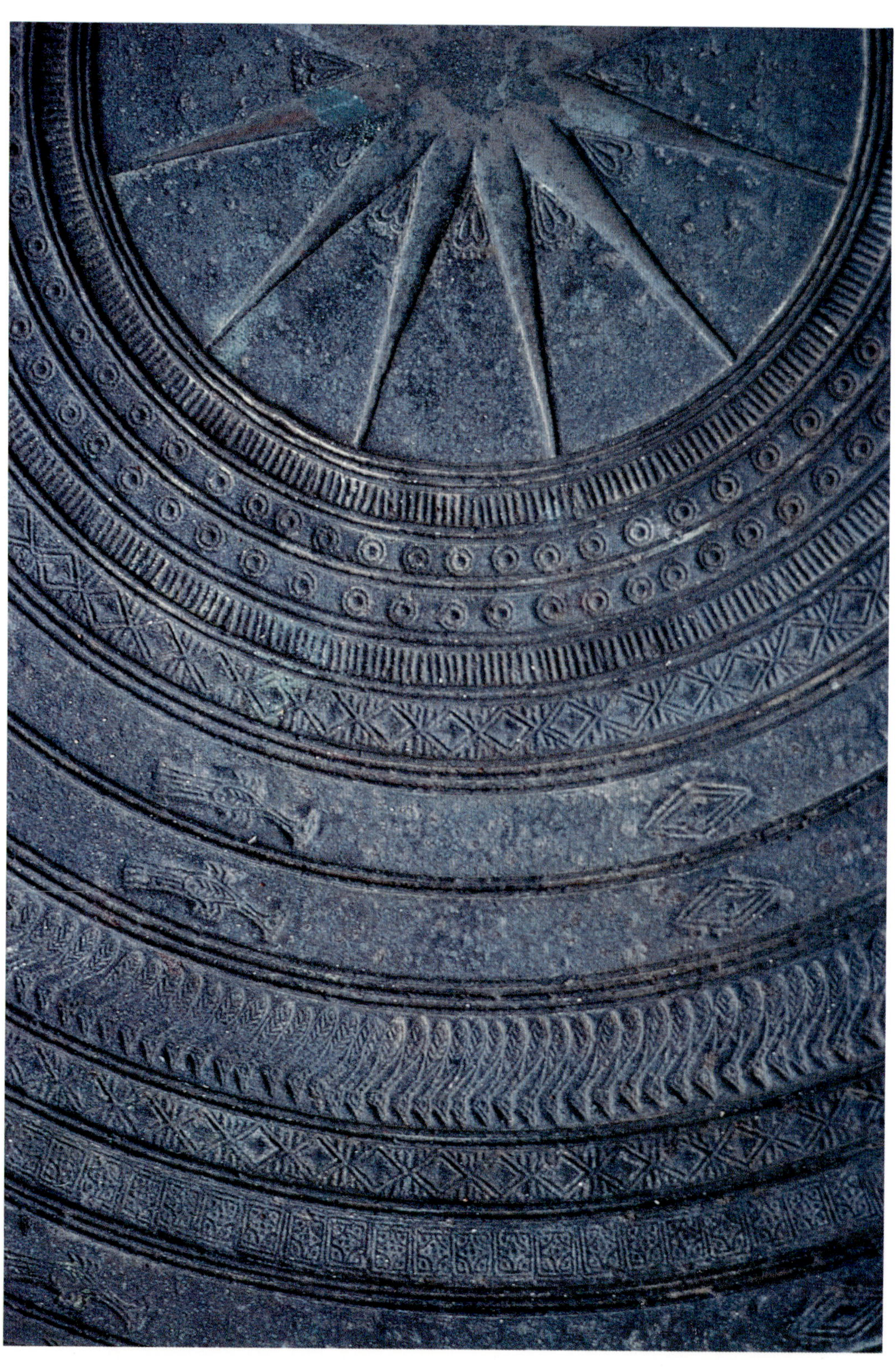

abode of these spirits, the drums were given honorific names of address. They also were carried into war and sounded to invoke the spirits' support in battles. Sometimes the drums served as containers for treasured possessions of individuals or the clan (under communal ownership); by this function they became a recognized sign of wealth among the Karen peoples.

Drums older than those in the collection were often buried with their deceased owners, to accompany them in the afterlife. By the eighteenth century, however, this practice became largely symbolic: only the frogs that decorated the tops of the drums were removed and buried with the owner. In fact, some of the frogs on the Mauna Kea's drums were affixed to replace original frogs buried as offerings.

In addition to the sculptural frogs, the tops of the drums are decorated with bands of concentric circles that issue from a central star with varying numbers of points. Some researchers suggest the star represents a stone flung into a pond and the concentric circles the rippling aftereffects. Indeed, the subject matter of the designs within the circular bands, both plant and animal, consists of life forms that have aquatic associations. The frogs perched on the perimeters of the tops suggest that the drums' edges are the banks of a pond. On some drums, frogs lie one on top of another, perhaps to indicate spawning and fertility. The sides of the Mauna Kea's drums are decorated with traditional Karen symbols of wealth, most frequently small elephants in procession, and sometimes snails—a favored food in the region. These designs are in a very low-relief form of the *cire perdue* technique that required extremely refined casting skills.

Eventually, through conquest or as gifts and offerings from the hill tribes, these drums passed into the hands of the Thai and other dominant peoples of the region, who prized them greatly. Up to the last decade, the royal Thai family treasured frog drums (the bronze forms were usually embellished with gilt and lacquer in Thai collections), using them in processionals and to announce royalty.

Head of a Buddha

Thailand, 13th century, stucco, height 19 inches.

THE EARLIEST Thai art work in the collection, this Sukhodaya-style Buddha is slightly damaged but remains an excellent example of early classic Thai art. Prior to the thirteenth century, the central regions of Siam were still controlled by the Khmer, who patronized sculpture that was usually confined to subtractive techniques executed in sandstone; even when bronze was employed, the wax and clay molds were cut and carved, rather than modeled, so that forms were somewhat harsh and angular. The Mauna Kea's Thai head of a Buddha is made of stucco and demonstrates the Sukhodaya-period preference for additive techniques and materials that produced soft and round forms, as opposed to the sharp forms that earlier prevailed.

The Buddha's head shows the three standard *lakshana* that convey the superhuman powers attributed to the Buddha. Other facial features reflect the symbolism used in Thailand during this period: the head is egg-shaped; the chin is meant to resemble the seed of a mango; the nose is slightly hooked, to suggest the beak of a parrot; the eyebrows are extremely high, bow-like curves; and the eyes are shaped to exaggerate the lotus petal outline into double curves. The curves of the mouth and hairline echo and intensify these rhythmic shapes and suggest a nervous and sinuous energy. The elongation and attenuation of the facial features also reflect Thai ideals of ethnicity.

The hair is the most detailed feature of the head, a pattern of tightly spiraled curls that symbolize the sun. The whorls of hair depict movement in a clockwise direction—the direction of ritual circumambulation traditionally followed by Buddhist worshippers at their shrines. This and other symbols in Thai Buddhist arts evince the survival of ancient forms of sun and fire worship, which may also have been the reason many shrines and sculptures were gilded. Originally, this Thai sculpture was painted and gilded; the gold leaf that remains suggests the lick of a flame, a fiery power flickering across the face.

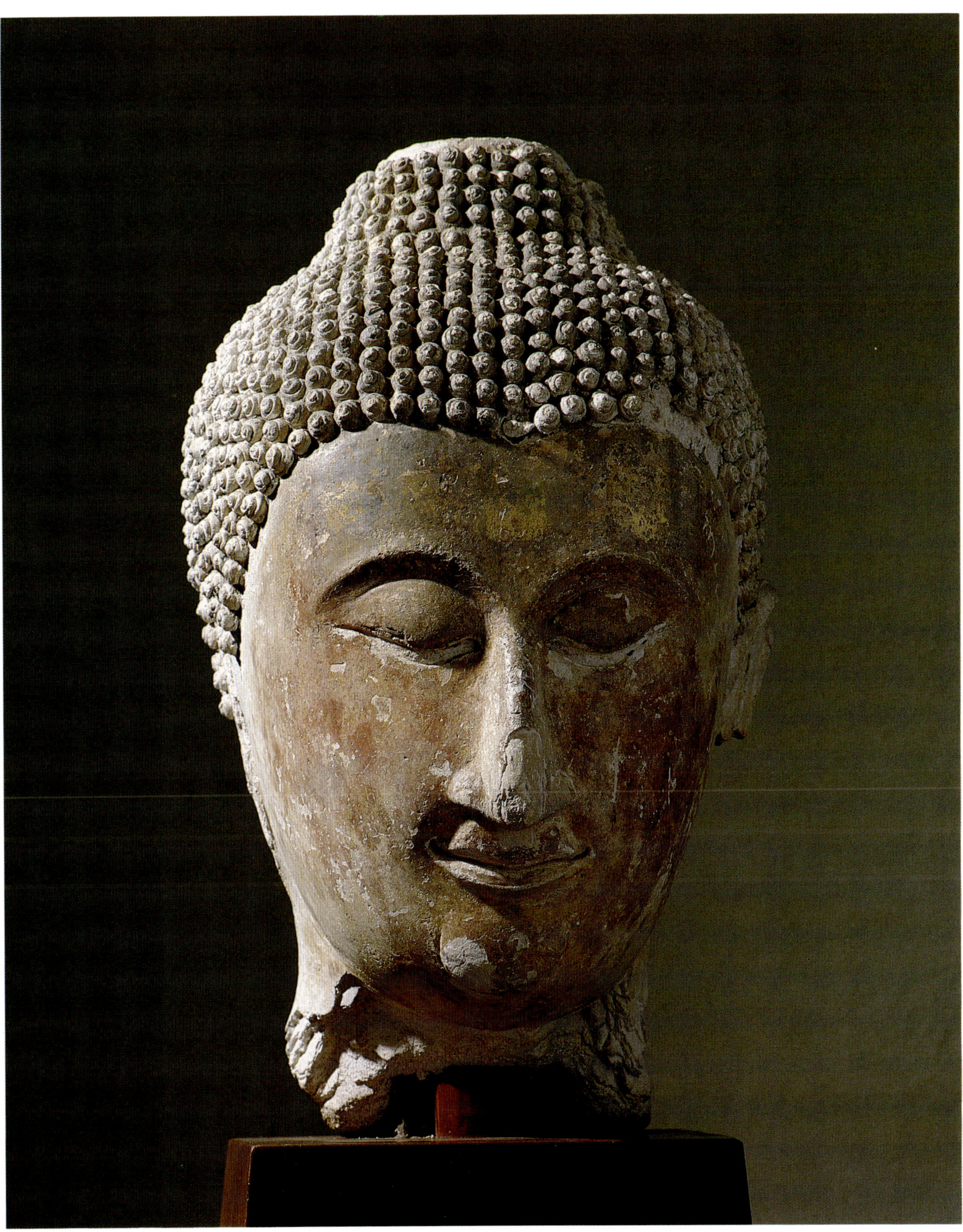

Standing Divinity on a Fabulous Bird

Thailand, 18th century, wood and polychromed mirrored glass mosaic, height 93 inches.

THE MAUNA KEA'S Thai wood sculpture of the Ayudhya period (which followed Sukhodaya) is rare in two ways. First, most Ayudhya kingdom treasures were destroyed during a chaotic takeover and burning of the capital city by the Burmese in 1767. Second, relatively few wooden sculptures were created during this period, which carries the name of the prosperous, densely populated city that served as the Thai capital from the fifteenth century until it was sacked by the Burmese.

Ayudhya rulers maintained the Theravada faith but also took interest in the Hindu practices of the Cambodian peoples they conquered. This sculpture depicts the god Vishnu, a member of the Hindu trinity of deities, with attributes that identify his role as "the preserver." Vishnu is standing on the form of the divine Garuda, his emblem and vehicle, a mythic sunbird that is part man. During the later Bangkok period, the Garuda was chosen as the official emblem of the king of Thailand and, by extension, as the symbol of the Thai nation.

The sculpture once decorated a building in a monastic complex on the outskirts of the capital. These complexes usually contained one or more *stupa*s. The *stupa* form, which originated in India as a mound of earth over a burial or relic shrine, evolved to include huge structures of complex symbolism. *Stupa*s eventually became dominant features of the landscape in most Buddhist communities throughout Asia, though each region evolved a distinctive style. Built on elaborate substructures, Thai *stupa*s were bell-shaped, attenuated transformations of the Indian form. Monasteries adjacent to *stupa*s included richly decorated ordination and assembly halls, whose overlapping roofs were brilliantly colored, due to Chinese-inspired use of glazed tiles. This sculpture originally graced the gable of such a monastic hall.

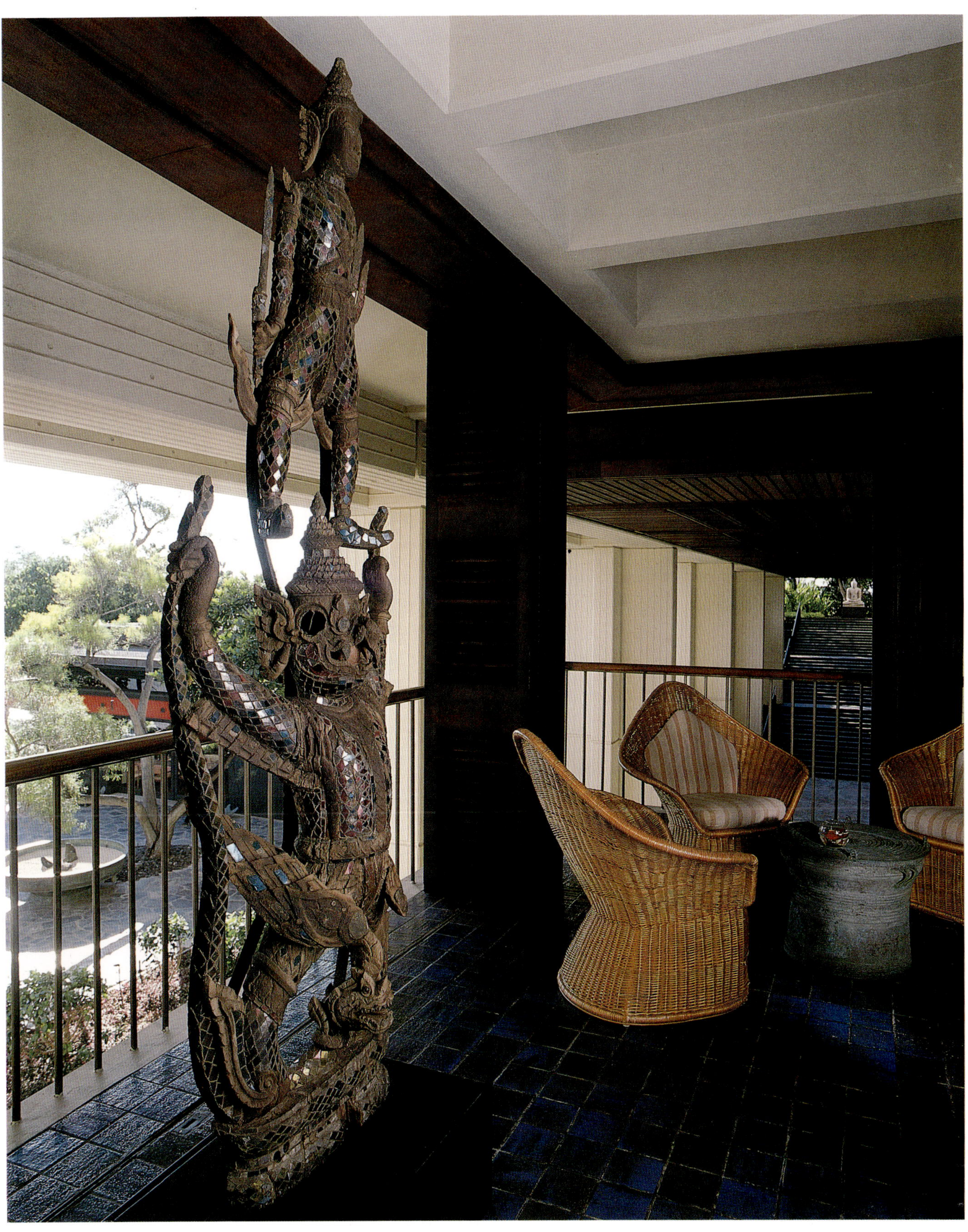

Pair of Buddhist Disciples

Thailand, late 18th century, gilt bronze with mirrored glass, height 40 inches.

THESE BRONZE figural sculptures, which greet guests at the Mauna Kea's main entrance, were cast using the *cire perdue* technique during the last quarter of the eighteenth century, after Bangkok became the center of Thai culture. The sculptures, however, are excellent examples of the "national style" of Thai art that developed during the lengthy Ayudhya period.

Instead of rebuilding Ayudhya after its destruction by Burmese invaders, a new capital was established, in part because a Theravada interpretation of the doctrine of impermanence deemed it more meritorious to construct new temples and palaces than to reconstruct those that had completed their predestined term of existence. The new capital was first established at Thon Buri, on the right bank of the river at Bangkok; in 1782, the capital was transferred to the left bank, present-day Bangkok. The architects and artists called on to create the new capital sought to maintain the respected Ayudhya style. Therefore, approximately twelve hundred bronzes and other works of art, reclaimed from Ayudhya and elsewhere, were taken to Thon Buri/Bangkok and rededicated in new settings. They, in turn, became models for a new era of Thai art.

Both sculptures represent disciples of the Buddha and, as such, show only one *lakshana*—the elongated earlobes that convey royal birth. Originally, these bronzes may have knelt on either side of an image of the historic Buddha. Their hands are raised in the *anjali mudra*, a reverential gesture that in secular contexts is a sign of greeting.

At first impression, the pair appear to be mirror images, but closer examination reveals many differences. Seen in profile, one nose subtly arches upwards, while the other is comparatively aquiline. Likewise, the monastic robe of one figure is patterned in geometric and floral designs in a very low relief, while the other's garment is enlivened front and back by a multiplicity of tiny Buddhas seated in meditation. The differences probably indicate that the pair are idealized portraits of the donors, devout Buddhists who wished to show themselves adoring Shakyamuni, just as many Renaissance altarpieces include portraits of donors in the same visual field as sacred figures, bearing witness to their faith.

Although bronze is the basic material of the sculpture, it is virtually invisible under layers of black lacquer and gold leaf. The lacquer served as an adhesive bond for the gold leaf. Use of gold is common in surface decoration of Thai Buddhist sculpture, expressing a belief that enlightened beings had radiant appearances. The inlaid mirrored glass on the monastic garments, and the blue glass set into the eyes, further enhance the brilliant appeal of the sculptures.

Connoisseurs of Thai art sometimes describe the later arts of Siam as excessively conventionalized, repeating patterns without vitality. This criticism is leveled especially at arts of the Bangkok period that scrupulously maintained archaic styles. The Mauna Kea's sculptures offer evidence that talented artists of the period continued to create fresh and appealing images using Ayudhya methods and models. While they are extremely ornate, these bronzes achieve a mood and expression of humility that would have appealed to pious believers.

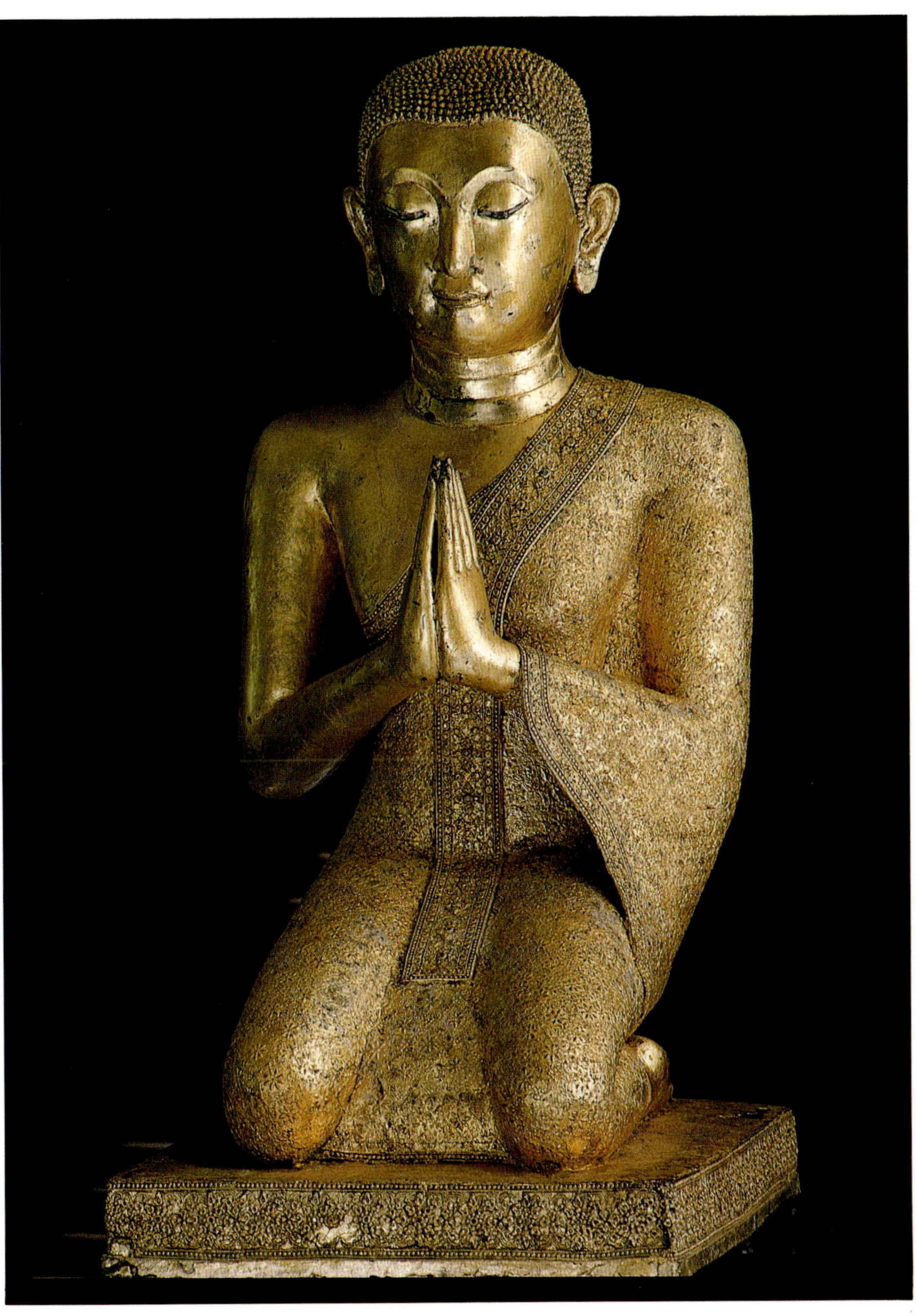

Votive Tablets

Thailand, 18th/19th century, gilt and painted wood, height 22 inches.

EACH of the many images of the Buddha on this pair of votive tablets depicts Shakyamuni stretching his right hand to the ground in the "calling of the earth to witness" gesture, the *bhumisparsa mudra*. The *mudra* derives from an incident said to have occurred during the time the young seeker spent beneath the *bodhi* tree. Just as Jesus was tempted by Satan during his meditation in the wilderness (and likewise St. Anthony, during his fasts), Shakyamuni was plagued by the god of illusion, Mara, who tried to distract him from his quest with seductive women and demonic visions. Finally, having failed to sway him by these means, Mara accused Shakyamuni of not having given alms in a previous existence. Still seated in meditation, Shakyamuni touched the ground with his right hand and called on Mother Earth to witness that he had indeed given alms and was worthy to triumph over evil. Mara was thus defeated and Shakyamuni went on to become enlightened.

Thai Theravada Buddhists often had votive tablets such as these created in quantities, to fulfill the need to perform an act of merit. Tablets were made of various materials, sometimes clay mixed with the ashes of a deceased Buddhist priest, and usually were enshrined under a *stupa*, along with venerated relics. The repetition of images is linked to the miracle at Sravasti, one of the few recounted miracles in the Buddha's life, when Shakyamuni filled the sky with an infinite number of glorious Buddhas, each like himself.

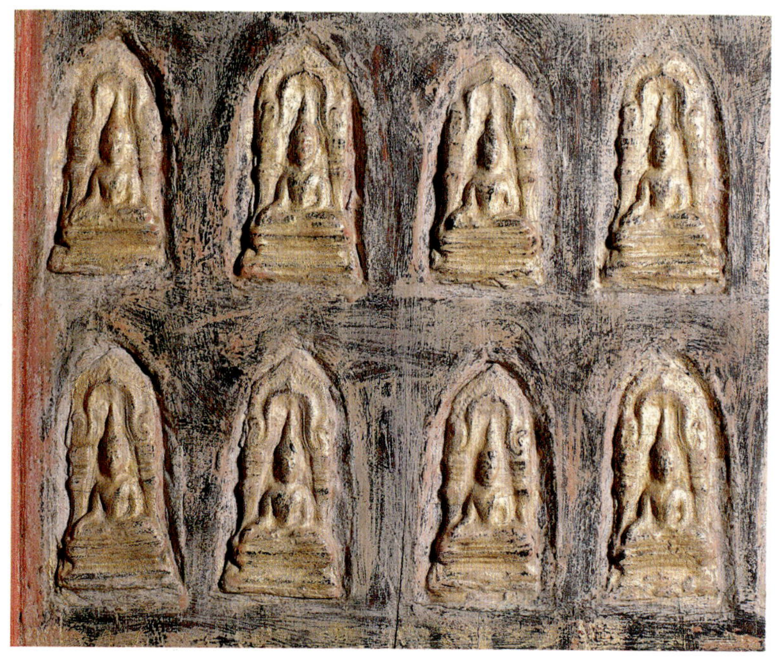

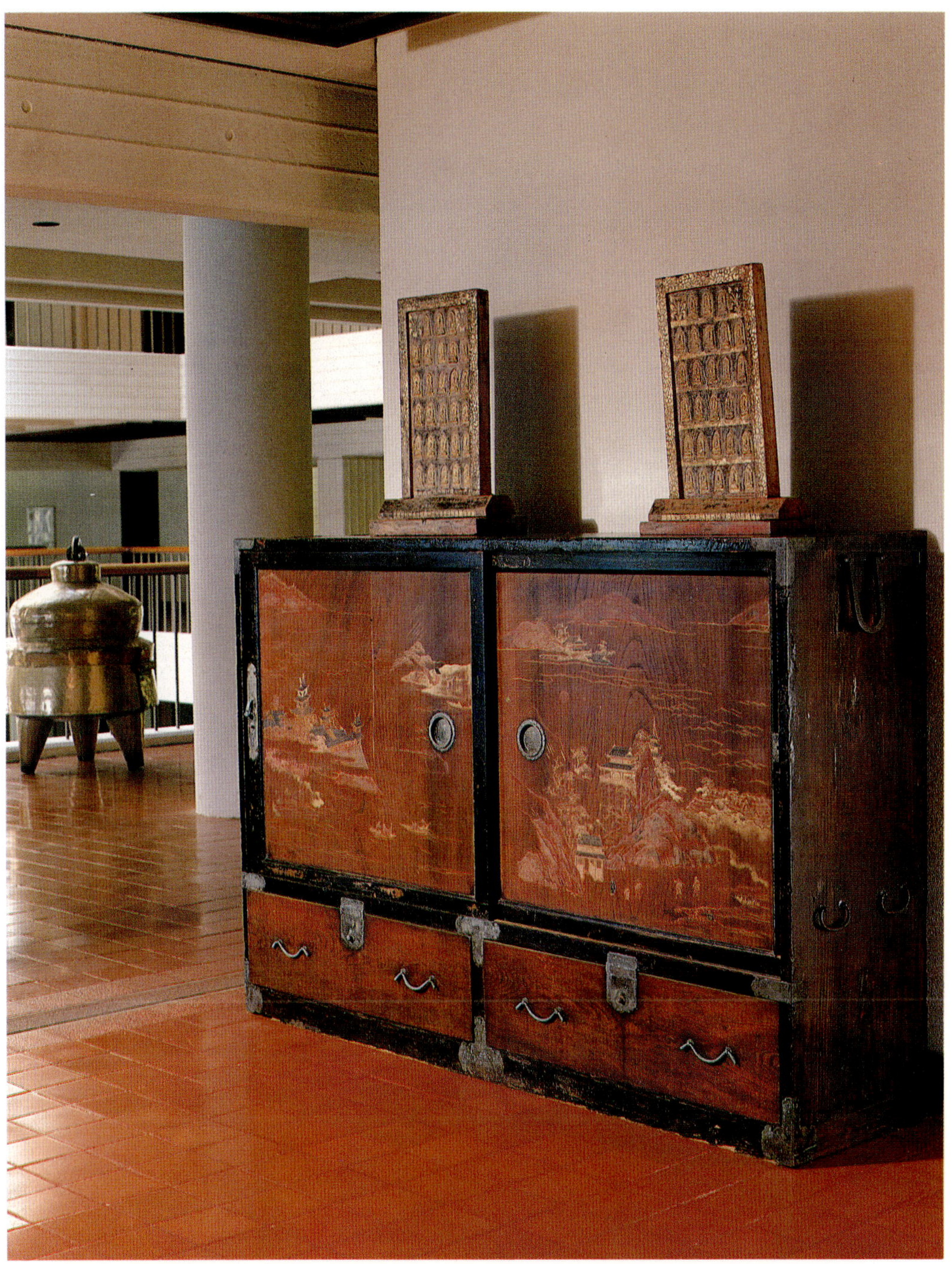

The votive tablets seen here atop a Japanese chest (*tansu*) were commissioned by followers of the Theravada school of Buddhism to honor the historic Buddha and to earn personal spiritual favor.

Buddhist Altar

Thailand, 18th/19th century, wood, height 66 inches.

THE MAUNA KEA'S Buddhist altar once may have graced a Thai monastic assembly hall or served as a private shrine in the residence of a wealthy and pious individual. Carved of teak, the altar is incised with intricate openwork designs in decorative rather than symbolic motifs. A foliated and pointed arch on the front frames the interior as if it were a proscenium. Behind it rise five, tiered plinths, which would once have functioned as pedestals for small devotional images and floral offerings. The upper rear of the interior probably originally held a relief-sculpture Buddha image; the painted image there now, which depicts the Buddha in a paradisal setting, is a later addition.

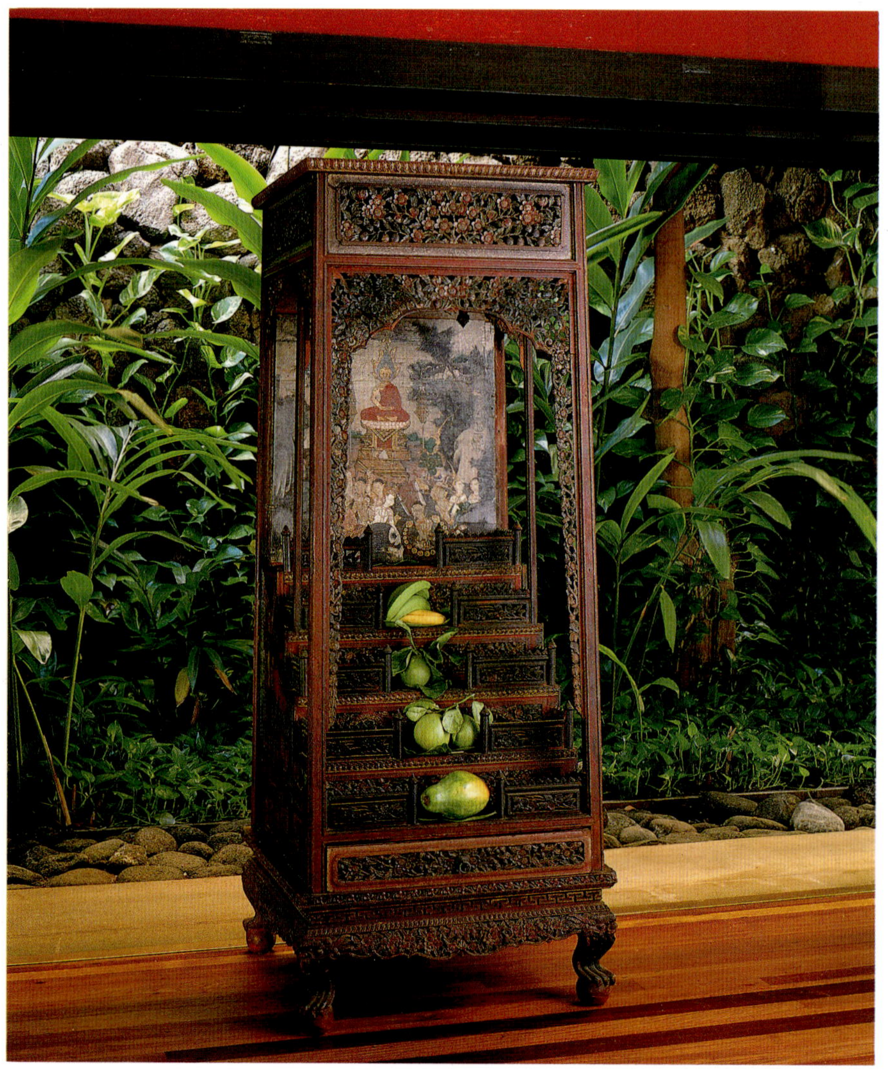

Sutra Chest

Thailand, 18th/19th century, wood with gold and black lacquer, height 41 inches.

THIS LARGE, square sutra chest is noteworthy for its lacquered and painted decoration. From the Chieng Mai region of northern Thailand, it once would have been used in a temple sanctuary. Although its surface is well worn, it is still possible to detect in the painting on the front panel a Buddha seated in meditation under a *bodhi* tree and a pair of heavenly beings hovering in adoration of Shakyamuni and of his teachings—the chest's sacred texts. The sutras once stored here were probably Thai versions of those teachings, written in the Indian format on long, narrow palm leaves rather than in Chinese scroll form.

The lacquer technique, *lâi rot nâm* (decoration that emerges by washing the work with water), used on the sutra chest was extremely demanding. First, the wooden panels were covered with at least three coats of black lacquer, each smoothed until flawless before the next was applied. Then the intended design was transferred to the panels by powder stencil through pinholes in paper, and a water-soluble yellowish sediment was painted over areas that were to remain black, the drawn areas left in reserve. Next, a clear lacquer was applied to the entire surface, followed quickly by application of gold leaf across the entire surface. Finally, after drying, each panel was washed with water to remove the unwanted gold leaf and yellow sediment. The result: a crisp design in gold sparkling against a black lacquer background.

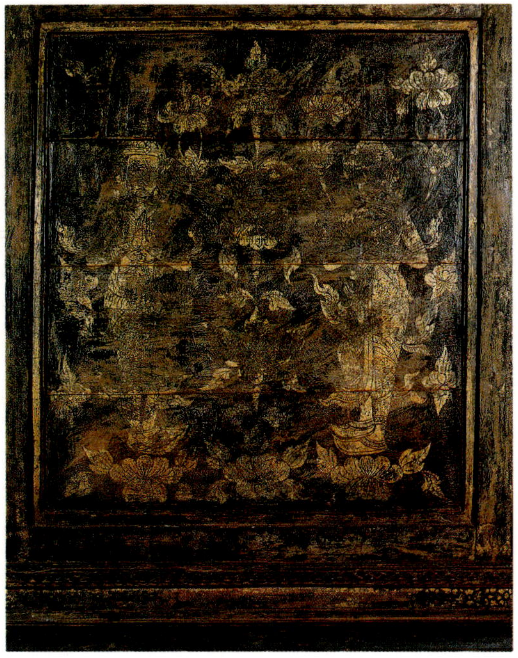

Temple Sculptures

Thailand, 18th and 19th centuries, wood, mirrored glass, and gilt, lengths 92 inches (dragon) and 108 inches (fish); heights 56 inches (18th century bird) and 72 inches (19th century bird).

TEMPLE SCULPTURES such as these four from Thailand were created to satisfy Theravada Buddhist requirements for piety and were displayed in various ways at monasteries, either on top of long masts or in association with the temple's altar and ritual gongs. These sculptures differ in subject and style from other Thai art in the Mauna Kea collection because they demonstrate the interest that arose in the eighteenth and nineteenth centuries, in Bangkok and other cultural centers, in art and architecture of Chinese style (*chinoiserie*). Works of this style were highly ornate, reflecting Thai interpretations of Chinese taste.

Two sculptures are based on the Chinese phoenix, the Feng-huang, a composite creature that is part peacock and part pheasant. In Imperial China, the Feng-huang was associated with royalty and eventually became the traditional symbol of the Chinese empress. It is likely that the link to royalty led to the Feng-huang's serving as a kind of Chinese surrogate for the Indian Garuda, the divine bird-man that is featured in Hindu stories as a vehicle for Vishnu and that eventually became a symbol of the Thai nation.

Just as the Feng-huang was a symbol of the Chinese empress, the mythic dragon was a symbol of the emperor. Rather than an evil or frightening creature, the Asian dragon is an auspicious, revered mythic beast of the heavens. The lithe and sinuous dragon in the Mauna Kea collection is nearly eight feet long and is displayed on its original tripodal support. During the recitation of Buddhist sutras, a metal gong suspended from the dragon's protruding tongue was struck to punctuate the chanted teachings. The teakwood from which the dragon was carved is almost completely hidden by surface embellishments of black lacquer, gold leaf, and tiny pieces of inlaid mirrored glass. Glass is also used for the dragon's eyes and teeth.

Another large temple sculpture, a nine-foot-long fish, is similar both in its decoration of inlaid mirrored glass on a gilt, teak body and in its function at the altar. This fish was carved so that its mouth grasps a red sphere, nominally a pearl, that stands for the luminous jewel of wisdom that Buddhists hope to attain. A gong would have been suspended from this pearl for use during ceremonies.

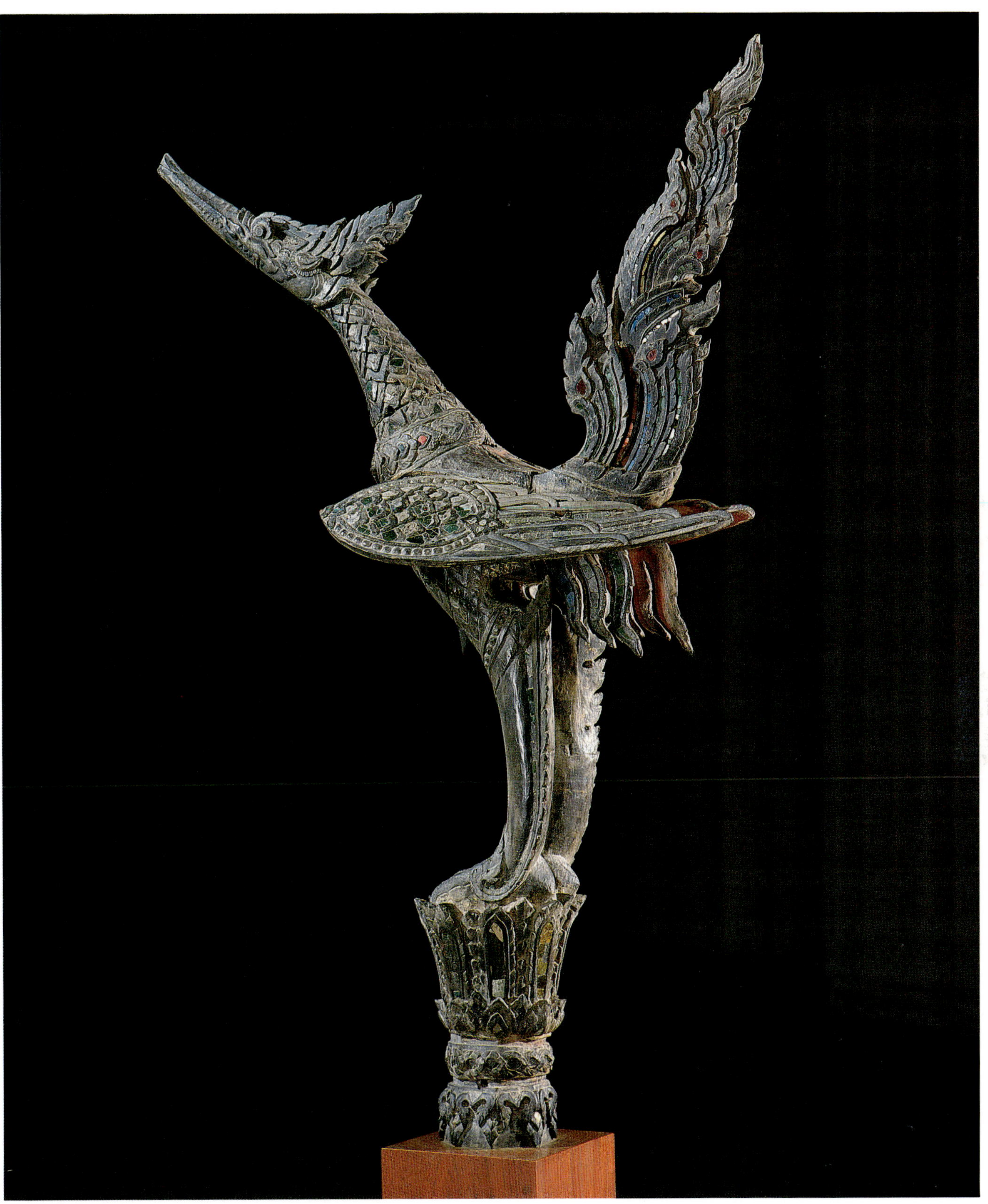

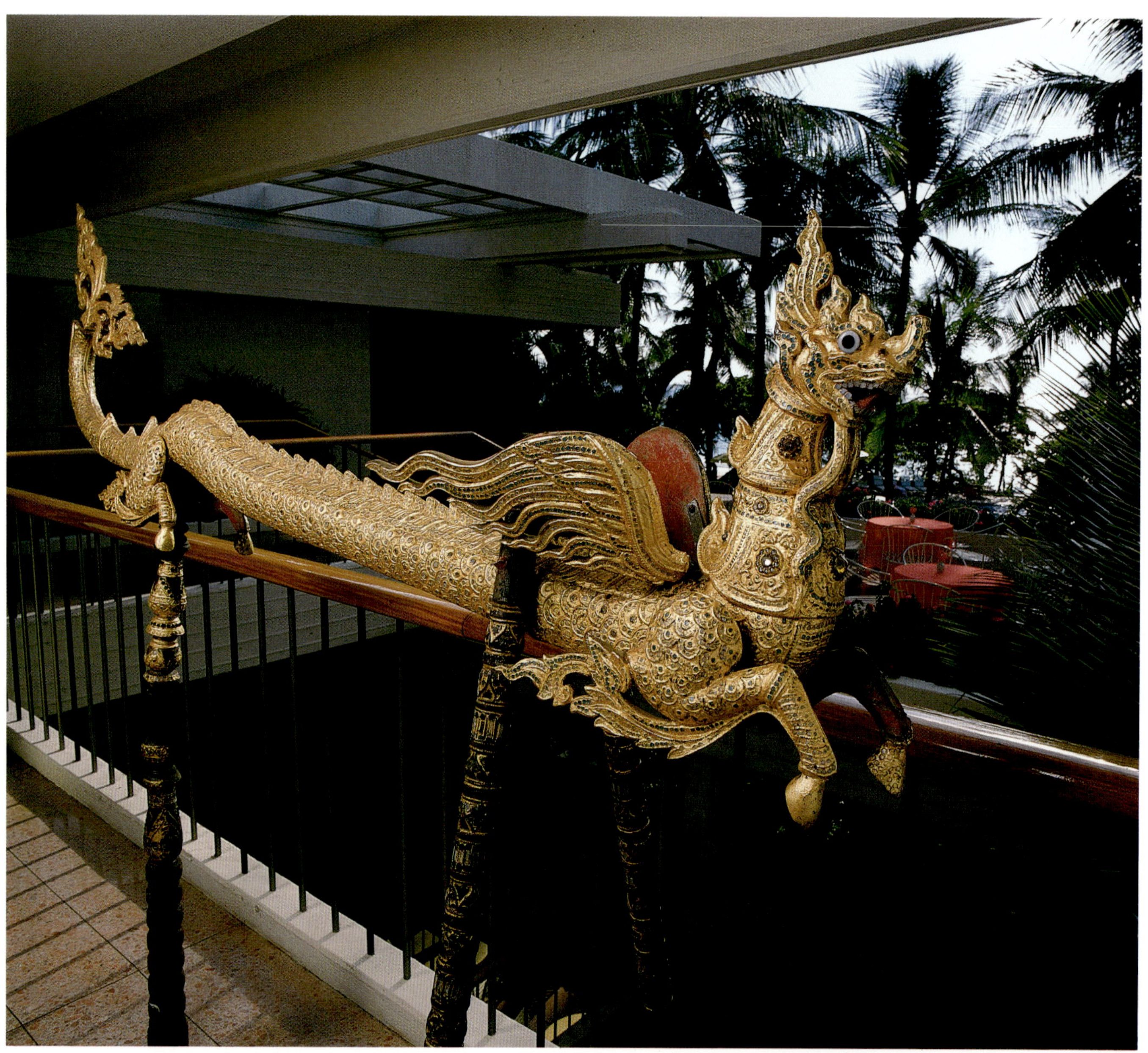

This nearly eight-foot-long dragon, created in Thailand as a temple offering, illustrates the sense of fantasy that arose during the eighteenth and nineteenth century Bangkok period as a result of Chinese influence. A gong was once suspended from the dragon's protruding tongue.

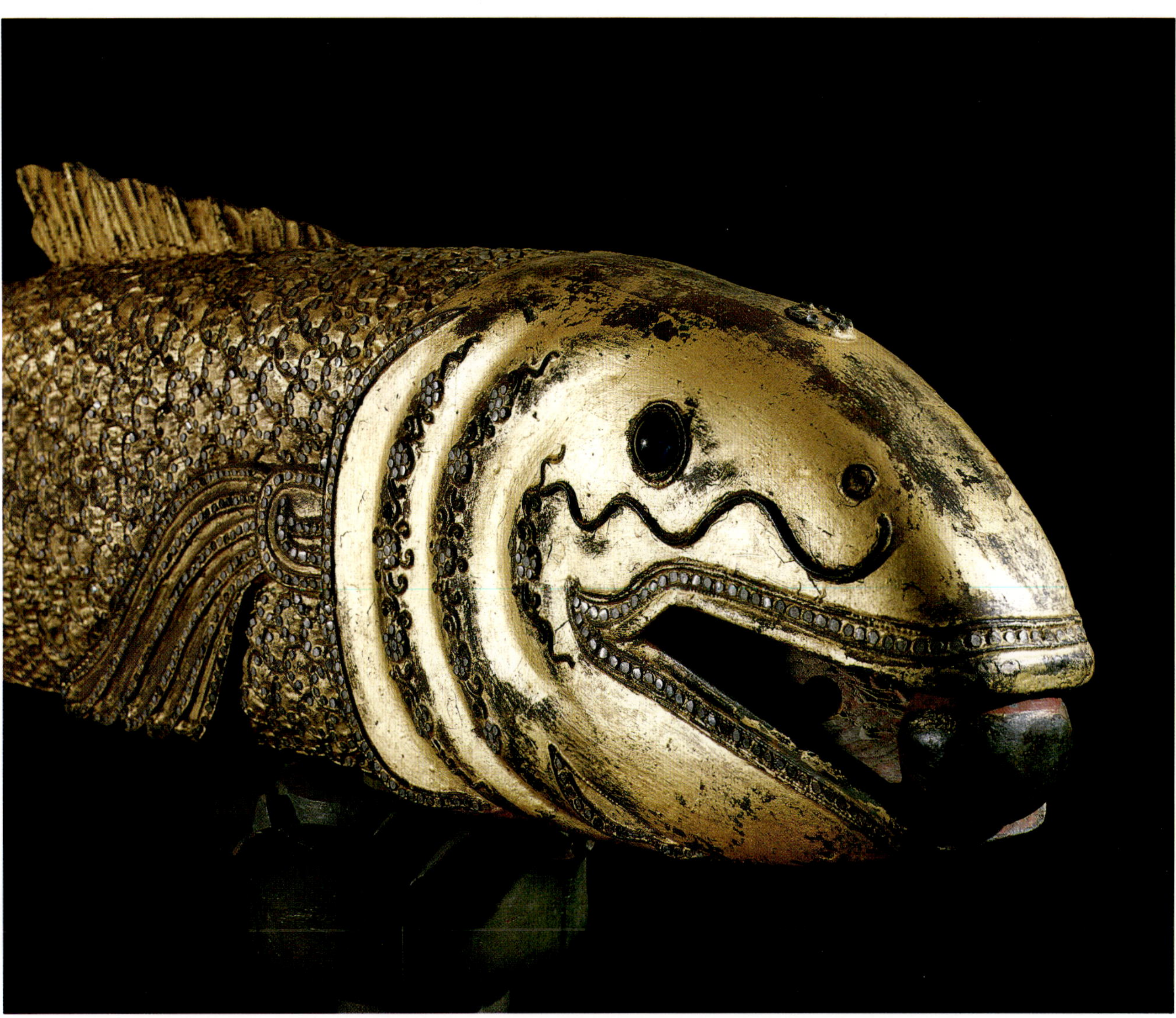

The red "pearl" captured in the mouth of this late-eighteenth-century Thai carp alludes to the jewel of wisdom—the enlightment—sought by Buddhists. Carp are often featured in temple decoration because their reproductive capacity makes them an auspicious symbol of regeneration.

Betel Nut Containers

Thailand, 19th century, lacquered wood, height 46 inches.

PRIOR to its acquisition for the Mauna Kea's collection, Thai craftsmen created this sculptural unit by combining four visually related betel nut containers. All four are Bangkok-style, late-nineteenth-century receptacles, carved or turned on a lathe and then lacquered in red, black, and gold. They bear curvilinear floral ornamentation and are fine representations of Thai lacquerware.

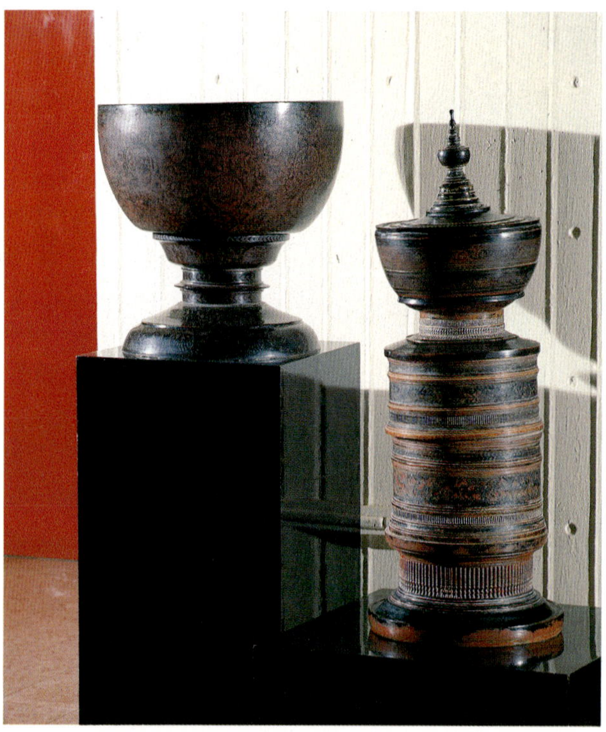

The Mauna Kea's pedestal bowl (left) and betel nut containers (right) exemplify the distinct Thai style in use of lacquer. The lacquer medium originated in China and was adapted by the Thai to serve the unique artistic style of their culture.

Like the preparation and use of snuff a century ago in the West, the chewing of betel nut traditionally involves a series of steps, tools, and containers. These vessels once would have stored the nuts themselves (fruit of the betel palm, *Areca catechu*); leaves of the betel pepper vine (*Piper betle*), in which to wrap the nuts; tobacco, lime, and cloves; and implements for cutting the nuts into small pieces. Used in Southeast Asia since at least the thirteenth century, as reported in one of Marco Polo's travel diaries, the aromatic and astringent fruit is known to have somewhat intoxicating and stimulant properties. The early explorer and other Europeans who witnessed the chewing of betel nut were distressed by the red lips, red saliva, copious expectoration, and blackened teeth of the practitioners.

Pedestal Bowl

Thailand, 19th century, dry lacquer, height 24 inches.

DISPLAYED adjacent to the betel nut containers is an impressive "pedestal" bowl constructed by means of a distinctly Thai variation of an ancient Chinese dry lacquer technique. In China, countless layers of lacquer-soaked cloth, ending with silk, were stretched over a clay or wood core that could be removed afterwards. A lacquer-paste coat, modeled to give a smooth surface, formed the final layer. This laborious technique was especially useful for creating huge, lightweight sculptures that could function as portable icons in ritual processions, especially in Buddhist ceremonies. To produce Thai lacquerware, such as the Mauna Kea's red and black bowl, craftsmen inventively transformed this process by using a woven wicker framework as the support and overlaying it with multiple sheets of paper dipped in lacquer (in lieu of cloth). The floral design on the surface was incised on the smooth final layer of lacquer paste before colored lacquer decoration was applied. It is believed that this dry lacquer material and technique preserved the bowl from damage by termites and other insects.

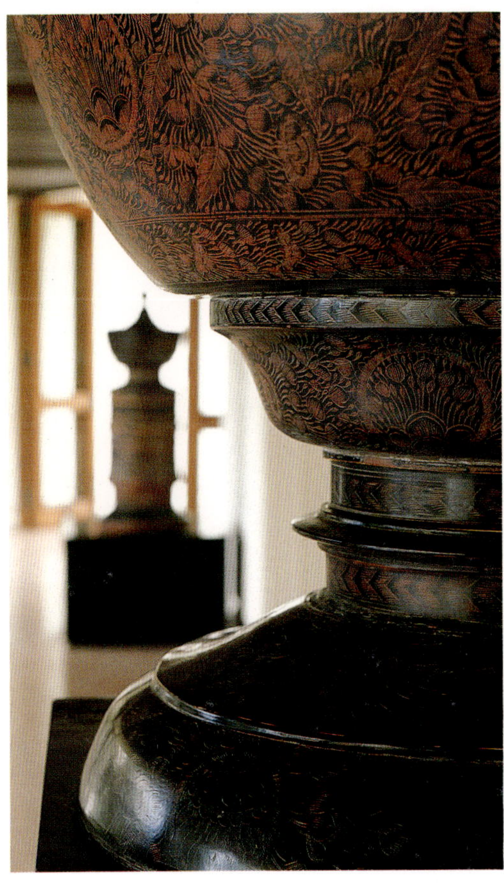

Thai craftsmen used red, black, and sometimes gold lacquer to decorate containers and bowls. They prepared their colors from mineral and earth pigments imported from China in powdered form from the eighteenth century on; cinnabar produced this deep red hue.

Crouching Goat

Thailand, late 19th century, painted and lacquered wood and metal, height 15 inches.

THIS RED GOAT with white, metal horns originally crouched at the entry of a provincial Buddhist temple. There, monks stepped on the goat before entering the sacred precinct of the assembly hall, thereby transferring their sins onto it. Like the votive offerings from India, this sculpture was probably an offering to the temple, and the selection of a goat image may have been a way to identify the donor. Most probably its patron was born in the Year of the Goat, the seventh stage in the twelve-year zodiacal cycle.

While many aspects of Western culture had entered Thailand long before this sculpture was created, there is no evidence of Western influence in this work. Rather, it is a fascinating example of folk art emanating from Thai animist superstitions. Coincidentally, there is a Biblical scapegoat (Leviticus 16.20): on the Day of Atonement, the high priest will transfer the sins of the people to the scapegoat by laying his hands on it; afterward, the goat will be driven into the wilderness to carry away those sins.

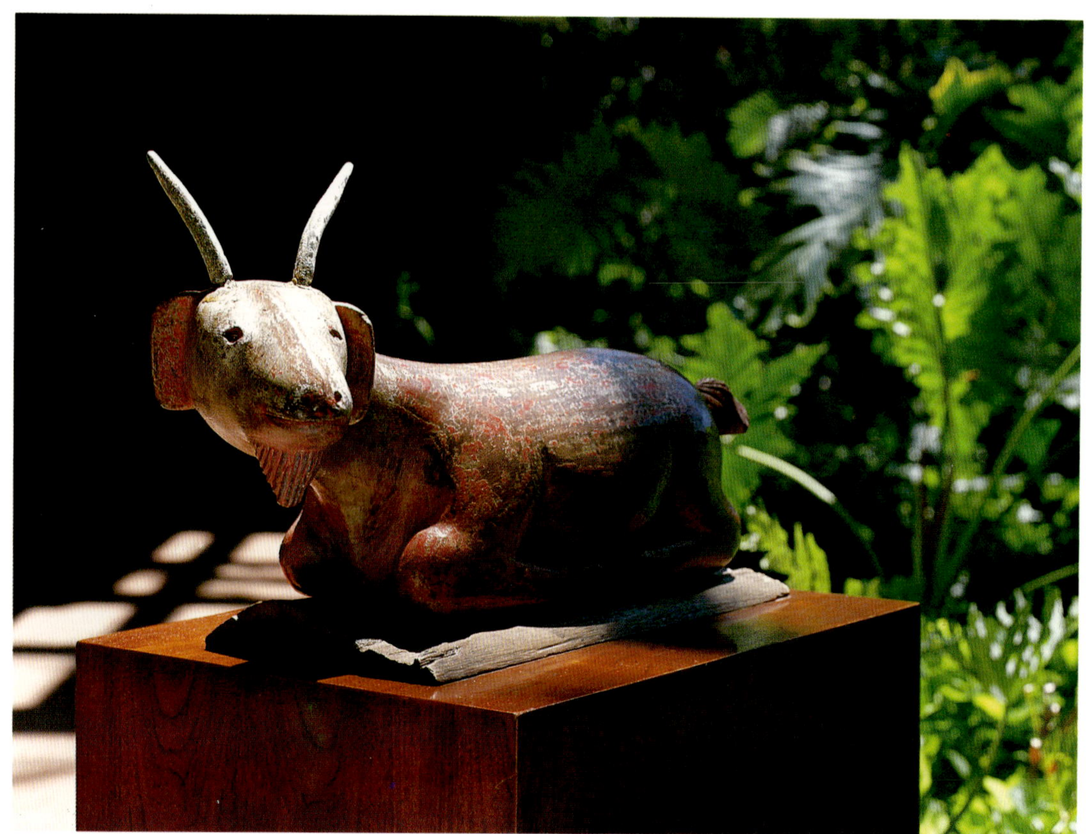

Thai Guardian Pair

Thailand, 19th/20th century, bronze with mirrored glass, height 62 inches.

PERMANENTLY installed at the promenade entry to the Beachfront Wing of the resort, these bronze sculptural "guardians" were cast by the *cire perdue* method, and their richly patinated surfaces glitter with polychrome mirrored glass mosaic. The figures come from the northernmost region of Thailand, near Chieng Mai, and their postures, symbolic of constant vigilance, suggest they were created to commemorate a military victory. These and many other works were removed from royal structures and monasteries in the vicinity of Chieng Mai during the 1960s, when construction of vast dams and irrigation systems threatened to submerge the buildings that housed them.

These fantastic winged creatures with leonine bodies derive from West Asian sources, as do the winged lions that appear in Christian arts by the fifth century. In the West, the winged lion has served as a symbol of the evangelist St. Mark and of the city of Venice. In Asia, as early as the third century B.C., the lion frequently represented the royal birth of the Buddha (another of his honorific names was Shakyasimha, the Lion of the Shakya Clan). The modeling of the earliest Indian lions was influenced by Persian conventions rather than inspired by observation of the animal itself, with the result that they were often depicted with wings. From India, the tradition of the winged lion passed to China, where the mythic and increasingly abstract and fantastic beasts were understood as Buddhist "Defenders of the Doctrine" and set up to guard the entry of temples. Winged lions also became symbols of royalty, fusing with the older Chinese royal symbol of the winged dragon.

The Mauna Kea's guardians are more closely related to Chinese lion forms than to Indian ones, and perhaps they arose from non-Buddhist images of the *Qi Lin* (also spelled *Ch'i-Lin*; in Japanese, *Kirin*), a mythic creature of remote antiquity, leonine, with a dragon's head and flame-like appendages from its shoulders. In China this creature was sometimes used to convey traditional ideas of yin and yang, representing the unity of male and female principles. These bronze guardians bear dragon heads, fierce expressions, and wings, and they are differentiated sexually by their genitalia, implying a perfect unity and enhancement of their protective roles. Unlike the *Qi Lin*, however, which was usually depicted with cloven hoofs (and sometimes horns), these sculptures have claws.

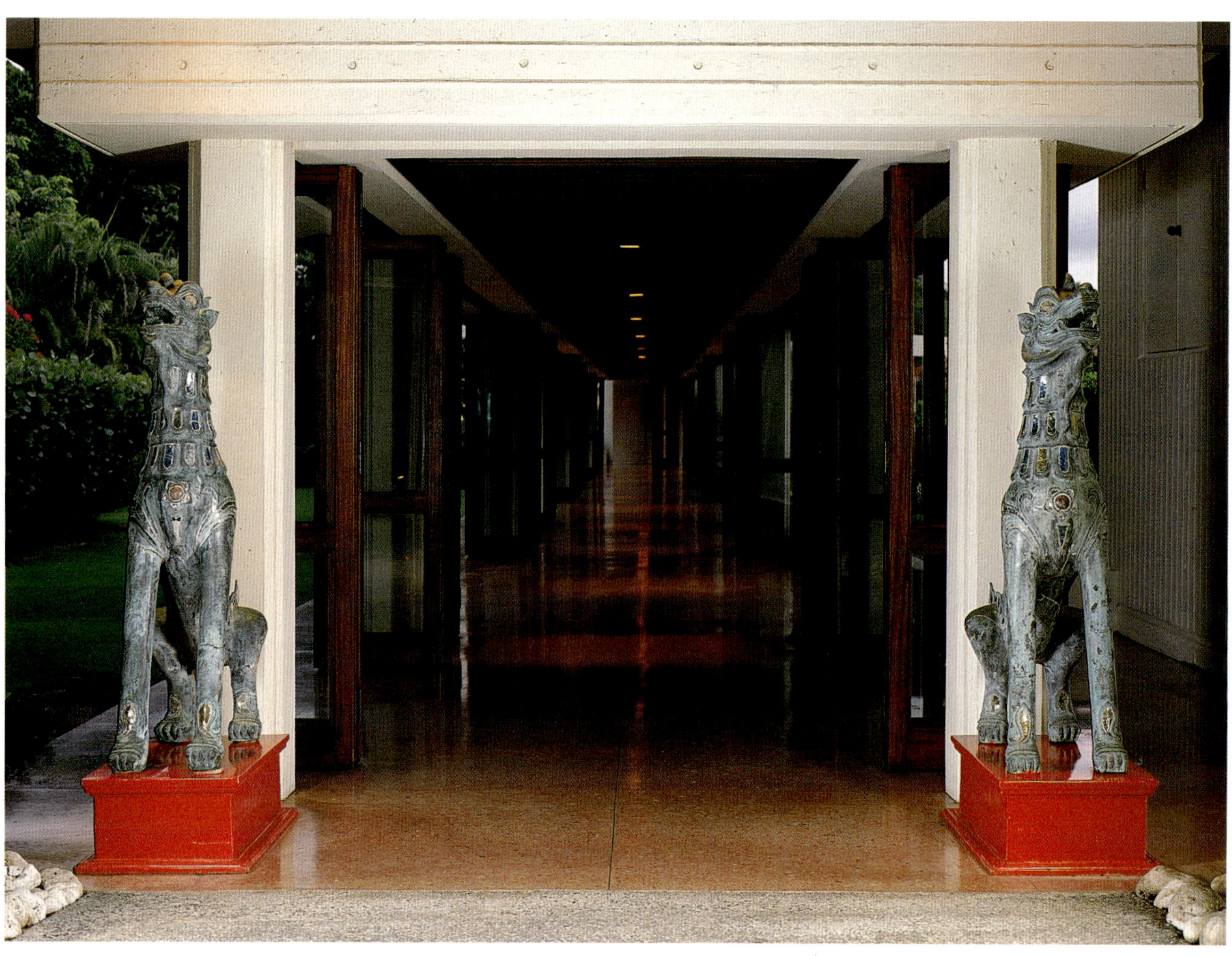

The Mauna Kea's monumental "winged lion" guardians flank the entry to the Beachfront Wing. This addition, completed in 1968, was planned by the architectural firm Wimberly, Whisenand, Allison, Tong and Goo, with Peter Wimberly in charge of design. The firm also designed the eighth floor of the main building, which was completed in 1973. Both additions continue the style established by the hotel's original structure.

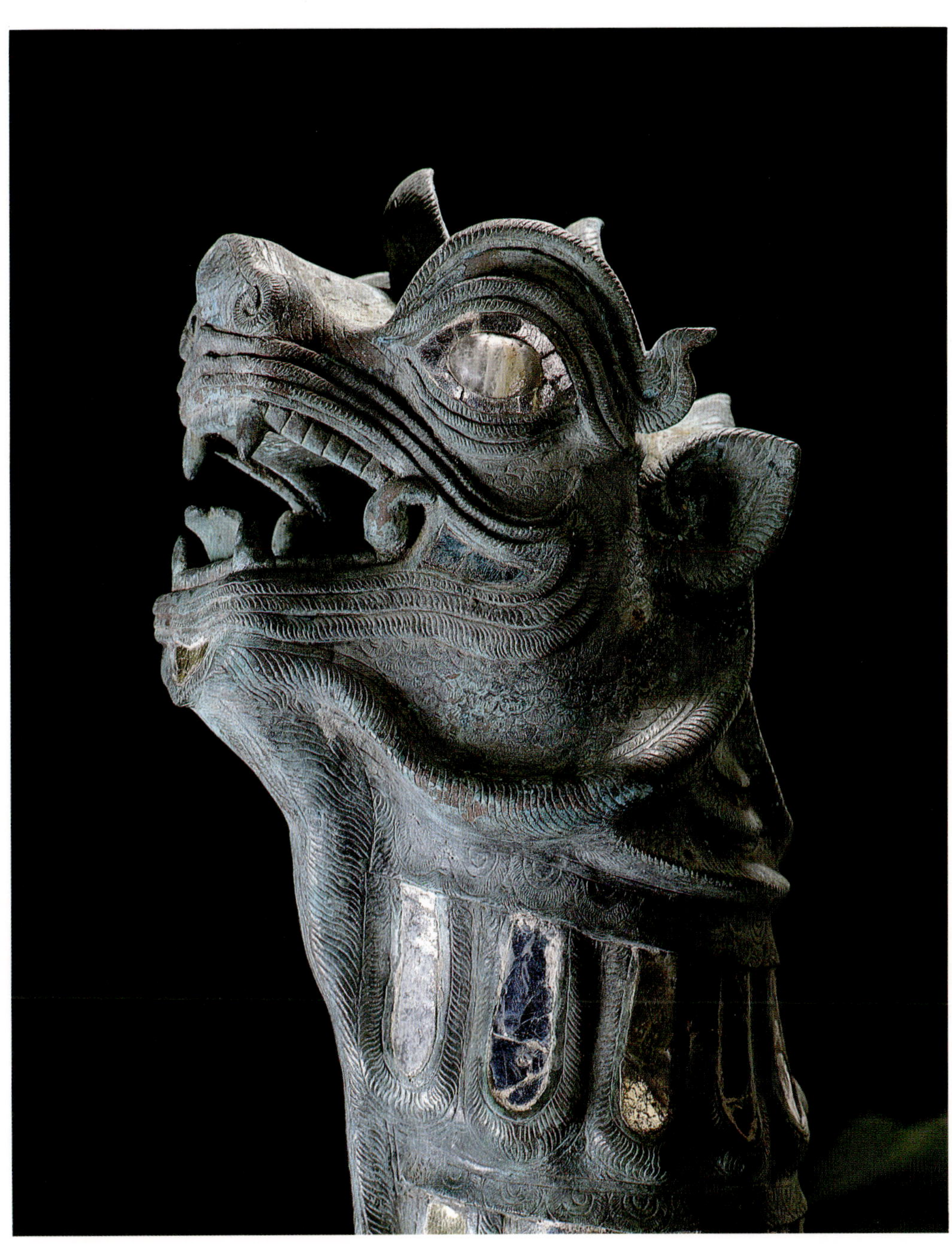

CHINA AND JAPAN

WHILE the impact of Chinese art, culture, and taste is reflected in works of many cultures in the Mauna Kea collection, the collection holds only a limited selection of Chinese works of art. This is the result of Rockefeller's acquisition plan, which was to collect works of art for the resort only from their countries of origin. Unfortunately, at the time of hotel planning and construction, in the early 1960s, the political atmosphere in China was volatile—on the verge of the "cultural revolution"—making it difficult to travel there.

The Chinese have traditionally called their country the Middle Kingdom, perhaps in reference to their cultural independence and their crucial role in the development of culture in most Far Eastern countries. Over the course of its long and complex history, China's political and cultural influence has extended to encompass most of central and eastern Asia, including parts of Korea, Manchuria, Mongolia, East Turkestan, and Tibet. Unified by their written language, despite their many spoken dialects, Chinese literary, religious, and philosophical traditions create a sense of consistency in the arts. While all arts are practiced in China, calligraphy and painting are usually considered superior to other forms. The Mauna Kea's Chinese furnishings convey the extraordinary artistic skills of the culture, showing how these skills were used to enhance even utilitarian objects. Chinese furniture designers were not only expert technicians and craftsmen but also serious artists who created works of high aesthetic quality.

Japanese culture has its earliest roots in indigenous animist beliefs that came to be known as Shinto. The Shinto religion revolves around ritualistic devotion to beneficent nature deities and worship of the emperor, who was considered a descendant of the Sun Goddess. Shinto ceremonies emphasize maintenance of ritual purity and seem remarkably similar to ancient Semitic views that were the source of Jewish, Christian, and Islamic ritual. When the literate and technologically advanced cultures of mainland Asia first entered Japan, via Korea, in the sixth century, it was through Buddhist missionary practice. These missionaries brought a Buddhism that had been transformed in China from Indian traditions. Suddenly, the insular, tribal, and aristocratic Japanese were exposed to the sophistication of civilizations thousands of years old. Buddhism subsequently became the dominant religion, although indigenous Shinto beliefs were maintained by adapting them to Buddhist concepts.

The Japanese works of art in the collection reflect the fusion of animistic and Mahayana Buddhist beliefs in an aristocratic culture. Shinto influence inspired respect of raw materials, such that artists strove to preserve rather than transform natural form, as if spirits still dwelt within their materials. These artistic ideas affected both Shinto and Buddhist cosmology. For instance, certain deities in the complex pantheon of Mahayana were equated with Shinto deities. Even the Buddha essence at the center of the universe, referred to as *Dainichi* ("Great Sun"), was considered an aspect of Shinto creation stories and a parallel to the Sun Goddess.

Unlike China, where three-dimensional arts were judged less expressive than the two-dimensional arts of calligraphy and painting, Japan has honored sculpture as a medium of fine art. Also, Japanese artists occasionally signed works of sculpture, ceramic, textile, lacquer, and other media, another notable difference from Chinese tradition.

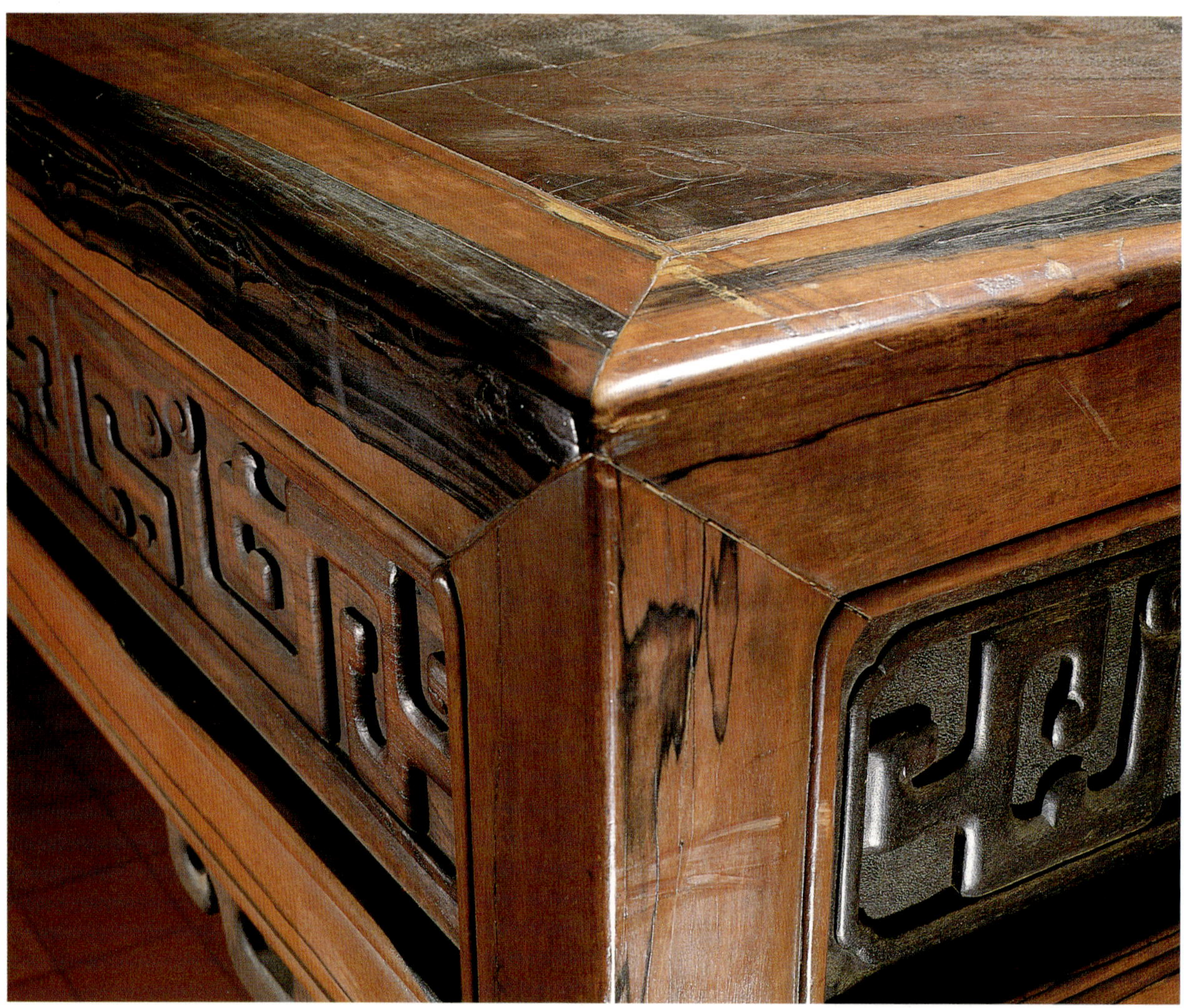

This detail photograph of an antique Chinese table shows the careful crafting of the table's mitred, box-like frame.

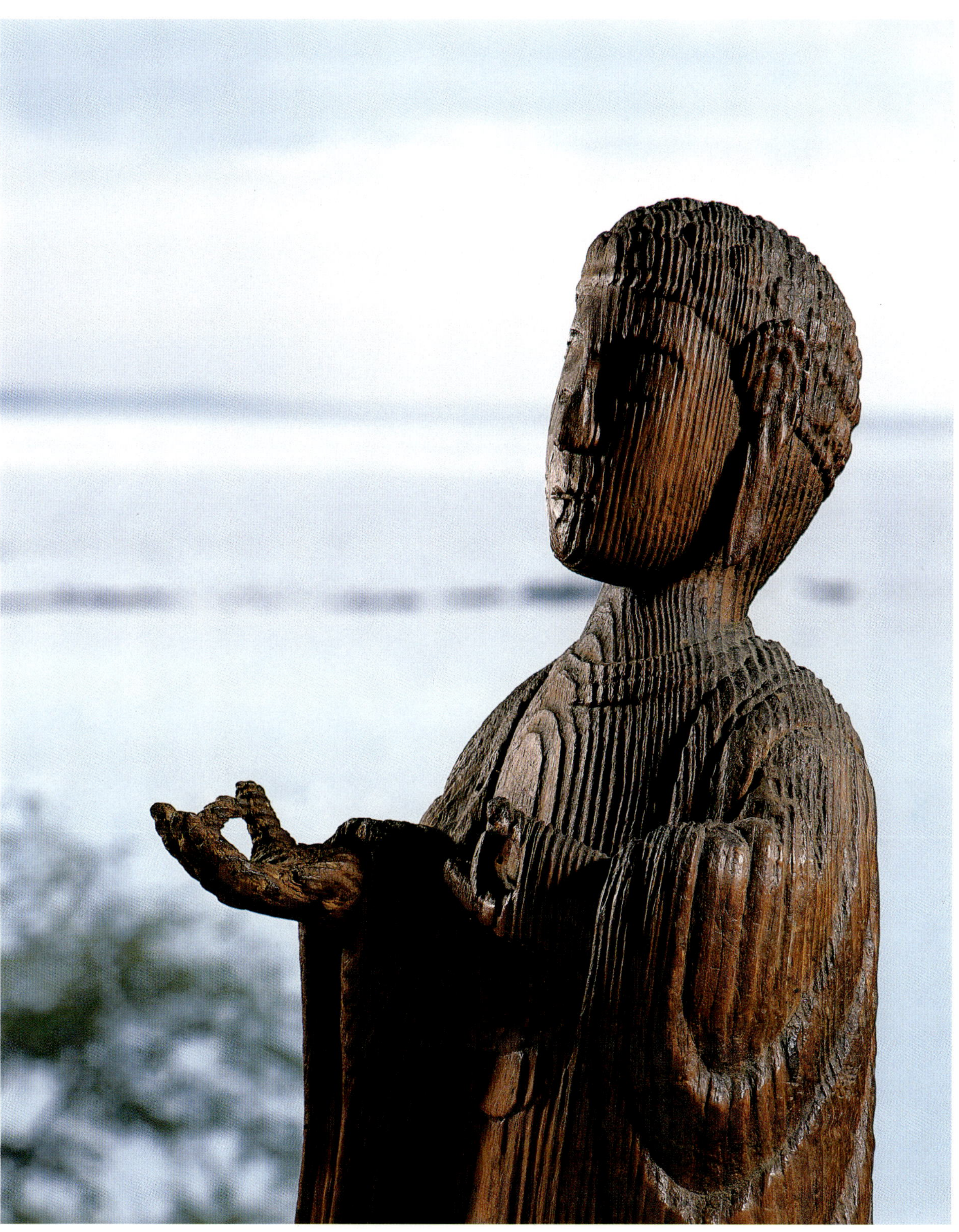

The rough carving style exemplified by this *circa* 1300 Japanese Buddhist sculpture was widely practiced in the Kamakura region of the country.

Altar/Scholar's Table

China, 18th/19th century, wood, height 44 inches, length 168 inches.

ONE of the many antique Asian furnishings in the collection, this large, oblong table of the late Qing dynasty retains the sculptural character of earlier Chinese furniture in that it resembles Chinese furnishings depicted in important paintings from the Song dynasty (A.D. 960–1279). The table's intricate joinery and elaborately carved decorations contrast with its simple hardwood frame, creating a balanced design.

The table's frame, an impressive fourteen feet in length, is made of a choice type of richly grained rosewood with lovely streakings and mottlings in the amber color most admired by the Chinese. The box-shaped frame surrounds rectangular apron panels carved in relief; connecting brackets are carved in swirls with ties tenoned into the frame. The brackets and apron pieces are teak, and the table top is constructed of a series of persimmon slabs. Several types of traditional joinery were used, including tongue-and-groove, dovetailed clamp, and miter, such that each part of the table seems organically connected to the next. The whole piece stands on solid, square legs that end in feet carved in a scroll form that Chinese cabinetmakers refer to as "horse-hoof."

The table's historical function has been debated. Its size, simplicity, and finish distinguish it from other Chinese altars of the period, which were usually more ornate, lacquered red, gold, and black, and decorated with metal trim. Inscriptions on the table's legs, however, indicate that at one time it was used as an altar, possibly in a grand private residence rather than a temple. Originally, it may have been made to serve a Chinese scholar as a library and viewing table. Its extraordinary length suggests this function, offering sufficient surface area for calligraphy and painting or for the display of handscrolls.

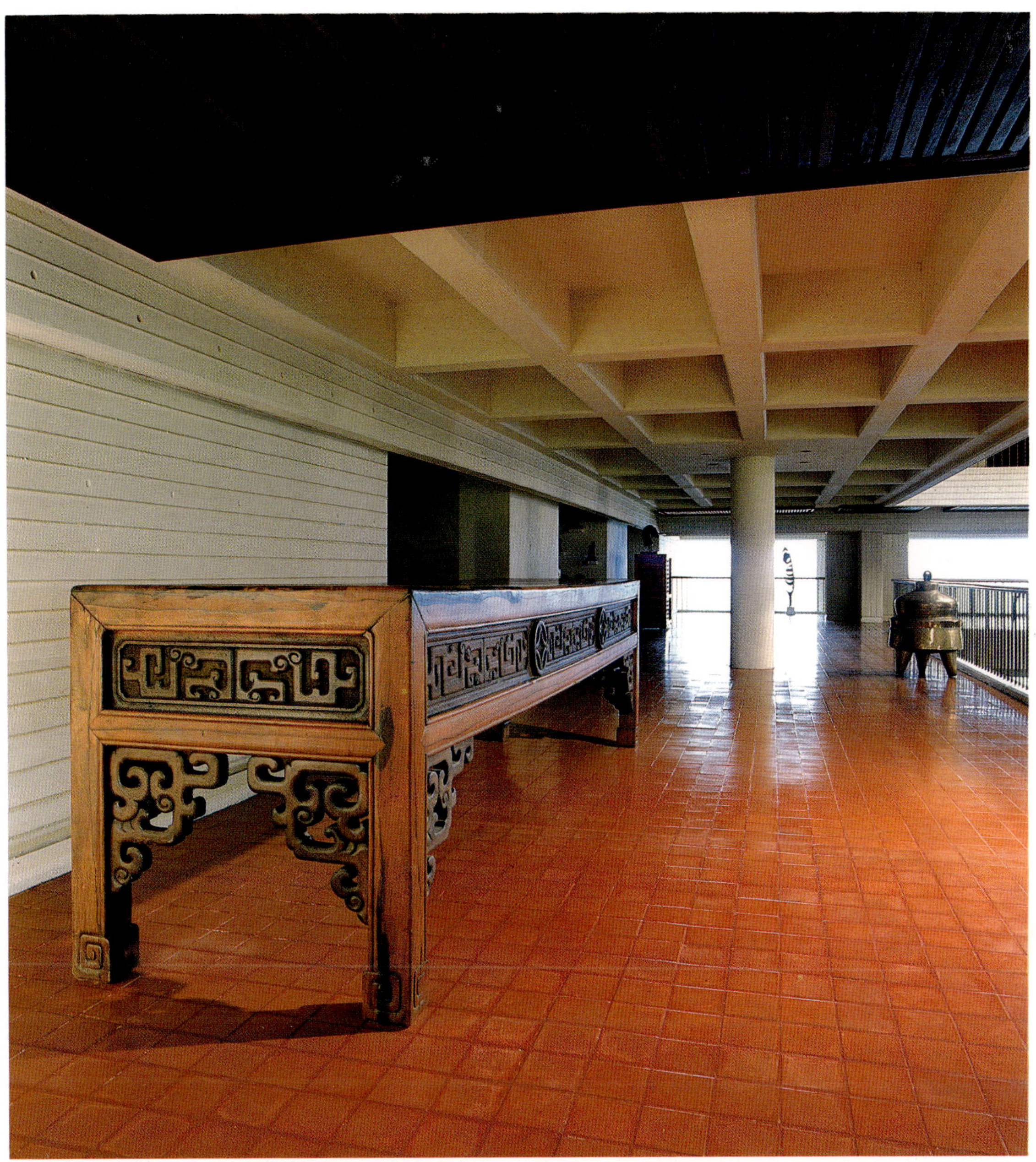

This huge table was constructed in the frame-and-panel technique that originated in ancient China, where it was also used in making chairs and sleeping platforms. Chinese characters inscribed at the base of two legs suggest that the table functioned as an altar at some point in its history.

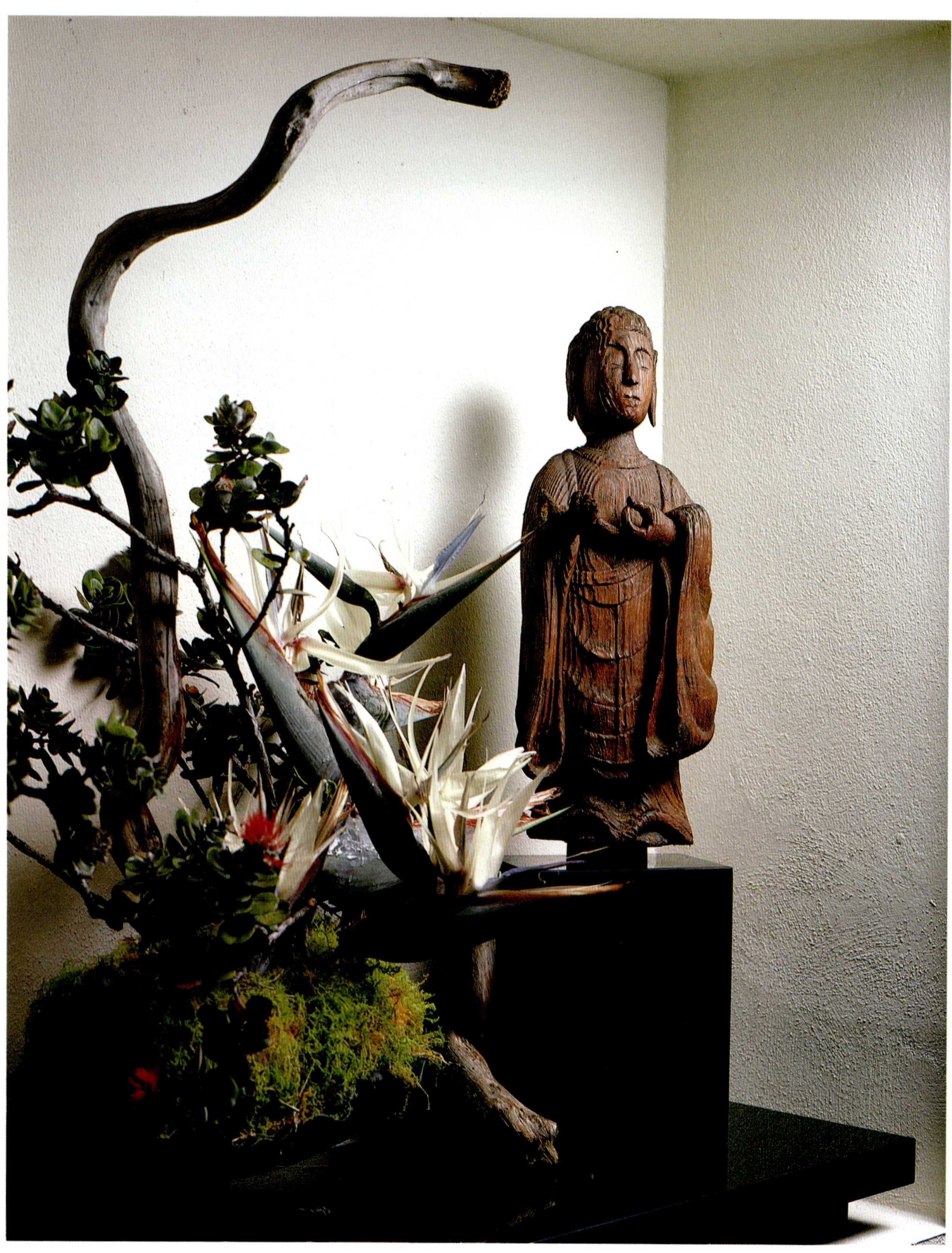

The Mauna Kea's Kamakura-period sculpture is displayed in a niche in the main lobby that derives from the *tokonoma*, the aesthetic and spiritual center of the Japanese house in which a work of art and a flower arrangement typically appear. The floral design was created by Barbara Meheula, the resort's director of decorative arrangements.

Buddhist Sculpture

Japan, *circa* 1300, wood, height 25 inches.

THIS small but impressive Buddhist statue is the earliest work in the Japanese collection; it was carved during the Kamakura period (A.D. 1185–1333) when, incidentally, rule by shogunate first developed. The unpainted statue's style belongs to a Japanese sculptural tradition that began before the Kamakura and before the development of Zen Buddhist sects. Nevertheless, its rough texture and emphasis on wood grain corresponds to Zen (Chinese: Ch'an; Sanskrit: Dhyana, meaning "meditation") delight in artifice that appears natural, a feature of Zen art in the tea ceremony as well as in garden design. Rippling grains in the wood are artistically carved patterns that seek to appear natural. Even chisel marks are allowed to remain in the rough-hewn *arabori* style of carving displayed in this sculpture.

While the figure was perhaps intended to represent Shakyamuni, the absence of clearly defined *lakshana* (there is no *ushnisha* or *urna*) suggests other possible identifications. For example, the figure's hands are raised in front of his chest in the *dharmacakra mudra*, the gesture of teaching, or turning the Wheel of the Law of the Buddha. This *mudra* occasionally was used to depict a revered Buddhist patriarch or priest. This association is strengthened by the figure's garment, a robe with long sleeves that reach nearly to its feet. The lack of well-defined facial features suggests that the sculpture commemorates the character of a deceased patriarch or priest rather than a living master. Images created posthumously used posture and emotive association, rather than a precise visual record of countenance, to express character. Thus in this sculpture the head is slightly tilted but erect, conveying alertness through its upward movement; the lips are pursed in a thinly carved line, as if about to address disciples. The relatively coarse and immediate style of the sculpture suggests it was not created by a professional artist but more likely by a devoted disciple.

Documentation of the sculpture's creation is unfortunately too vague to determine whether the image is of Shakyamuni or of a Zen patriarch or priest. The form, style, and expression of this work, however, typify the brusque Zen style that had significant impact on Japanese arts of later periods.

Japanese Guardian Pair

Japan, *circa* 1500, wood, height 19½ inches.

LEONINE guardian sculptures from the Muromachi period (A.D. 1334–1573) stood in the Japanese Imperial Palace as well as in temples and shrines. Large, bronze guardians typically were positioned at entryways. The Mauna Kea's pair of wooden guardians, however, served inside a temple. It is likely they were stationed near the inner sanctuary as weights to hold aside altar curtains. Guardian sculptures such as these were often commissioned by a group of donors as votive offerings to a shrine.

During the Muromachi period, the Ashikaga family created a new hereditary shogunate, returned the seat of government to the city of Heian (present-day Kyoto) from Kamakura, and continued the patronage of the arts. The pair of temple guardians at the Mauna Kea are excellent examples of arts of the period and of revived interest in Chinese subjects, the result of renewed contact with China following Chinese expulsion of the Mongols. While their subject is clearly a revival of Chinese iconography, these pieces evidence Japanese enthusiasm for arts displaying exaggerated expression—especially grotesqueries—popular since ancient times when bizarre masks enlivened court dramas. The skillfully conceived grimacing faces of these guardians reflect this interest. At one time, both works were painted in polychrome, which would have heightened the guardians' ferocious bearing.

The creation of leonine guardian pairs was guided by precise iconographic conventions seen in these examples: one has a horned head and an open mouth, the influence of continental chimera-like subjects; the other is without a horn, its mouth scowling but closed. This fifteenth century pair display a certain severity; works of the seventeenth and eighteenth centuries were more playful.

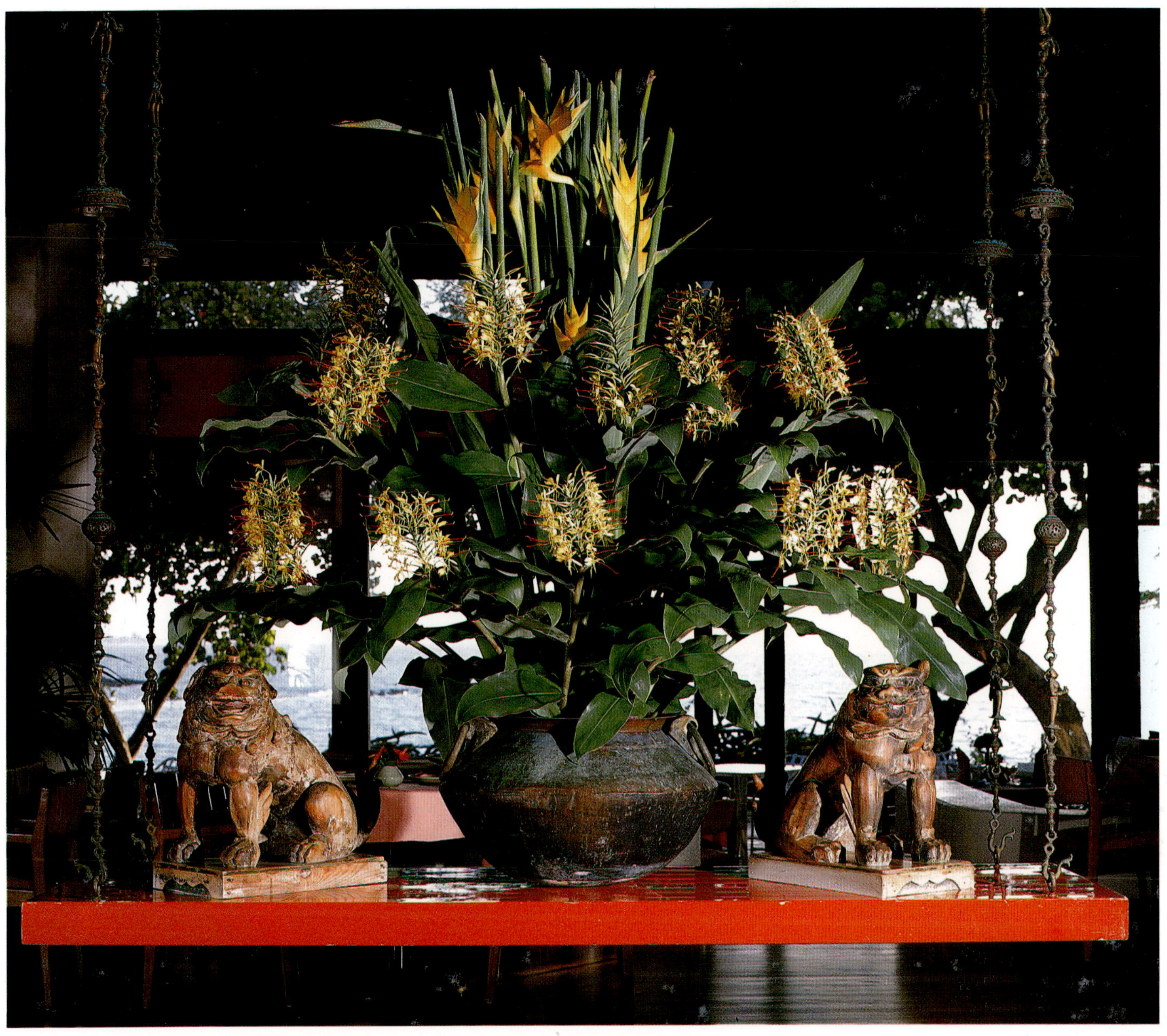

While they once held back altar curtains in a Buddhist temple, the resort's Japanese guardians now perch on a lacquered platform in the Pavilion restaurant. A brass figural chain from India suspends the platform from the ceiling. (Floral arrangement by Barbara Meheula.)

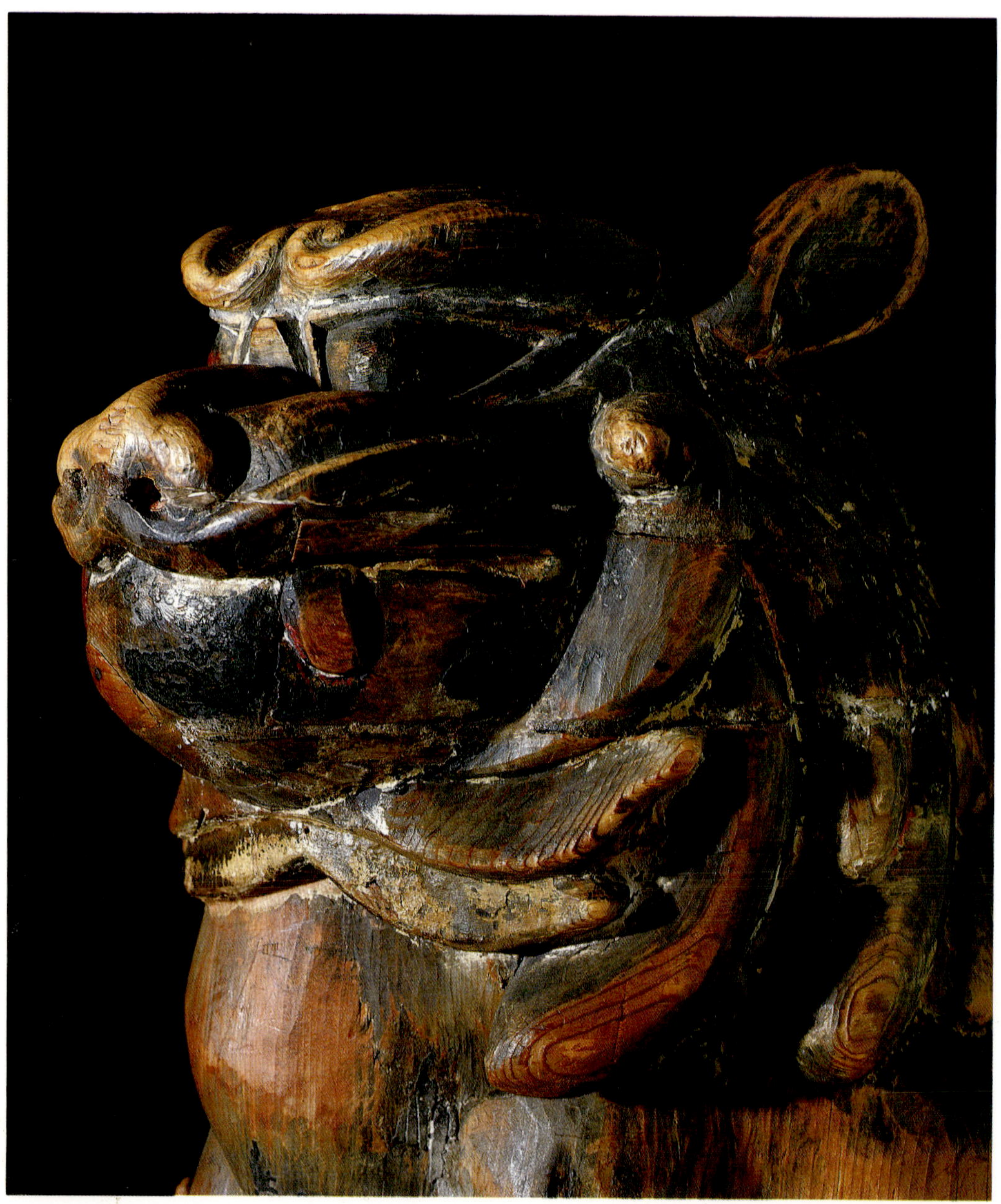

The head of this small, *circa* 1500 wooden guardian shows traces of the sculpture's original polychrome decoration. Unlike larger stone and metal guardian lions commissioned by aristocrats, the Mauna Kea's images were probably donated to a shrine or temple as votive offerings of a group of commoners.

Votive Horse Figures

Japan, 18th century, wood and mixed media, heights 50 inches and 54 inches.

THESE horse sculptures possess a strikingly real presence, testimony to the importance of artistic illusionism in eighteenth century Japanese art. Juxtaposition of different materials accentuates the play on reality: the horses' bodies are carved and lacquered wood; the saddles and stirrups are metal, leather, and padded textiles; their hair is horsehair. And, like Buddhist sculptures centuries before, their eyes are carved crystal, painted on the back so that their gaze seems to shift with the viewer, enhancing the illusionistic effect. Many European artists learned from similar Japanese arts that they could conjure up new aspects of realistic illusion by combining materials to stress a real presence; Degas, for instance, draped a blatantly metallic ballet dancer in an actual chiffon tutu.

These horses were created during the Edo period (A.D. 1615–1868), when shoguns ruled from the then remote village of Edo (present-day Tokyo), ostensibly in the name of the emperor. The horses are votive temple offerings, likely made on behalf of children of

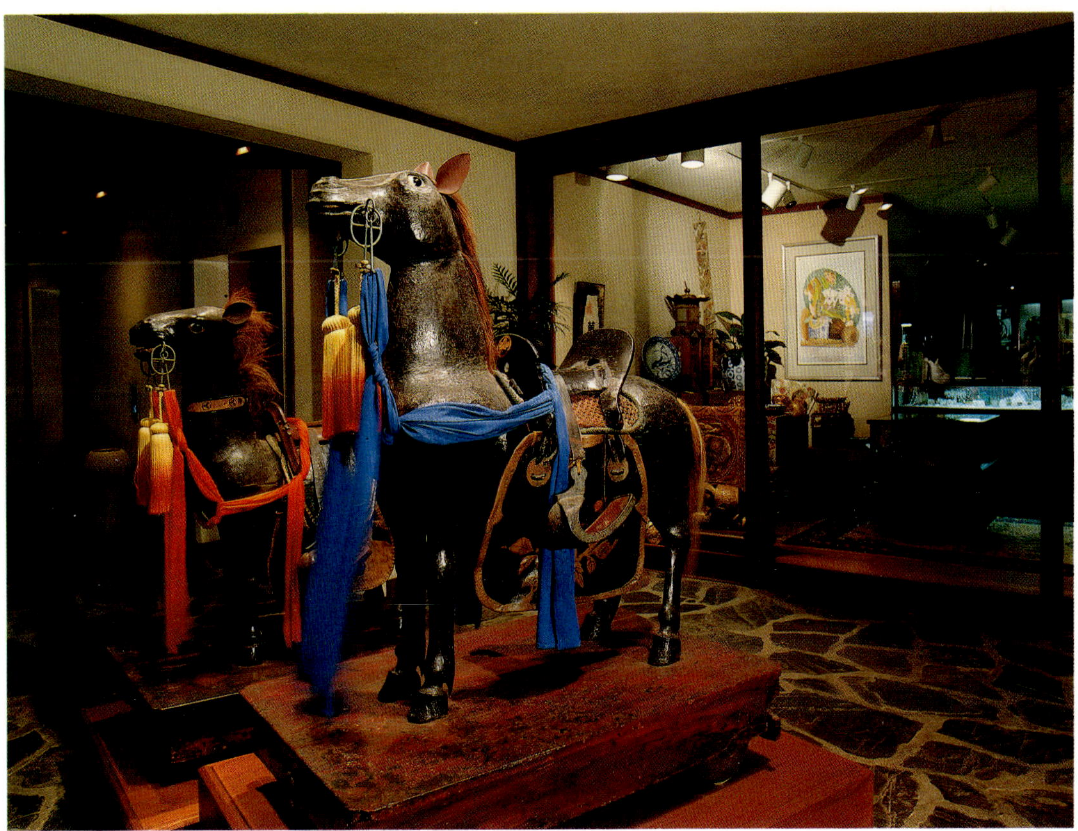

the aristocracy, and may have been ridden by children in parades and ceremonial processions. Both are equipped with wheels for this purpose.

The horse is a frequent and traditional subject in Japanese art, first seen in the fourth to sixth centuries A.D. on cylinders of clay (*haniwa*) that surrounded imperial tombs. Horses in funerary arts often appeared without riders, perhaps as magical surrogates for the live animals sacrificed in ancient rites to appease spirits of agricultural fertility. The popularity of the horse as a subject was revived during the Kamakura period when patrons of the arts from the warrior class commissioned equestrian works. During pageants, samurai warriors sometimes rode on ornate saddles created of lacquered wood with inlaid mother-of-pearl; trappings and other accessories were also important artistic productions. In the sixteenth and seventeenth centuries, renderings of well-groomed horses became a motif for monumental works of art, such as six-fold screens for feudal lords' castles.

Horse images also figured prominently in both Shinto and Buddhist arts during the Edo period. The Bodhisattva of mercy and compassion, Kannon, was sometimes presented as Bato (horse-headed) Kannon, her headdress surmounted by the figure of a horse, signifying her role as savior of all animals. In Shinto folk arts from the thirteenth century on, horses were featured on votive plaques or hanging scrolls, *Ema*, that decorated roadside shrines. (*Ema* literally means "horse pictures.") Sometimes such *Ema*, the offerings of commoners to various deities for farm productivity or successful animal husbandry, were suspended from eaves of provincial Buddhist temples. As an indication of the superior potency of horse images as votive offerings, the Japanese continue to refer to such arts as *Ema* even when the visual motif is not a horse.

Japanese Chests (*Tansu*)

Japan, 18th and 19th centuries, wood with lacquer, heights 31 to 59 inches.

AN EXTENSIVE group of furnishings in the resort collection comes from Japan. These works represent many types of domestic furniture and at the Mauna Kea serve as display pedestals for other objects, including *jizai* (page 100) and Buddhist sculptures. Some of the chests are relatively small, with multiple sections, and may have been used by Buddhist monks as cabinets for scriptures, Buddhist images, and a few personal possessions. These *tansu* are unpainted, their surfaces burnished to accentuate the wood grain and color. Other cabinets are quite large and likely were used in private residences of the upper class. Many of these chests were fitted with metal handles or with wheels. During the Edo period, fire was a constant threat in the capital city (now called Tokyo) and in other large cities built almost completely of wood, and the handles and wheels facilitated quick evacuation of possessions.

Several lacquered chests are also of particular interest. One large *tansu*, possibly used to store kimonos, has a pair of sliding doors painted in polychrome lacquer and gold (page 63). The paintings show panoramic landscapes seen from above, through cloud forms. One painting depicts a Buddhist temple compound, including the Kondo (or "golden hall"), where images were worshipped, and a multi-storied pagoda, which commemorated venerated relics. The other sliding panel depicts a feudal lord's grand castle rising on stone foundations and, across a body of water, a small roadside Shinto shrine marked by its free-standing gateway, the *torii*. That Buddhist and Shinto monuments should appear together is not unusual in Japan. Even today the owner of such a chest might maintain two adjacent shrines in his residence, one for Shinto rites and one for Buddhist.

Two other lacquered chests are fine examples of the prized Negoro lacquer technique, which originated at the Negoro temple in Wakayama province. Negoro lacquer is created by brushing many coats of black lacquer on finished wood, carefully smoothing each coat. Over this, a final lacquer coat is added in a deep vermillion hue, but here the brush strokes are intentionally brusque so that a hint of the black shows through, a subtlety that appeals to Japanese connoisseurs. Many types of furnishings and vessels were decorated in this manner for Buddhist monasteries as well as secular environments.

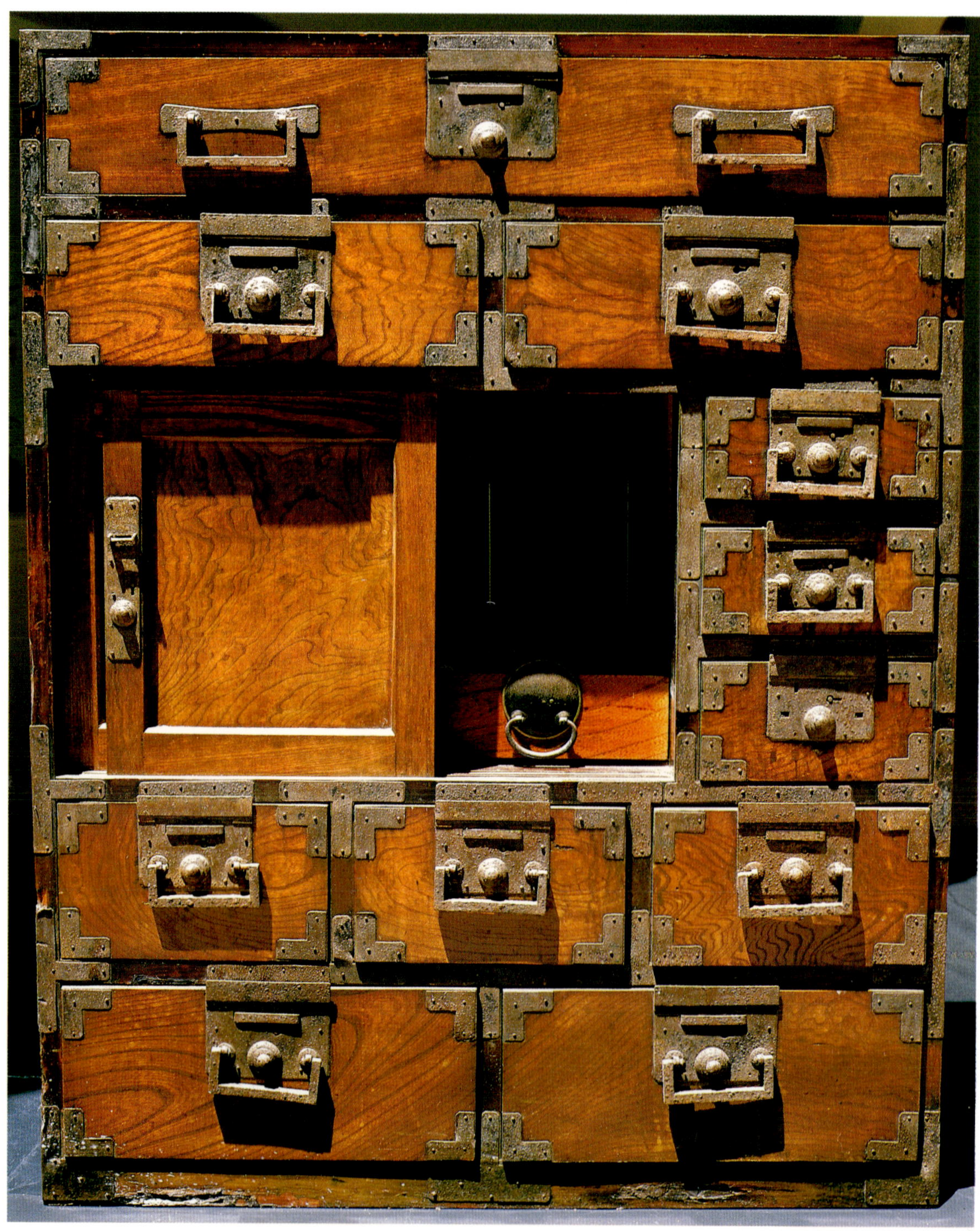

This eighteenth century Japanese *tansu* is well proportioned, skillfully executed, and beautifully finished—a display of fine cabinetry. The fine craftsmanship of metal decorations and the careful arrangement of drawer pulls, nail-head covers, and other hardware shows concern for detail in creating an overall aesthetic.

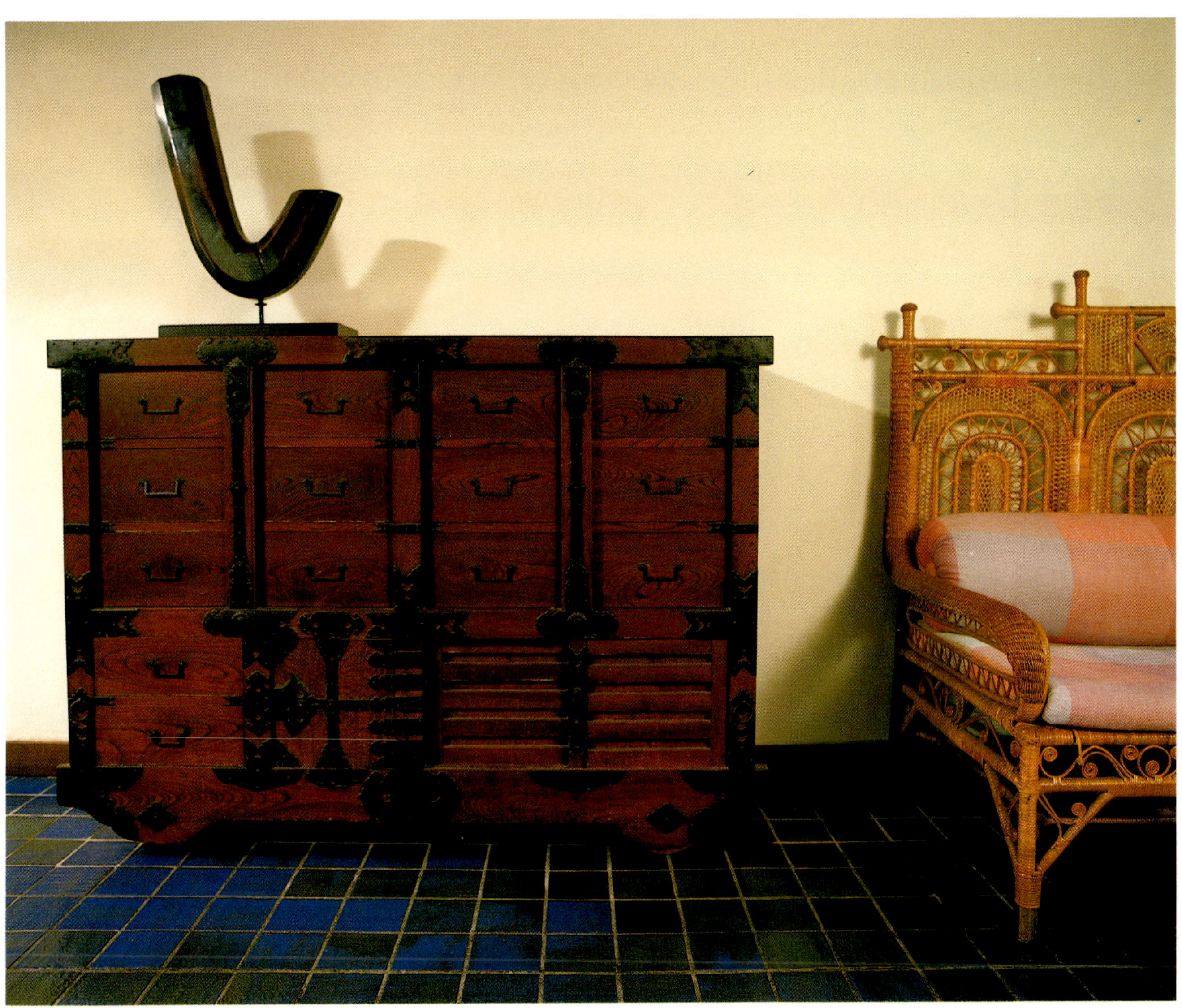

The wheels underneath this burnished *tansu* provided its original owner a means to move quickly in the case of fire, a serious threat in the wood structures of Japanese cities. The wood hook, called a *jizai*, was attached near the rafters in a home and used to suspend cooking pots over the hearth.

Head of a Rakan

Japan, early 19th century, wood, height 15 inches.

THE SUBJECT of this *hinoke* cypress sculpture of the late Edo period is a Rakan (Chinese: Lohan; Sanskrit: Arhat), a Buddhist patriarch, especially one associated with the original disciples of Shakyamuni. This Rakan's long earlobes identify him as a disciple of the Buddha and of the same high caste.

The head is a fine example of *yosegi* (joined-block technique), an ancient Japanese woodworking method seen in many works at the resort. When this method of laminated sculpture was first perfected in the eleventh century, it was predominantly used for creating huge Buddhist images that would otherwise have been impossible to carve from a single tree trunk because of the sculpture's planned height or girth. The technique is also pragmatic: a hollow, laminated sculpture reduces the possibility of the wood splitting because of fluctuations in temperature and humidity over time, a frequent problem with aged wooden sculptures carved from a single block. Five pieces of wood were joined in creating the Mauna Kea's head.

Yosegi sculptures tend to be the product of ateliers rather than the work of individuals. Since pieces were made separately and joined later, often many skilled apprentices produced individual sections—specializing in certain forms—under the supervision of one master sculptor. This system facilitated mass production of sculpture, and on occasion groups of Rakan were produced in numbers ranging from ten to five hundred. Extraordinarily accomplished master sculptors sometimes were granted honorific titles of rank by Buddhist temples. The skilled joinery of the head displayed at the Mauna Kea is evident on inspection of various areas, especially the clearly defined parietal and frontal bone sections, which are made from separate pieces of wood.

Art honoring Rakans appears in many Buddhist sects and was particularly popular with Zen Buddhists, as a Rakan is not a deity but a human whose achievement could be emulated. Rakans epitomized self-discipline, wisdom, and holiness. They were honored for achieving enlightenment through meditation and were believed to have had the ability to prolong their lives to serve the Buddha. Their portraits were therefore often found along the walls of Zen temples. Facial features in these renderings were sometimes grotesque or heavily proportioned, almost obese, like the Mauna Kea example. Such rotund images, invented by the Chinese and emulated by the Japanese, deviate from usual conventions for depicting spirituality, but in the iconography of China and Japan, an unattractive visage became a convenient symbol of an individual's achievement and nobility of character: the more respected the patriarch, the more the features departed from accepted norms of beauty. No irises or pupils are indicated in this image, as if their presence would suggest an involvement with the world of the senses rather than internal concentration.

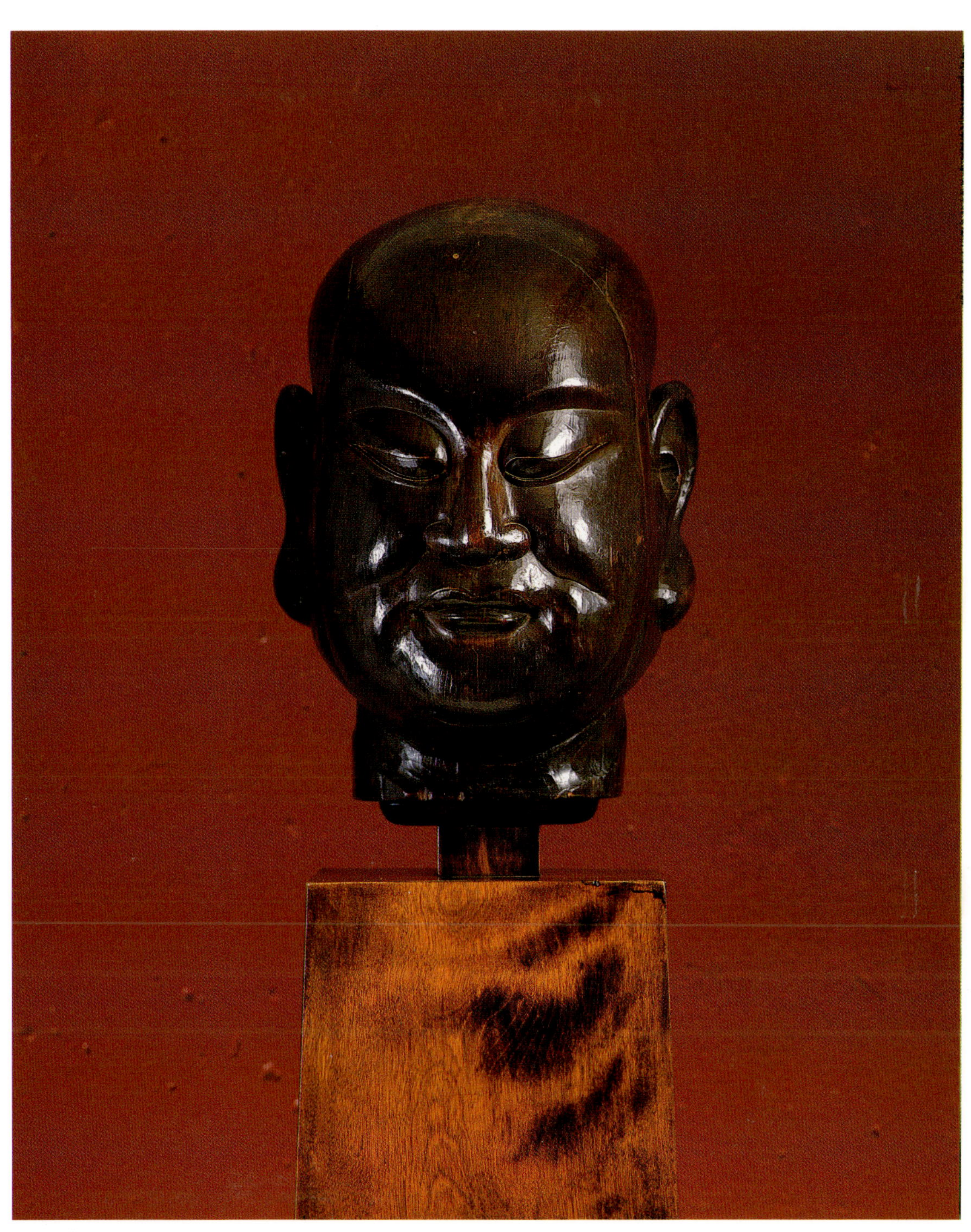

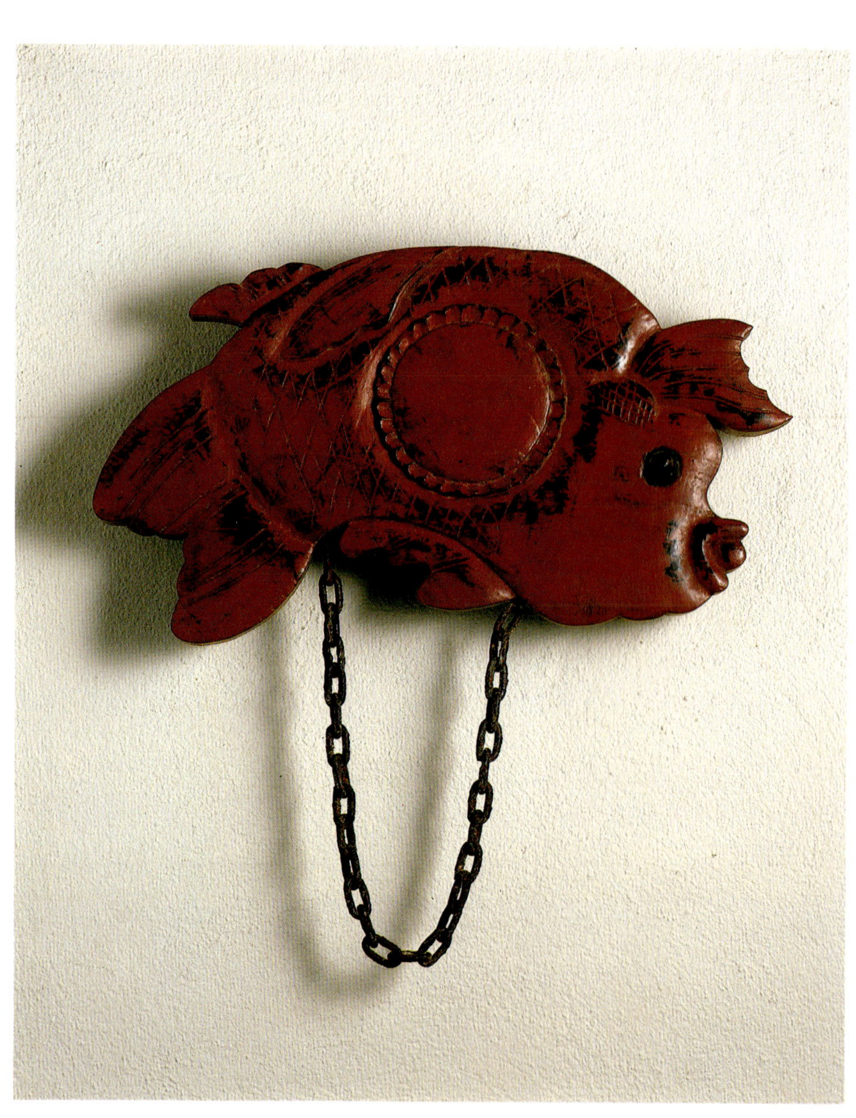

Gongs, Knockers, and Drum

Japan, 19th century, bronze and wood, heights 9 to 14 inches (gongs and knockers) and 24 inches (drum).

A NUMBER of nineteenth century Japanese works at the resort evince the island nation's continuing taste for Chinese art subjects, including the ubiquitous fish and the mythic dragon. These works include gate knockers, temple gongs, temple drums, and free-standing sculptures. Some are lacquered red, a propitious color favored by East Asian Buddhists.

The fish most frequently portrayed are the *tai* and *koi*. The *tai* (snapper) was associated with Ebisu, the popular household god of work and prosperity who originally may have been a Shinto spirit and was absorbed into Buddhist belief. *Tai* images appeared as tokens of gratitude at festivals celebrating successful fishing expeditions. Depictions of Ebisu (with a fishing pole in one hand and a large snapper in the other) were frequently carried on fishing boats. The wooden gate knockers in the collection depict *tai* in both realistic and abstract forms. Such knockers were struck with a mallet by visitors to a home to announce their arrival. The presence of *tai* at a home's entryway signified wishes of prosperity for resident and visitor alike.

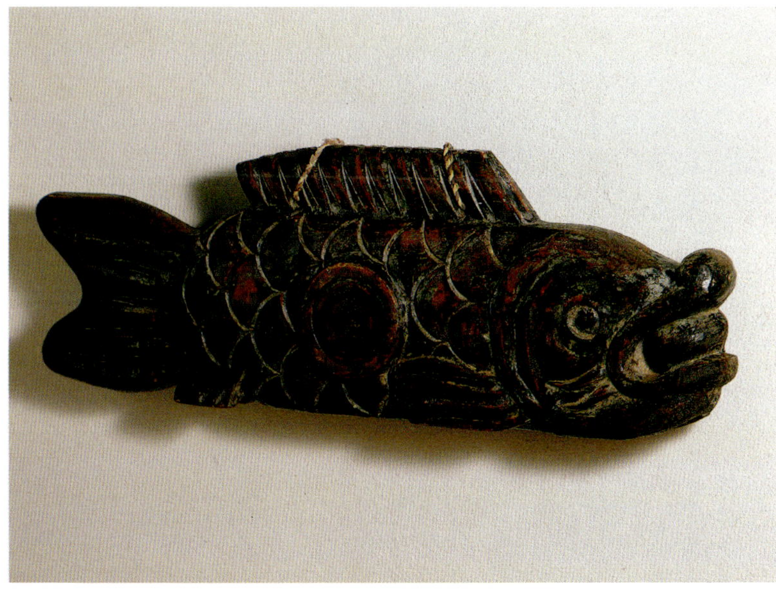

The shape of this nineteenth century Japanese gate knocker resembles that of a carp.

The *koi* (carp) is an even more frequent motif in Japanese art and is closely related to the dragon in East Asian mythology, where the two creatures are sometimes interchangeable. According to one popular belief, a *koi* successful at leaping a waterfall and ascending a river, a display of strength and will, could transform itself into a glorious dragon. In traditional Japan, this association with strength made the *koi* a sign of the warrior class—of the samurai mastering the trials of life. The warrior symbolism is still celebrated in contemporary Japan (and in Hawai'i) when kites shaped as *koi* are flown on May fifth, "Boys Day." These long-standing associations determined the form and pose of two large bronze *koi* displayed at the entry to the temple-like Pavilion restaurant at the Mauna Kea. These *koi* are poised for the leap over the waterfall, supporting themselves momentarily on their fins. Next to them is a huge bronze basin, nine feet in diameter, that may once have held living carp in a temple garden.

Koi are also an extremely popular subject in Buddhist arts, perhaps because they are known to live for more than a century and are therefore associated with longevity. Inside Buddhist temples, *koi* forms were used as gongs struck during services; outside, they served as decorative roof finials. A large number of *koi* gongs are displayed at the Mauna Kea, some constructed of wood and others of bronze.

A large, lacquered wooden drum in the collection is considered a descendant of Chinese temple drums. Carvings on the drum depict a pair of open-mouthed dragons grasping a large pearl between them—the pearl a symbol of the Buddhists' eternal pursuit of the luminous jewel of enlightenment. The dragons' heads emerge from a hollow ovoid body, which is the resonance chamber of the drum; the sound of the drum is amplified through openings at the sides and bottom. The scaly forms of the heavenly dragons are seen in spaces between carved cloud patterns on the drum's body. This type of red-lacquered temple drum would have been suspended near the altar or laid on specially shaped, ornate silk cushions; struck with a padded stick, it was used to beat rhythm during rituals. Four smaller dragon forms, wooden drums, are seen in the resort's Pacifica Collection, along with bronze fish gongs.

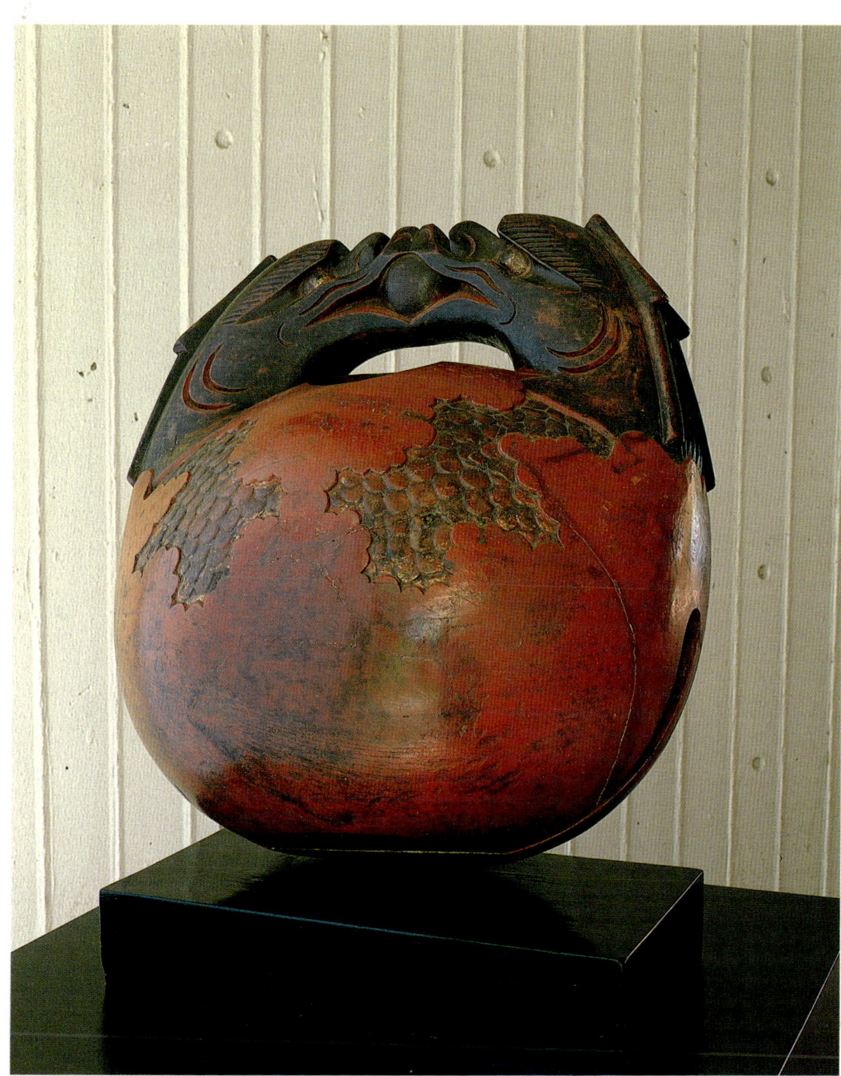

In its original home, a Japanese temple, this lacquered wooden drum was struck to punctuate Buddhist services. Both of the dragons on the drum pursue a symbolic pearl. The dragons' form and the ovoid shape of the drum derive from Chinese prototypes.

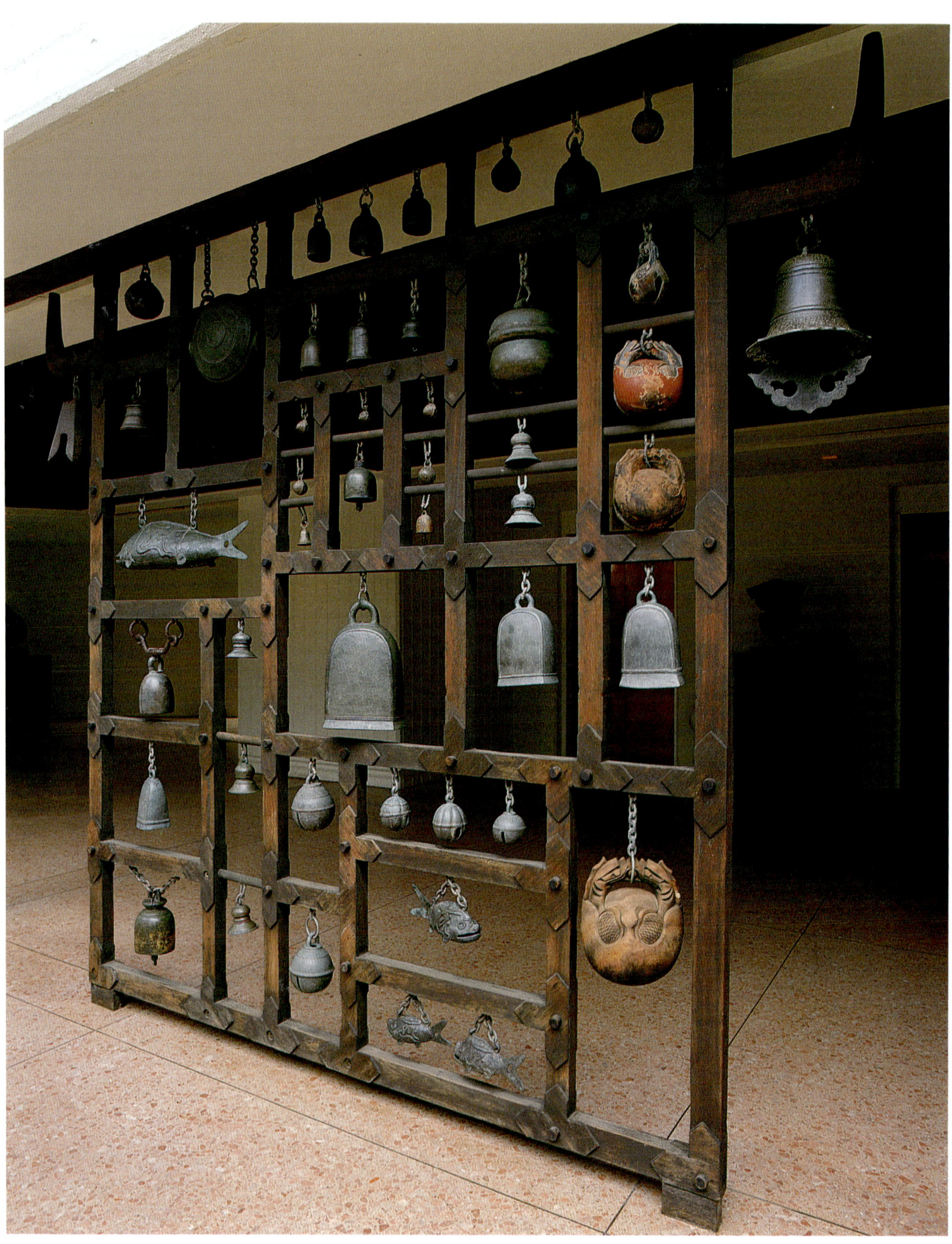

The Mauna Kea's Pacifica Collection includes chimes, bells, and gongs—musical sculptures—from Asian countries such as India, Thailand, and Japan. The display vehicle was constructed by sculptor Edward Brownlee; its form was inspired by the free-standing *torii* gateways that mark the entries to Shinto shrines.

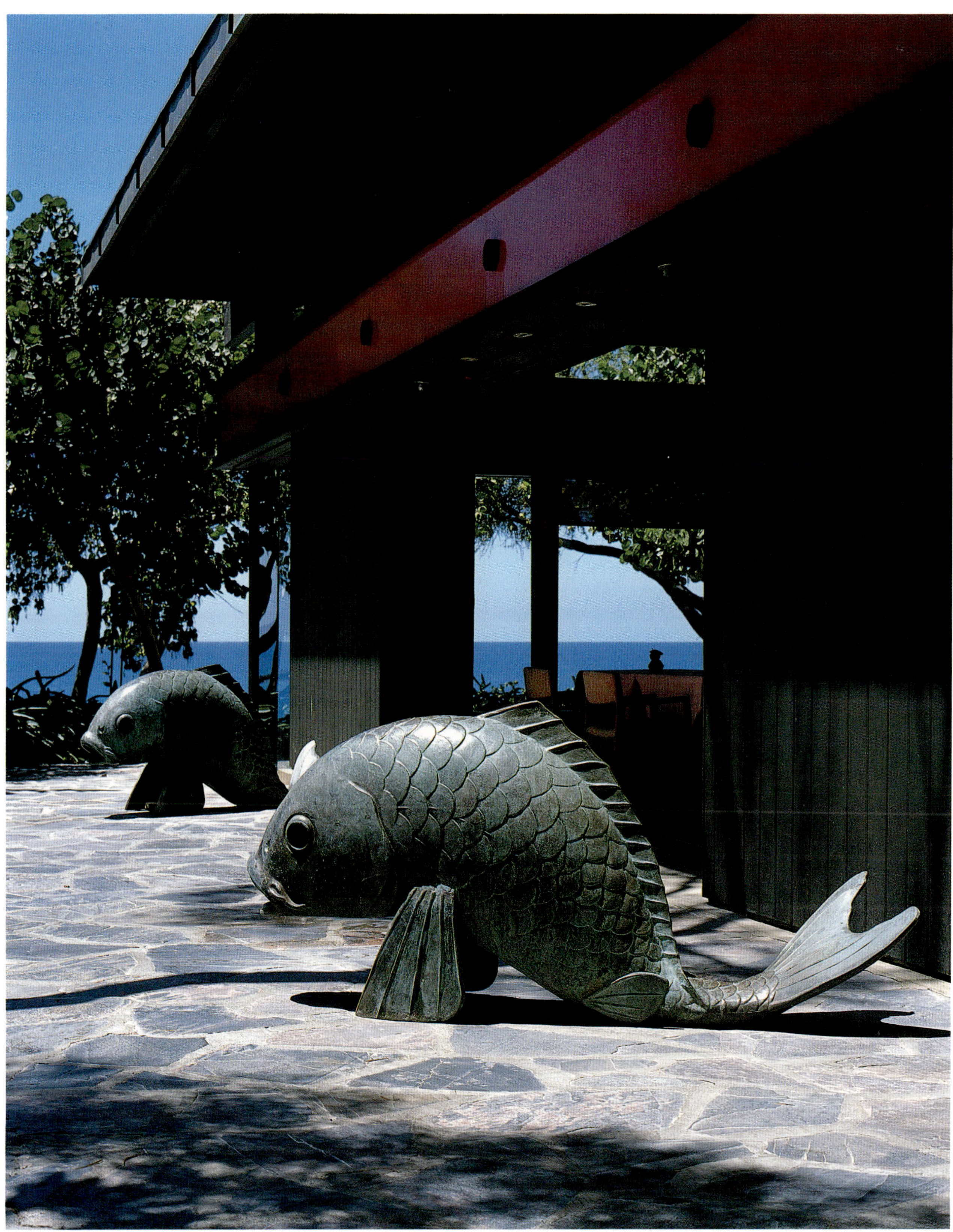

The Japanese have historically revered *koi* (carp) for their ability to navigate dangerous rapids and to leap waterfalls. Such feats made *koi* the traditional symbol of the samurai warrior; to this day, the *koi* symbolizes "Boys Day," a festival celebrated annually since the eighth century.

Hanger-Hooks and Iron Pots (*Jizai*)

Japan, 19th century, wood, iron, and bamboo, heights 17 to 23 inches (hanger-hooks) and 46½ to 61 inches (iron pots with attached chains and bamboo).

A SELECTION of iron pots and wooden hanger-hooks used for Japanese open-hearth cooking during the Edo period are displayed at the resort, their shapes and presence more suggestive of contemporary sculpture than mere kitchen tools. All these implements reflect a long-standing Japanese interest in applied design. Instead of seeking simply to beautify the functional through artistic decoration, the Japanese believe applied design is an art in itself. A refined sense of aesthetics characterizes all aspects of the traditional home, from architecture to furnishings and implements. This Japanese admiration of unadorned beauty in part derives from Zen and from the associated form of tea ceremony, *chanoyu*.

In Japanese country homes, foods were prepared over a charcoal- or wood-burning open hearth. Unembellished iron pots hung from an assembly of functional parts: horizontal bars and fasteners used to adjust the pots' height over the hearth were connected to bamboo-covered chains that hung from hooks near the rafters, producing a strong horizontal–vertical contrast. While each part of the pot-and-hanger assembly has a different name, the parts are referred to collectively as *jizai*.

Designs employed in the horizontal adjusters include fish shapes, specifically the *koi* (carp) and *tai* (snapper). Other motifs derive from sculptured renditions of Japanese written characters, *kanji*. Design of the massive wooden hanger-hooks, while never figurative, alluded symbolically to household deities, in particular two from Shinto beliefs, Daikoku and Ebisu, gods of work and prosperity. Daikoku and Ebisu are also two of the seven traditional gods of good fortune, and most homes maintained places for their images. Two highly distinct *jizai* styles evolved under the names of these gods. Hanger-hooks with chevron-shaped caps above rounded forms are called Daikoku; the more austere and angular hanger-hooks are referred to as Ebisu. Both forms balance sculptural design against utilitarian function. The beauty of the pieces displayed at the Mauna Kea was enhanced by their daily exposure to smoke over two centuries of use; the smoke has darkened the wood so that grain patterns stand out through a lustrous patina.

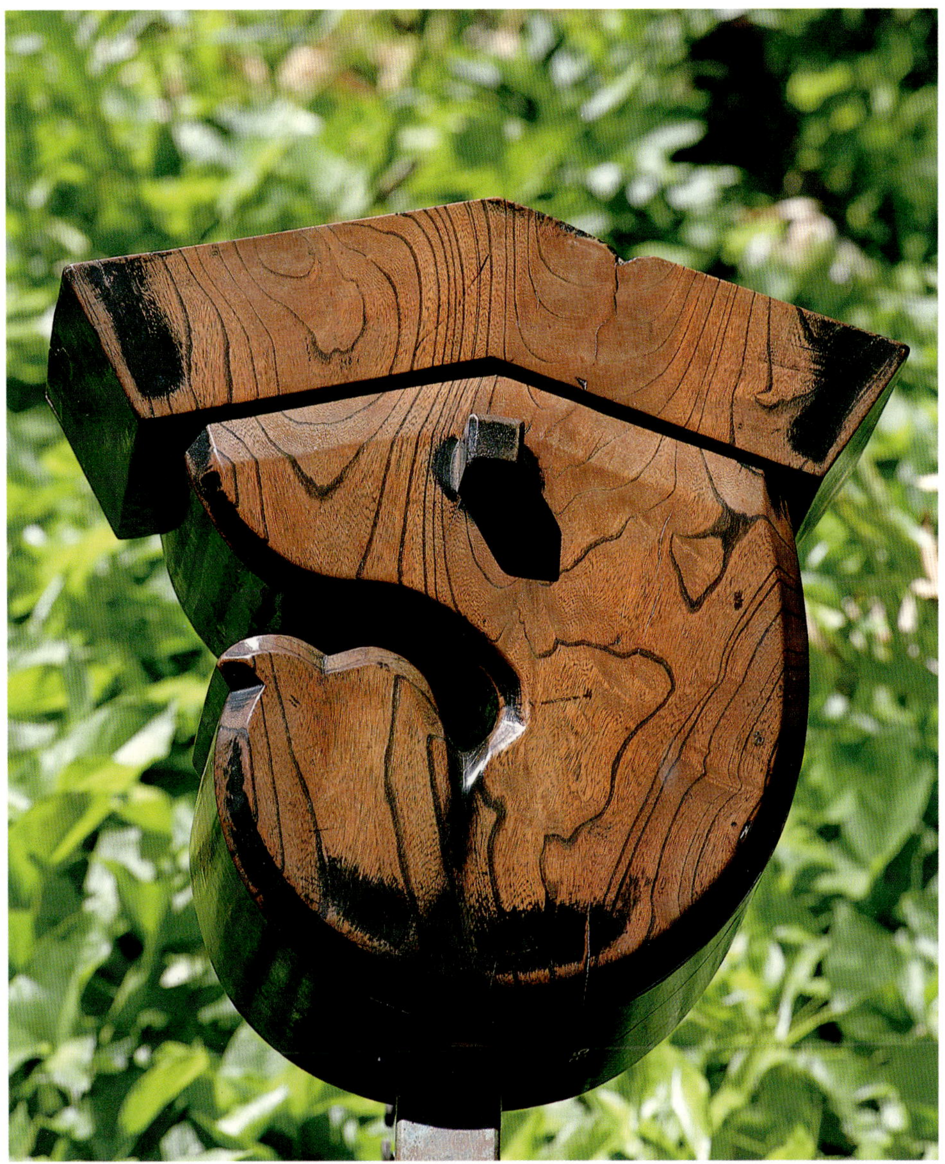

Wood hanger-hooks, such as the one shown here, were suspended near the rafters in rural Japanese homes to carry chains from which iron pots hung over the hearth. *Jizai* are now appreciated as valuable folk art, *mingei,* in Japan. This particular *jizai* form is called Daikoku, in honor of a god of good fortune; the cap-like shape at the top of the hook resembles the form of the god's hat.

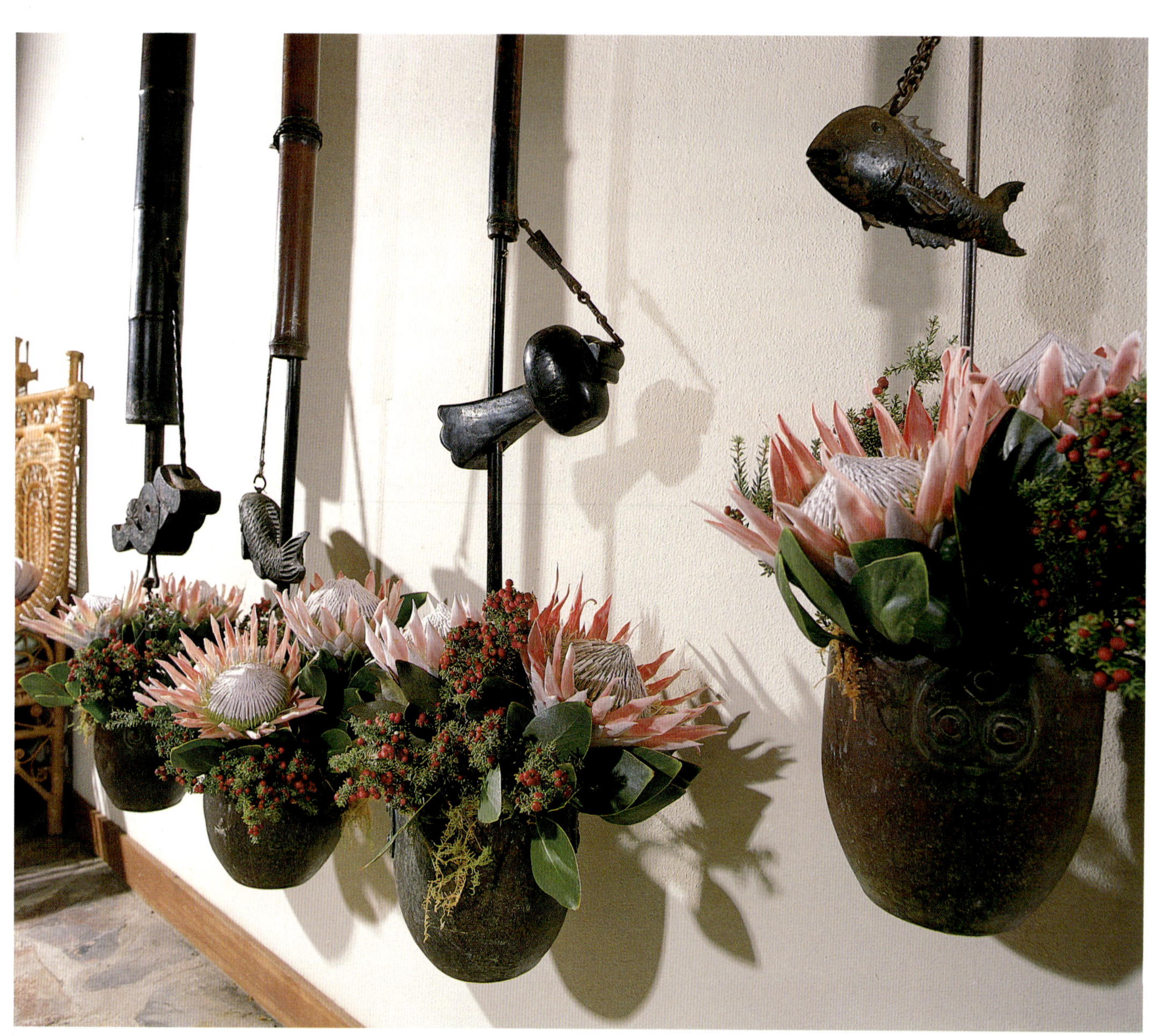

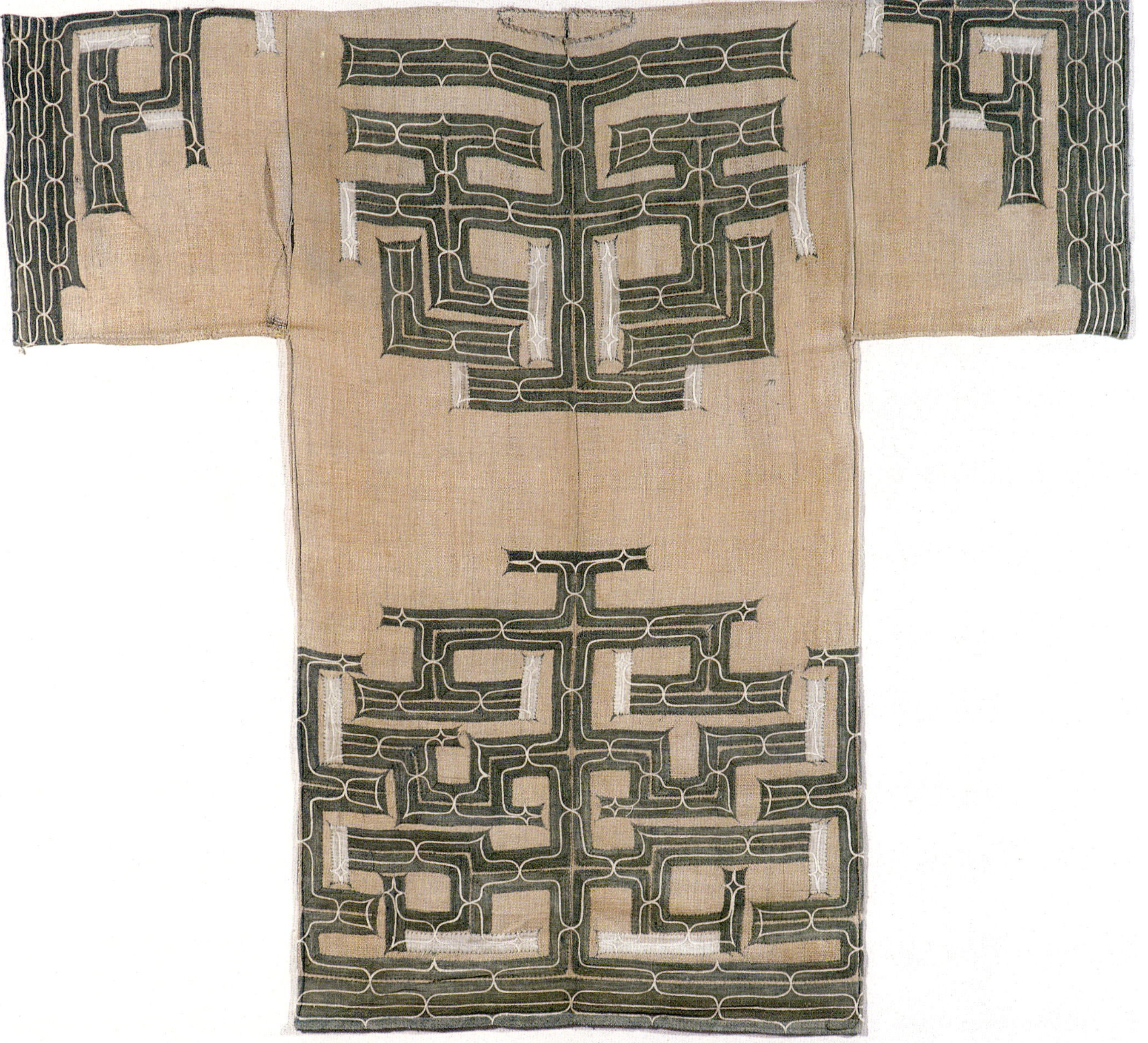

Ainu garments were acquired in trade and collected by Japanese seamen in the nineteenth century. The appliqués on these garments were believed to magically help ward off evil. The common pattern of tree-like branching forms may have represented a shaman's pathway for trips to and from the underworld.

Ainu Garments

Japan, late 19th century, cotton with applique and embroidery, lengths 43½ to 52½ inches.

FIVE GARMENTS of the native Ainu people, who now live only on Japan's northernmost island of Hokkaido, form a unique grouping within the Japanese collection. Like many other tribal people, the Ainu wore clothing that expressed their unity as a people, and thus the Mauna Kea's coats are extremely similar—in fabric, style, size, color, and decoration. While tribal chiefs and shamans had distinctive garments, Ainu clothing was otherwise quite homogeneous, though men wore garments of finer cloth and more complex decoration.

The five coats are made of cotton imported by the Ainu in the nineteenth century and are cut in a style similar to the Japanese kimono but much shorter, reaching at most to mid-calf. In all cases, the cotton background cloth is overlaid with angular appliqués; in contrast, curvilinear, characteristically Ainu designs are embroidered over the appliqué. Some of the embroidered designs are raised, couched over bits of bark to lend the coats textural interest. The decorations are conventionally placed at the neck, sleeve, and hem openings, probably to ward off evil believed to enter the body at these points. Earlier garments were woven from wool or grass fiber, or sewn from fish and animal skins.

These coats bear overtly botanical patterns or motifs that resemble tree forms. The tree forms may be related to Ainu shamanistic beliefs: leaf forms springing from branches could represent magically safe routes that shamans took to the underworld and, therefore, were protective emblems of these journeys and communications with spirits.

Visually, the designs on the coats relate to an ornamental, wavy-line pattern found on pottery created by the Ainu into the early twentieth century, as well as on pottery of the neolithic Jomon culture. Scholars also suggest the patterns resemble ancient Chinese motifs, traditional Polynesian designs, and the arts of pre-European American peoples. Textiles such as these have proven valuable in the study of trans-Pacific migrations.

The origins of the Ainu people are unknown. Anthropologists and archaeologists conjecture that they descended from the earliest known inhabitants of the archipelago, a Caucasoid people who migrated from central and northern Asia and developed the Jomon culture perhaps as early as the eighth millennium B.C. (The Ainu today exhibit linguistic and cultural ties to tribal peoples who inhabit southeastern Siberia.) Thousands of years later, in the second century B.C., they were supplanted by the Iron Age people of the Yayoi culture, a Mongoloid people who are more likely the direct ancestors of the Japanese. (The Ainu are physically distinct from the Japanese in bone structure and quantity of facial and body hair.) Since the first century A.D., they have occupied only the island of Hokkaido, where relative isolation has helped somewhat to preserve their racial characteristics, religious beliefs, and material culture. Even as late as the eighth and ninth centuries,

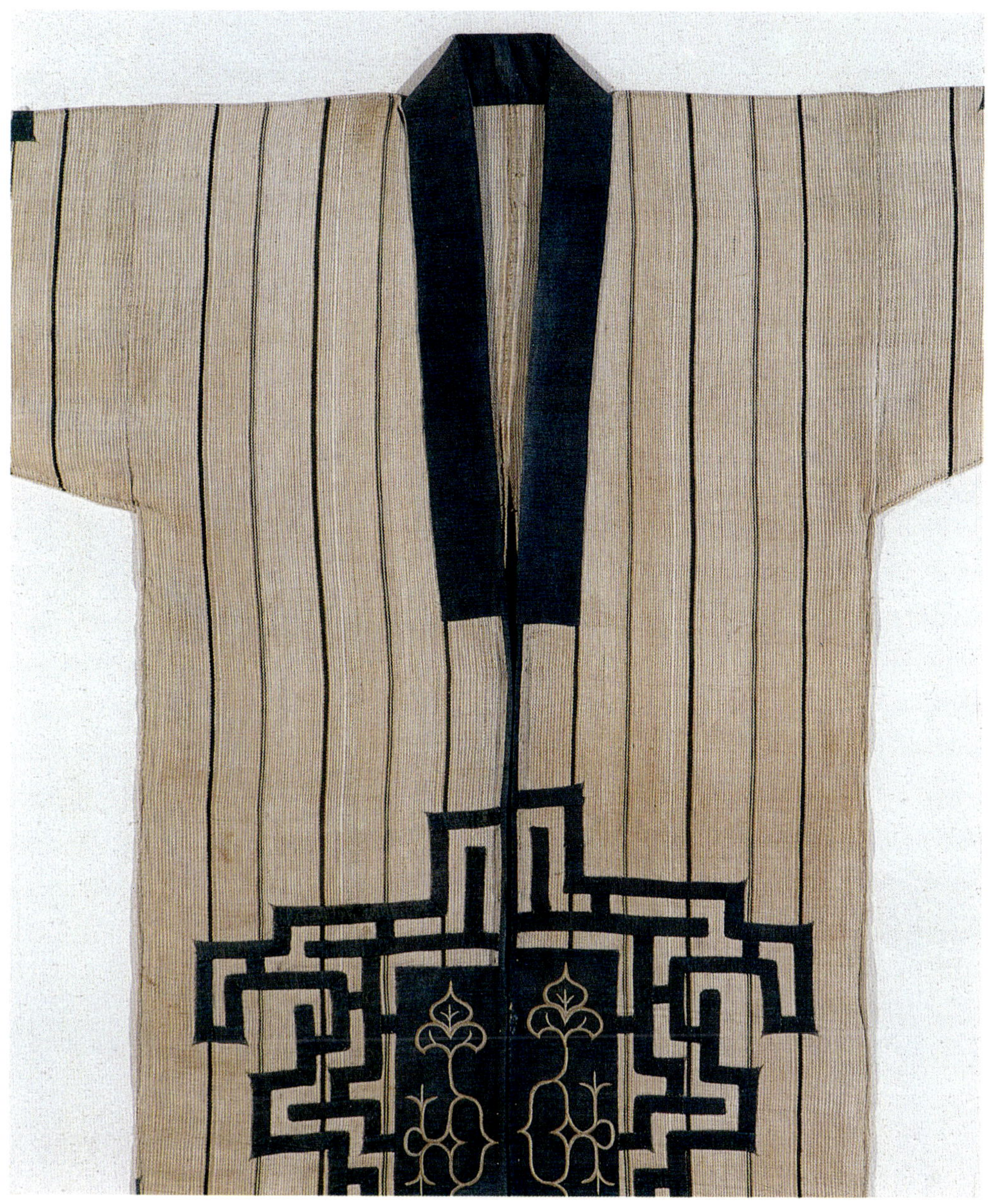

the Ainu were unpacified tribes that raided Japanese settlements. For the past five hundred years they have been only superficially influenced by the Japanese, and they have maintained a fishing and hunting culture into the twentieth century. Their shamanistic religious orientation is manifest in ritual ceremonies, body amulets, fetishes, totems, and designs on the garments in the collection. Today approximately twenty-five thousand Ainu exist, dwelling primarily on Hokkaido. However, the number of pure Ainu may be far fewer, as this figure likely includes all members of households in which the father alone is Ainu.

Four-Panel Screen

Japan, *circa* 1965, gold on black lacquer, length 124 inches.

A HIGHLY nontraditional four-panel screen by the widely acclaimed contemporary calligrapher Shiryu Morita is the only twentieth century work in the Japanese collection. Morita was influenced by Zen artistic principles in producing this important example of Japanese modern art. Zen rejoices in contradictions and in shattering conventions, and Morita's choice of lacquer, a slow, laborious medium, for a large screen with bold cursive calligraphy suggests a certain iconoclasm.

Traditionally, lacquered objects such as cosmetic boxes, ink stone or medicine containers, fan handles, and Buddhist altar pendants were produced for the aristocracy. These objects, created by craftsmen using painstaking techniques, were usually idyllic in subject and style, lavish in color, and explicit in detail, if not somewhat stiff in execution. Lacquered screens were produced in limited numbers.

Morita's calligraphy in lacquer is bold, in the so-called "grass-style" (*sosho*), an unrestrained script that sweeps across the four panels. The characters translate to "Dragon knows Dragon," according to the artist; however, even the most literate Japanese would not be able to easily decipher the script. The supreme mythic creature in the universe, the dragon is cosmologically understood as the symbol of sunrise (and "Japan" in Japanese characters means "The Origin of the Sun"). The phrase may allude to the sense of unity and tranquility to be grasped by those kindred souls who have attained enlightenment through the practice of Zen.

The phrase exemplifies the Zen preference for short, direct statements of only two or three characters; these writings are usually found in an intimate scroll format rather than on monumental screens. While often quite illegible, *sosho* calligraphy is admired for its aesthetic content—the calligrapher's ability to express personality and style through brush strokes. The stroke of each character has some relationship to the standard form of writing and shows expressive force through the movement of connecting strokes. Corrections are not possible in this technique, which makes the cursive style even more of a feat.

Gold on black lacquer, as used by Morita, was traditional in arts created for the aristocracy; however, it was not used for the type of free calligraphy seen on this screen. Pre-Zen Buddhist texts were sometimes written in gold on a dark background; these writings were supremely legible. Morita, instead, applied gold in rough strokes that are intentionally difficult to decipher.

Morita's contemporary calligraphy was first displayed in the United States in 1954 at New York's Museum of Modern Art, in an exhibition that acknowledged the impact of Japanese calligraphy on American painting; the calligraphy was presented not to be "read" but to be enjoyed as a form of abstract art.

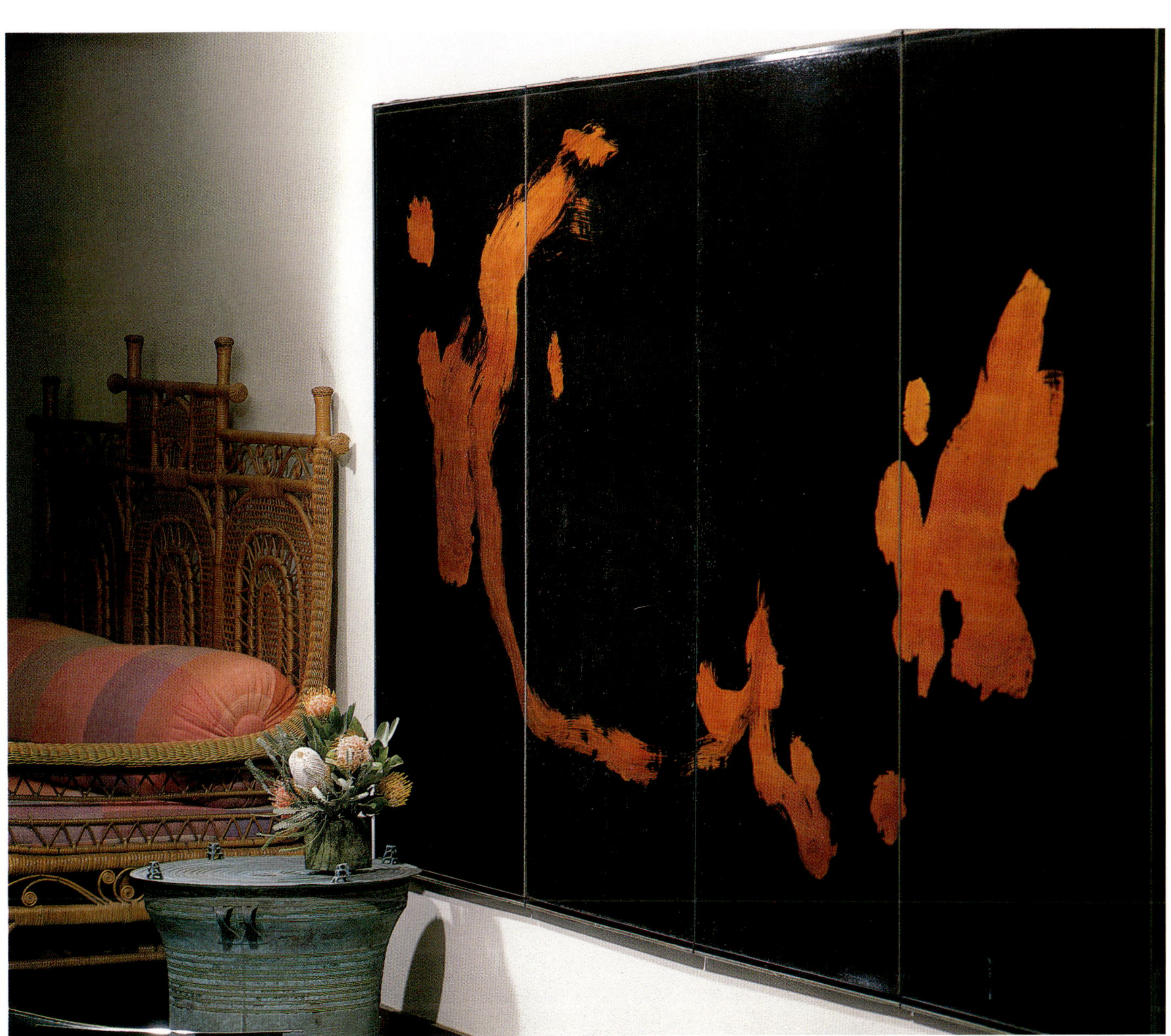

Oceanic Arts

THE PACIFIC OCEAN covers about one-third of the earth's surface; Oceania is an apt name for the thousands of islands that dot the central and south Pacific. The islands are grouped into three geographic and cultural regions: Micronesia, Melanesia, and Polynesia. The Mauna Kea's collection does not include works from Micronesia; Melanesia is represented largely through the arts of New Guinea and environs, and Polynesia through the arts of New Zealand's Maori peoples and of Hawai'i.

The people of Oceania share the bond of lives dominated by the Pacific, an existence where water, sky, fish, and birds are key cultural influences. Their arts also bear the shared artistic traditions of works produced through relatively simple technology in small social groups of isolated cultures. With the exception of the Hawaiian works expressly created for the resort, all the Oceanic arts displayed at the Mauna Kea derive from people of tribal or clan social groups, which valued oral rather than written traditions.

Unlike the beliefs of Buddhists and Christians, the beliefs of Oceanic peoples are not attributable to creedal religious views but rather to codes and legal systems passed down through oral tradition for many generations. These traditions were most often preserved through chants, and these chants, such as the Hawaiian *kumulipo* creation chant that describes the origins of life, often reveal a rich and complex theology. When eighteenth century European travelers described Hawai'i, it was the refined development of religious and artistic traditions that most impressed them; they found throughout the Hawaiian Islands sacred precincts with monumental temples and sculptures, sacrificial platforms, and towers used in communicating with the gods. Oceanic arts are primarily religious and, to a great extent, the nature of Oceanic religious beliefs has been deduced from them. In addition to conveying dogma, the arts in Oceanic societies provided a tangible way to honor deities through signs and symbols of their presence. Like the craftsmen of traditional Buddhist arts, Oceanic artists carefully maintained the stylistic codes and systems of the elders. The peoples of New Guinea and other Melanesian islands demonstrated a particularly conservative attitude towards change in artistic style, an attitude perhaps analogous to the preservation of constitutional law in a Western society.

A number of works in the Oceanic collection, especially those from Melanesia, were venerated in ways that to Western eyes might appear "demonic" or idolatrous. However, like Buddhists and Christians, Oceanic cultures have distinguished between the rendered image and the deity or spirit represented. Images signified the spirit and reminded worshippers of its presence, or afforded the spirit a temporary resting place; images were not intended to be the subject of devotion. However, acknowledgment of such fine distinctions by and large depends on a relatively sophisticated notion of religious intent. In Oceanic as well as in Asian and Western cultures, there is often a sector of the faithful that confuses the deity with its representation. In these instances, in Oceania or elsewhere, an image indeed functions as an idol.

Oceanic arts were spiritual as well as religious, conveying general and even universal ideas of spirituality, and were not confined to didactic religious history. As in the case of Buddhist figures, many Oceanic images communicate feelings and ideas beyond ordinary human experience, through a vocabulary of proportions, facial expressions, or gestures, such as the elongated limbs and spectral grimaces seen in Melanesian ancestral figures.

Many tribal peoples of the Pacific felt the immanence of the divine in all aspects of life, with the result that utilitarian objects often reflect their spiritual understandings and concerns. These objects express emotions and thoughts about the supernatural as effectively as sacred artifacts used for religious ritual.

Attributing provenance and chronology is problematic with Oceanic arts because the oldest examples of these arts were not scientifically categorized at the time of their collection. The oldest datable works were collected by the earliest European explorers in the late eighteenth and nineteenth centuries, and reside today in major ethnographic museums throughout the world. Most works at the Mauna Kea are from the twentieth century; fortunately, however, Rockefeller was able to select many works produced early in the century. Although changes in subject and style have occurred, the oldest surviving Oceanic arts and those created in this century retain a strong relationship. Accordingly, Rockefeller commissioned some works for the collection, not to rigidly imitate older forms but to honor and continue vital traditions.

Oceanic art works were considered primarily of ethnographic interest, but not "art," until the 1940s, when New York's Museum of Modern Art began a series of exhibitions. These shows were primarily inspired by the museum's presiding trustee and president, Nelson Rockefeller—the late governor of New York and vice-president of the United States, Laurance Rockefeller's brother. In 1957, Nelson Rockefeller opened New York's Museum of Primitive Art, the first institution to celebrate the arts of tribal peoples as such. The first scholarly publications to present "primitive arts" alongside the creations of major world cultures appeared during the early 1960s, at the same time that Laurance Rockefeller was acquiring his collection for the Mauna Kea. The Mauna Kea opened its collections to the public in 1965, four years before the Metropolitan Museum of Art held its first major exhibition of primitive art, consisting of collections from the Museum of Primitive Art. (These collections were eventually gifted to the Metropolitan by Nelson Rockefeller in memory of his son Michael, who disappeared in New Guinea in 1961 while on a collecting expedition.) Thus the resort was in the vanguard of a trend to present the arts of the native peoples of Oceania as valuable examples of creativity, spirituality and, above all, humanity.

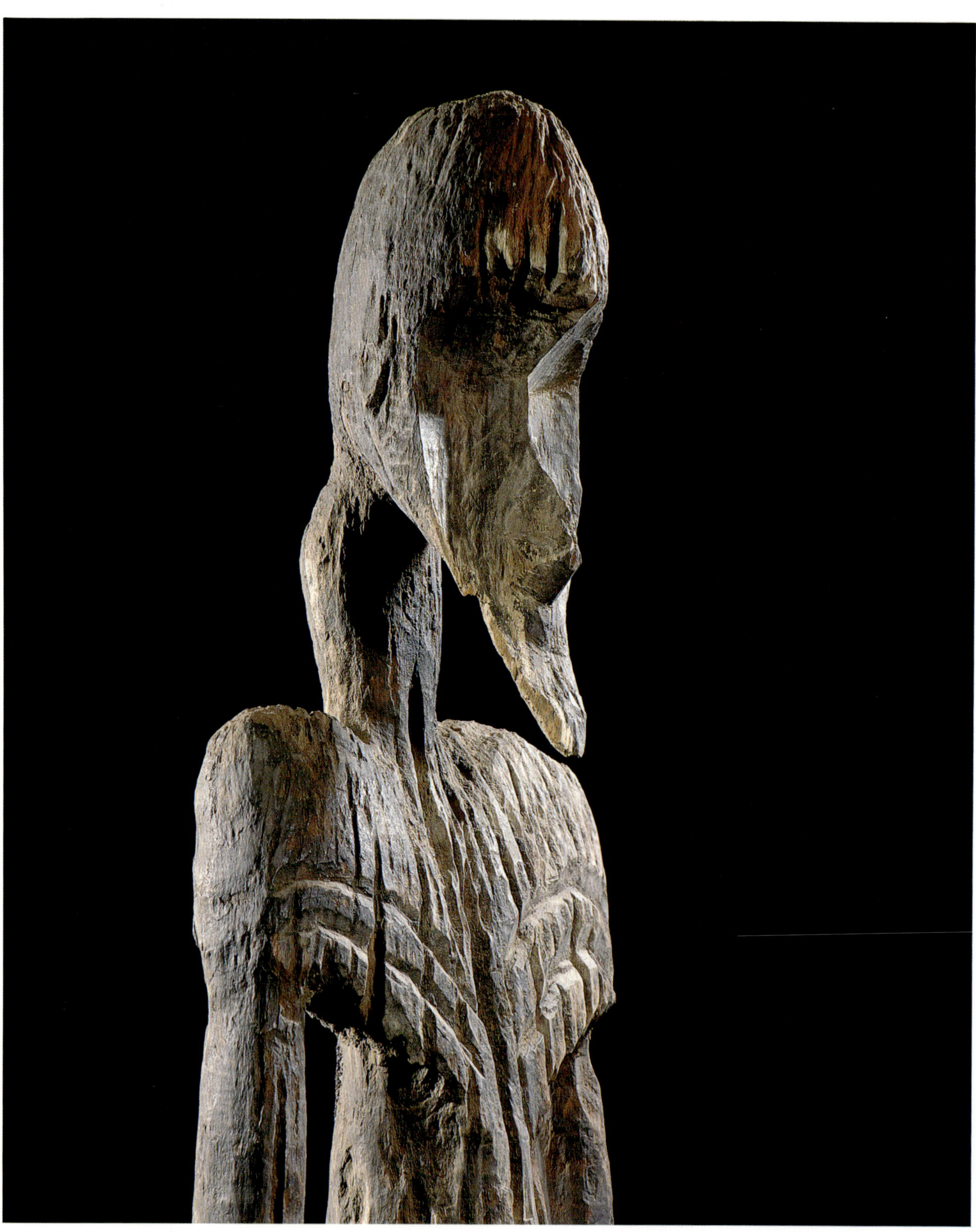

Scarification patterns on the chest and shoulders of this New Guinea figure suggest initiation rituals of death and resurrection. The patterns were perhaps intended to represent the bites of a monstrous creature and the strength and survival of the individual. The head resembles the skulls of venerated ancestors that were often displayed in ritual houses.

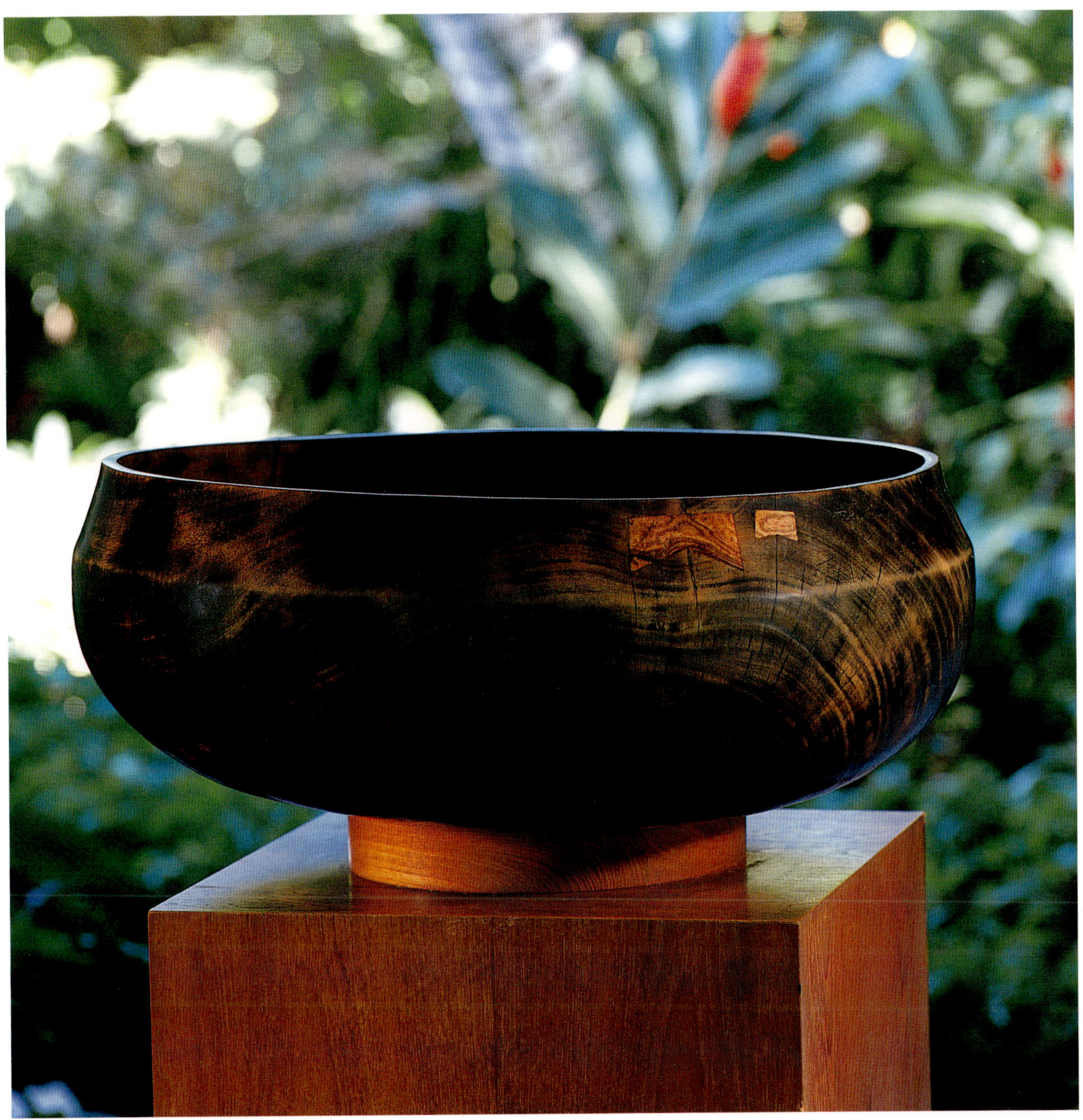

This highly sculptural nineteenth century bowl is the oldest Oceanic utensil at the resort and an excellent example of the Hawaiians' refined carving techniques. A very old, splined restoration is evident close to the bowl's rim, on the upper right of the photograph.

MELANESIA

THE ORIGINS of the black-skinned Melanesian peoples are uncertain; cultural anthropologists believe, however, that Asian peoples migrated to the South Pacific more than twenty thousand years ago and that Melanesia was populated by descendants of the earliest migrations. Those who settled Melanesia eventually dispersed into hundreds of tribes that, by historic times, waged almost constant warfare among themselves. Unlike Polynesia, Melanesia seems never to have had an aristocracy, nor any priesthood set apart from the people; all spiritual power resided in spirits and deities. Tribes were relatively egalitarian, and superior achievement, whether in war, arts, or agriculture, was the only real criterion for prestige and rank. Tribal leaders were chosen for their military and other social successes, with no special deference to heredity. This organization of sociopolitical life may partially explain the paucity of older works of art: objects were created to function only for the lifetime of the owner; even the ruler could not plan on dynastic heirs.

While varying from tribe to tribe, in style as well as in materials and techniques, Melanesian arts are unified through religious meaning, ritual function, figural subjects, and an emphasis on masks with exaggerated facial expressions. Objects used for secular purposes were frequently enhanced with religious cult designs, a phenomenon seldom found in Polynesia.

Melanesian arts also tend to be esoteric, their precise significance known and understood only by the tribe's so-called secret societies, an inner-group organization of initiates. These societies were actually secret fraternities, joined by all the young men upon coming of age. Women formed the primary audience for ritual performances in which the men, once initiated, shared in ritual knowledge. The secret organizations and their rites primarily served to maintain order and ethics within the tribal group and to mete out punishment for transgressors. The more important the issue, the smaller the group of individuals entrusted with knowledge and control over that particular sphere of concern.

Ritual performances with masks and images usually comprised reenactments of stories regarding the origins of sacred spirits and the social order they established. Creators of masks and objects for rituals were less concerned with aesthetic appeal than with effective and convincing function, as these works were tools in the education of the tribe and instrumental in maintaining control of the tribe through spiritual revelation.

Veneration of ancestral deities, for protective purposes, guided the anthropomorphic form of most works, but in styles that were usually quite abstract, as if realism were anathema and inadequate for representing spirits. Rituals that evolved from this veneration of ancestral spirits and deities, including those that prepared participants for warring and headhunting missions, used art forms that answered people's concerns for survival, success, fertility, and dominance.

The Mauna Kea's Melanesian collection is mostly from the tribal peoples of New Guinea, with other works of art from archipelagos such as the New Hebrides and the Solomon Islands. New Guinea is the center of Melanesia and, at more than twelve hundred miles in length, is the second largest island in the world. Some districts of the island have yet to be thoroughly explored, some of its peoples remain semi-nomadic, and its arts display a wider range of styles than all the islands of Polynesia combined. The diversity of this island, where approximately eight hundred languages are still used, characterizes all other Melanesian archipelagos.

Research in the field of Melanesian arts has progressed enormously during the past quarter century, but certainties are slow to emerge. Thus, although all the Melanesian arts in the collection have been assigned a provenance, many of the attributions are provisional rather than absolute.

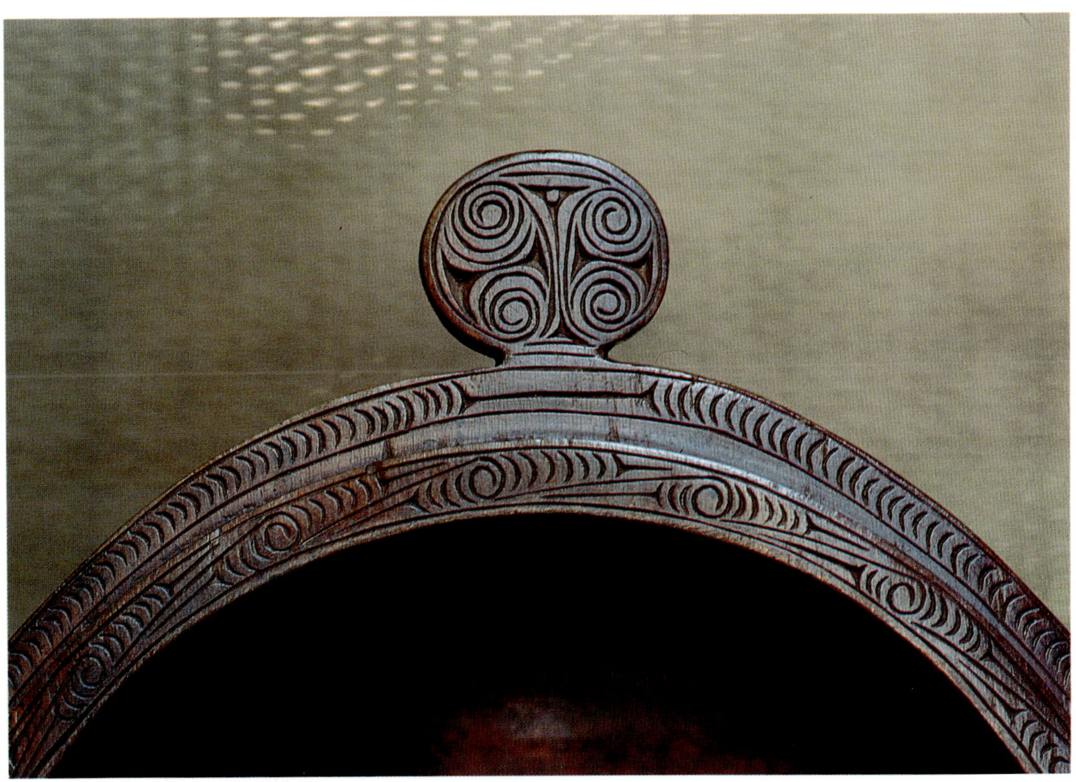

This finely carved bowl from the Middle Sepik shows the meticulous swirls that characterize the ornamentation of many Oceanic containers. The bowl was fashioned with two complete rims, one above the other, and its handle projects from the lower rim.

Abelam Ritual Masks

New Guinea, woven rattan, heights 17 to 33 inches.

THE MAUNA KEA'S collection of seventeen basketry masks comes from the Abelam tribe of New Guinea's Maprik region. The Abelam people dwell in relatively small villages in the Maprik Valley, which is approximately fifty miles north of the Sepik River on the flanks of the Prince Alexander Mountains. The Sepik region is home to many tribal peoples, some of which were not affected by foreign influence until fairly recently. People from the Middle Sepik are believed to be the progenitors of the Abelam. The Abelam cultivate yams as their main food supply and have created a complex system of rites dedicated to the yam and to fertility through an amalgam of spirits responsible for successful harvests. Abelam arts are prominently displayed in the Mauna Kea collection because these peoples evolved a unique and identifiable style of artistry that influenced other people of the Sepik region.

The masks were originally used in the tribe's initiation rites for adolescent boys, a complex process requiring ceremonies of different types spread over many years. These rituals of admittance to the men's secret society often involved real suffering for the initiate, including scarification and modified circumcision. Most anthropologists interpret Abelam initiation ritual masks as representations of the clan's female ancestral spirits, believed to be the original discoverers of the yam spirits that the Abelam venerated.

The Abelam grow yams of astonishing size, sometimes exceeding fifteen feet in length. The yams are the basis of sustenance, ritual, and social prestige for the grower, especially when entertaining neighboring clans in formal celebrations. As in most Melanesian cultures, prestige is the basis of an individual's economic and political power within the tribe. At harvest, yams are decorated with wooden masks and displayed in the tribe's ritual house, a pyramid-shaped structure that is the tallest in the village. A large facade painting decorates the outside; carved wooden images, whose shapes recur on the decorated yams, are displayed inside. The artists who create the wooden masks gain prestige if their masks prove ritually effective, as evidenced by a bountiful harvest the following season. While tribal leaders were renowned warriors, yam growers and mask artists could acquire status and power through nonaggressive behavior.

Women in the tribe were forbidden interaction with all masks and were allowed to see them only when public rituals were performed, and even then only from afar. The male performers were effectively invisible, their bodies hidden by garlands of fruit and leaves below the masks, so as to leave the spirits to dance together. The ritual initiation dramas were intentionally frightening spectacles of spectral forces, enactments of tales of spirits who devoured and then regurgitated the very sons who were being initiated. These dramas were accompanied by powerful drumming, wind instruments, and loud song.

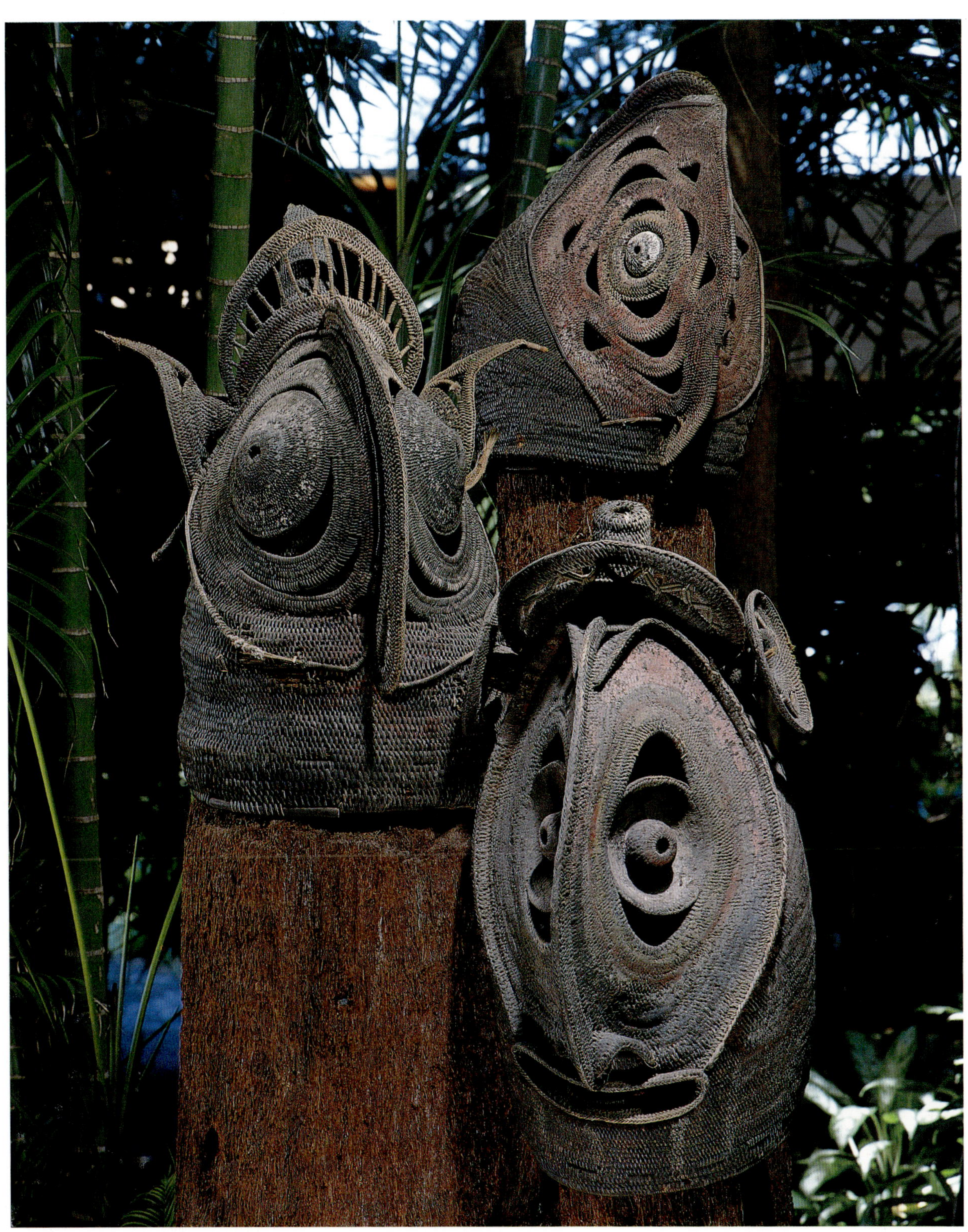

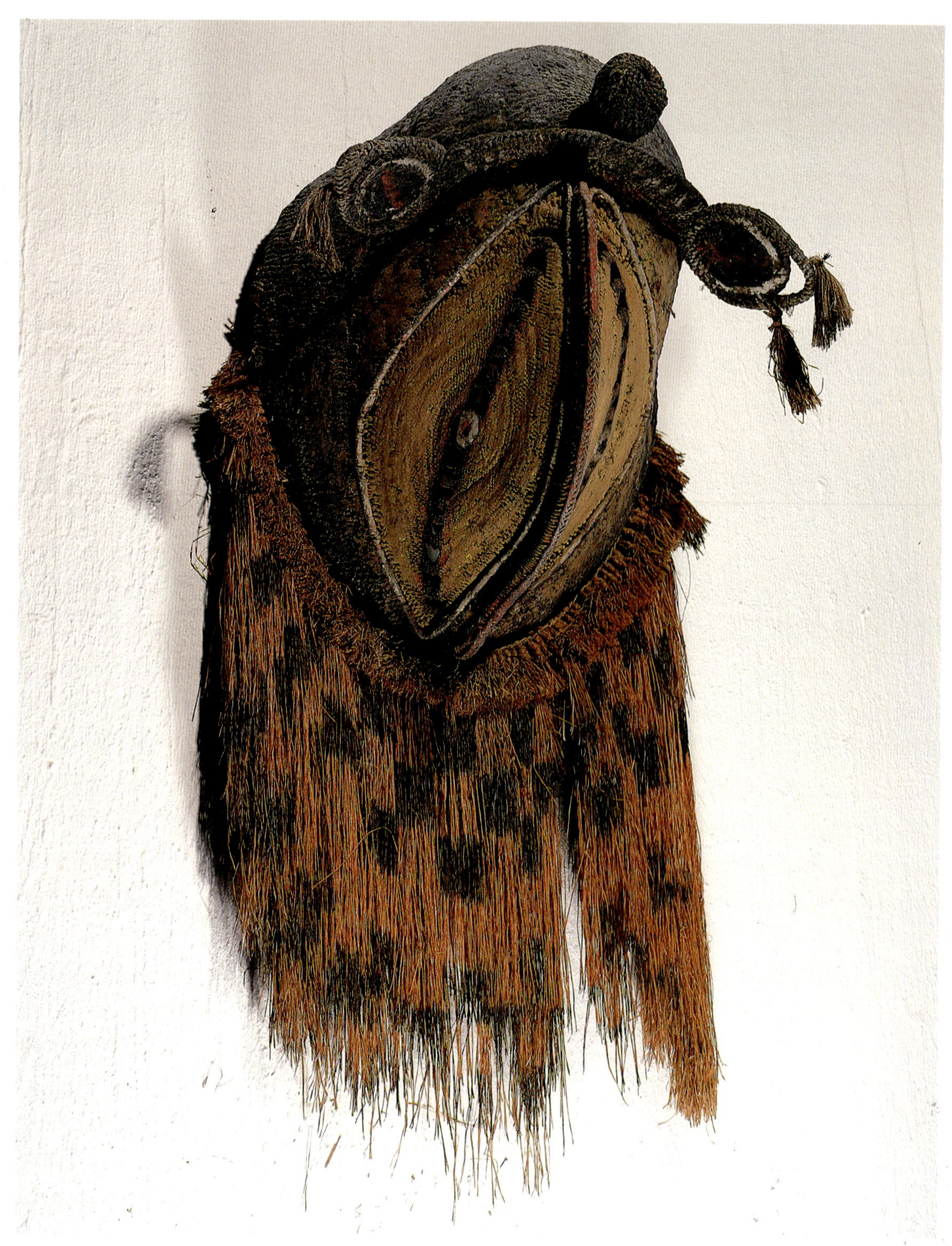

A beard of bark fibers painted in a geometric pattern adorns this striking Abelam ritual mask. While masks could depict either male or female spirits, in the Abelam social system only initiated males could participate in the yam-harvest rituals that utilized the masks. The yams themselves were grown by men, only, in areas kept separate from women's gardens.

Initiation was required not only to familiarize youths with the tribe's mysteries but also to teach them skills—the use of musical instruments for rituals, the methods of creating required costumes, and the techniques for making the masks themselves.

All the Mauna Kea's Abelam masks are constructed of rattan, woven and then dyed with vegetable pastes; flexible twigs tie parts together. The Abelam are generally known for colorful masks of bright red and yellow set off by black and white. The pigments used were sometimes scraped off after rituals and buried in the yam gardens to ensure plant fertility; the Mauna Kea's masks bear evidence of such scraping. The shapes of many masks suggest a bird's head, especially because of the extended and exaggerated noses and crest-like forms, some made of feathers, affixed to the masks. The exaggerated noses relate to Abelam ideals of beauty, for the nose was understood as the focal point of an individual's appeal. The eyes on most masks are circular or ovoid, and patterns in the surrounding wickerwork echo the eyes' form. Crown-like appendages and openwork projections for ears, or perhaps earrings, intensify the masks' bizarre appearance.

These Abelam masks show unity in subject, style, and function, as well as in material and technique. They also display subtle variations, however, which Abelam traditions expected and encouraged: inasmuch as masks bestowed prestige on their makers, a mask that literally copied another implied a less effective spiritual content and a less creatively endowed artist. Young mask artists were apprenticed at certain stages of initiation, often working under master sponsors in other villages with which their tribe had kinship ties. As each village maintained different conventions, even when only a few miles apart, apprenticeship exposed youths to a varied repertoire of forms, techniques, and decorations.

Masks are common to tribal and literate cultures. Peoples of India and of central and Southeast Asia often use masks in sacred rituals and celebrations. In Japan, masks figure significantly in religious dances, dramas, and other ceremonies. In Western culture, masks survive as descendants of ancient Christian rites performed during pre-Lenten carnivals and of pagan rites (such as today's Halloween) that depict demonic spirits. In function, the ancestral portrait heads kept by wealthy Western citizens from ancient Roman times through the early Christian period also relate to tribal masks. These venerated portraits resided on the family altar for use in rituals.

Ritual-House Mask

New Guinea, woven rattan and clay, height 58 inches.

THIS monumental mask, close to five feet high, was created by the Blackwater River people, who live on the delta of swamps and plains formed by the southern tributaries of the Middle Sepik. The Blackwater River people enjoy strong linguistic and cultural ties to the Maprik area and to the Abelam as a result of extensive trade contact via Sepik waterways. This mask was an architectural decoration on the gabled peak of a men's ritual house. As such, it would never have functioned as personal adornment for ritual but was permanently displayed, as a sculptural representation of an important clan spirit, to protect the people from natural calamity as well as from enemies.

The basketry technique used to structure this abstract head combined flat leaf strips with varnished creepers. The mask's basketry provided a framework over which a clay and lime mixture was applied, modeled, and subsequently painted with red, black, white, and ocher vegetable pastes. Typical of this region, the form juxtaposes concave and convex areas: the forehead bulges dramatically up to the sharp ridge line of the brow; an elongated concavity below the forehead represents the rest of the face. The nose is narrow, projecting from the center of the face almost to the chin, its flared nostrils emphasized with swirls. Below the nose, the narrow-lipped mouth appears sinister as it arches wide across the jaw, exposing jagged teeth made from reeds. The eyes are small, squat cylinders magnified by painted designs that widen as they move across the cheeks. These highly exaggerated features suggest that this mask was conceived specifically for viewing from below, appropriate for its function.

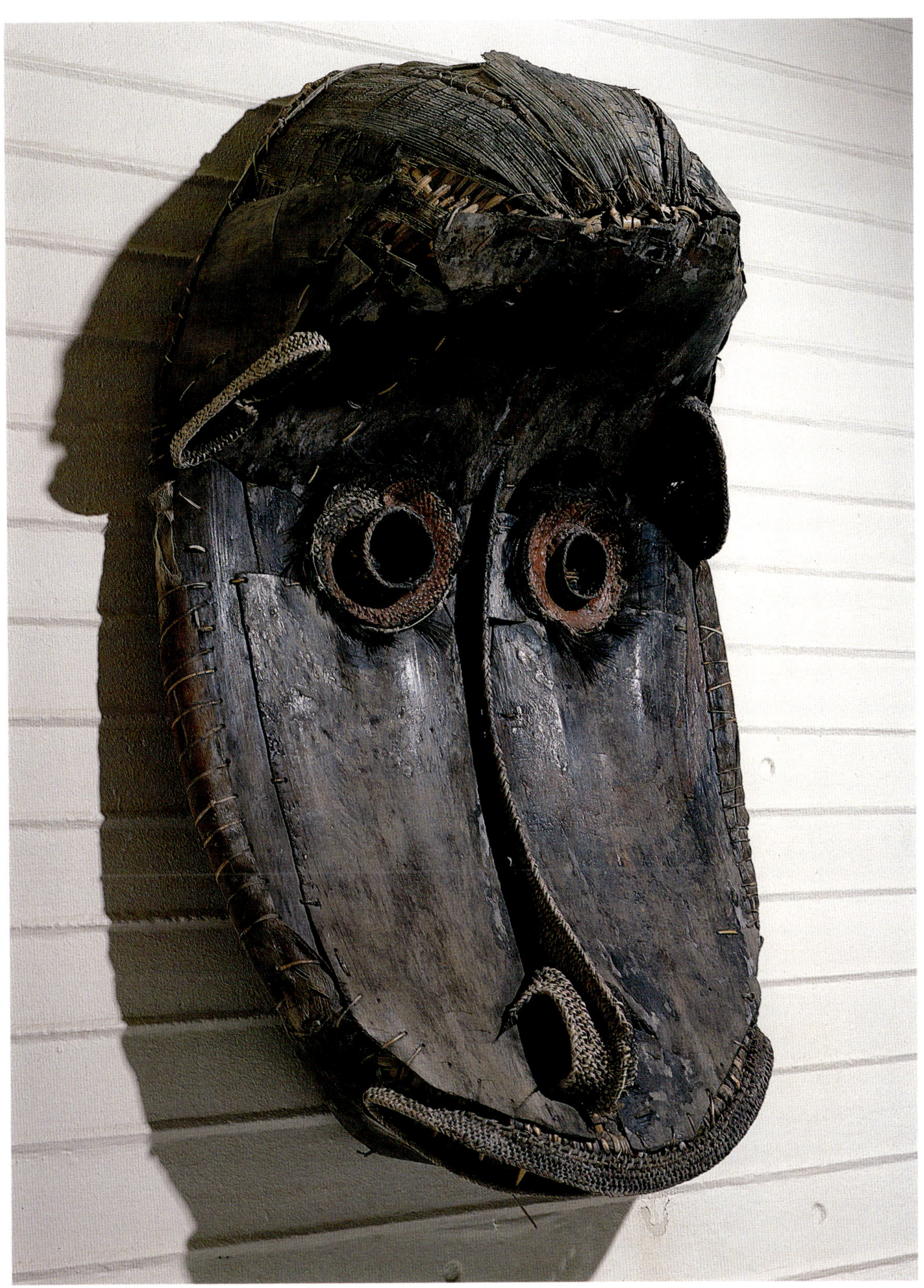

Group of Figural Sculptures

New Guinea and Vanuatu (formerly New Hebrides), wood, heights 18½ inches (mask) to 73 inches (ancestral figure).

INSTALLED in the resort's Main Building and Beachfront Wing, these Melanesian works include ritual-house sculptures, a memorial plaque, ancestor tablets, and a wooden mask. All of these arts demonstrate considerable technical achievements in figural carving. The rough forms for these sculptures were crafted using ax-like tools with stone or shell blades, stone hammers, and a variety of other cutting tools made from flaked stone, shells, and the teeth of animals, including sharks, rats, and wild boars. To achieve a smooth finish, the sculptors rubbed the rough forms on boulders and sometimes used river sand as an abrasive.

One important work in this group is displayed at the hotel's Terrace restaurant on a high pedestal where it can be viewed from below, silhouetted against the sky, much as it would have been in its original setting (page 18). Produced by the Sawos people of the Eastern Sepik region, the sculpture once served on a ritual house as a roof finial, an extension of the carved ridge board. A male figure perches on the cylindrical base; scarification marks are clearly incised on his shoulders and chest, as well as on his protruding abdomen and fleshy thighs. Above this round-faced male looms a large bird, probably a sea eagle, its rosette-patterned wings spreading out behind the man's head, as if it were about to carry him away.

Bird subjects were common in art of the Sepik, and the same iconography characterizes other New Guinea sculptures at the Mauna Kea. This bird was symbolic of clan prestige; by uniting it with the human form the clan evoked one spiritual being. In New Guinea, where individual prestige was of concern, this type of image was intended to encourage initiation candidates: initiates who successfully completed the hierarchy of ritual grades were identified with the clan's bird spirit and thus worshipped posthumously as significant ancestors. In pagan Roman culture, too, citizens sought wealth and prestige not only for temporal benefits but also to support those civic cults that assured them ritual honor for generations after death.

A gaunt, life-size ancestral sculpture from the region south of the Middle Sepik offers a sharp contrast to the relatively full-figured sculpture of the Sawos people (page 110). This Karawari River figure is elongated, its attenuated extremities providing no suggestion of hands or feet. The upper torso shows concentric arcs of scarification marks across the chest, repeating the curve of the shoulders. The facial features are vague, the deeply hollowed eye sockets surrounded by sharp planes that conjure up bone rather than flesh. The smoke-darkened hue of this particular sculpture was achieved by rubbing the figure with coconut oil while suspending it over a fire.

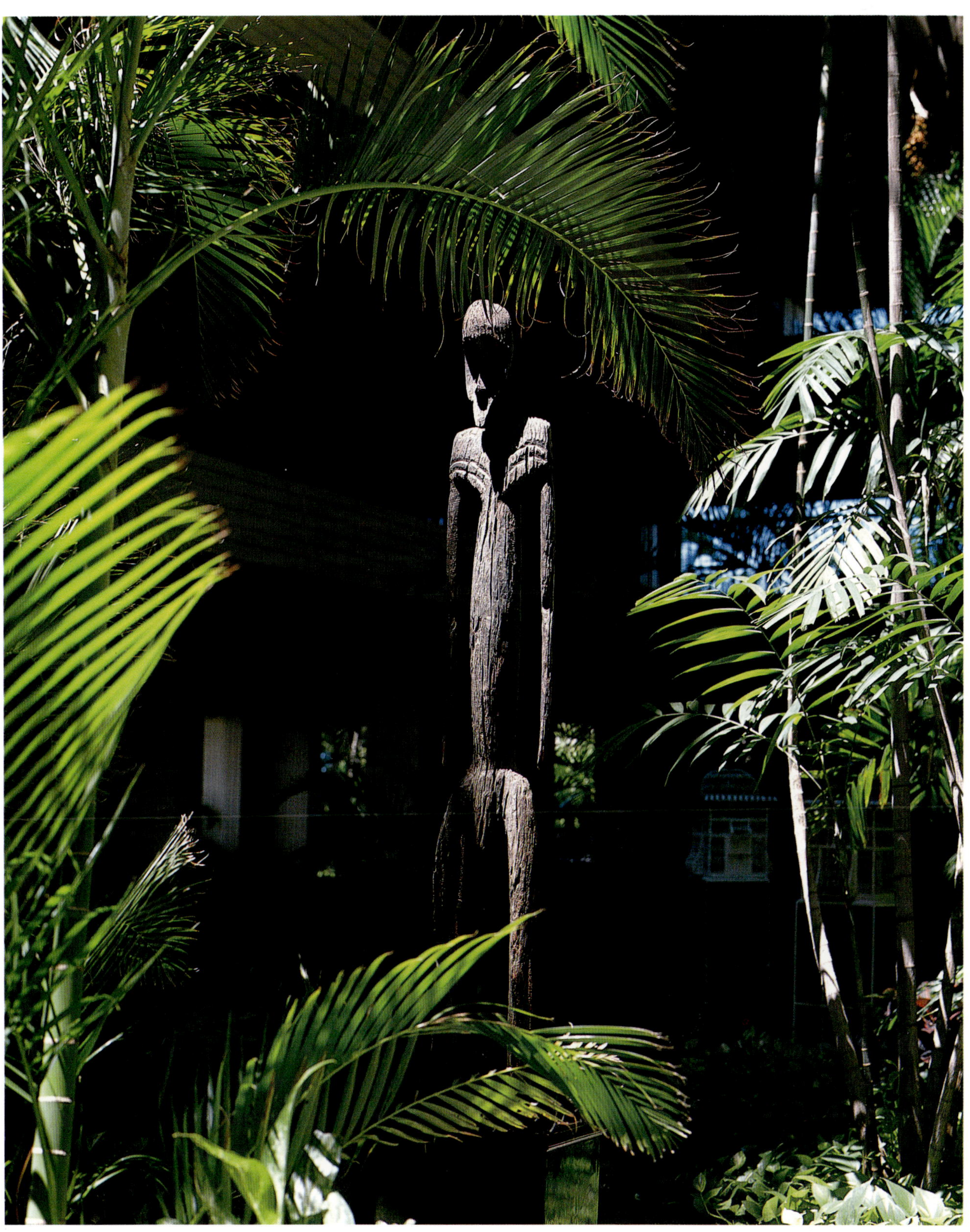

This attenuated and spindly Karawari River figure conveys a powerful sense of aloneness and bears an intriguing resemblance to the sculptures of European artist Alberto Giacometti (1901–1966). Since the beginning of the twentieth century, New Guinea arts, including those based on human form, have significantly influenced the development of Western modern art.

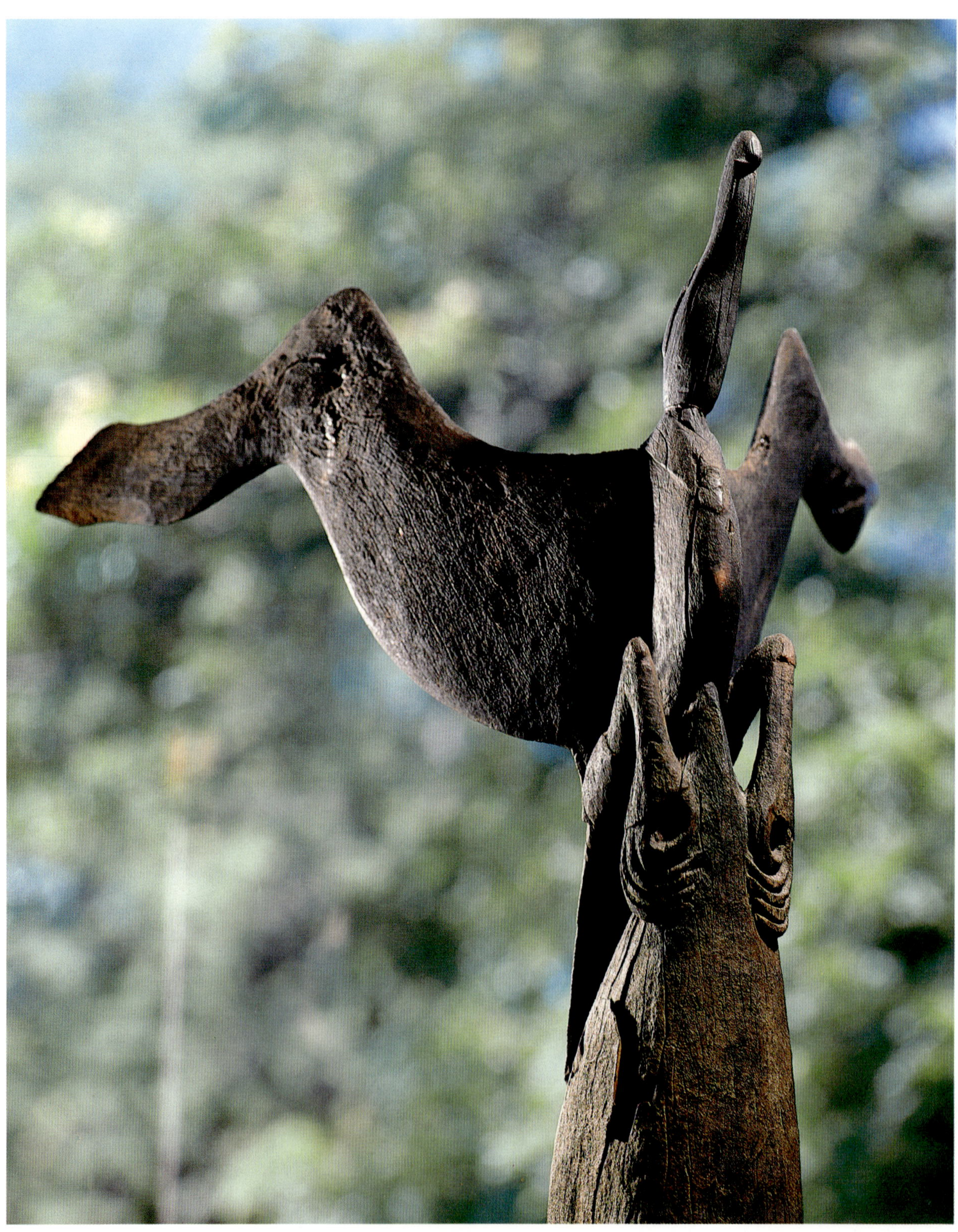

The predatory bird depicted in this Sawos sculpture is probably a frigatebird or sea eagle, a popular avian emblem. The Sawos, the Iatmul, and other peoples living in the Sepik River region of New Guinea created such sculpture as signs of village strength and prestige.

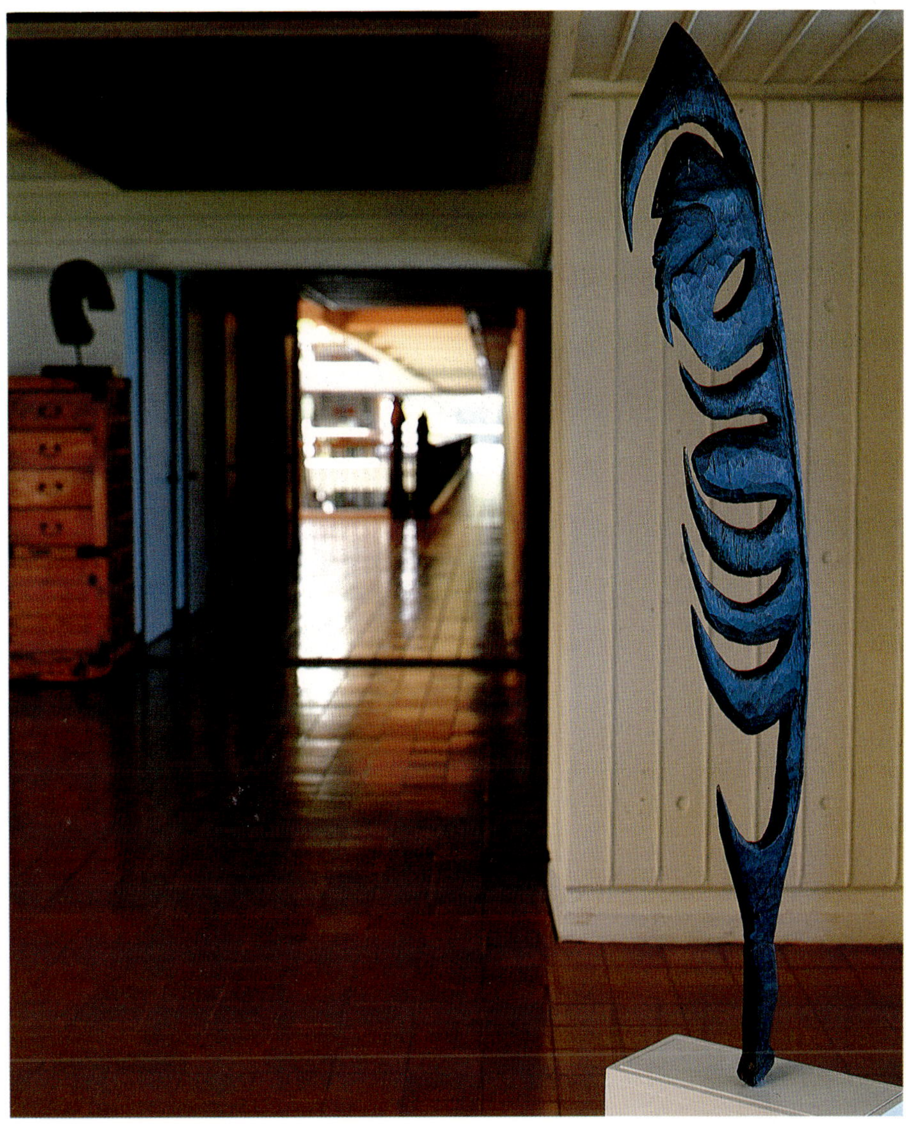

Another important ritual-house sculpture at the Mauna Kea also comes from the Karawari River area. The highly abstract sculpture seems to fuse human and crocodile forms. Veneration of the crocodile spirit led to frequent depiction of the creature in sculpture of many New Guinea peoples. The spiny ridges of a crocodile's back are usually emphasized in more literal representations of the animal. Here, the scaly protuberances are transformed into a series of sharply curving hooks that move downward from the top of the sculpture and upward from its base, guiding the eye to the rudimentary profile of a human head encompassed between them. The sculpture personifies a mythic spirit frequently seen in smaller sizes. This large variant is a clan oracle, a figure to be consulted before warring and hunting expeditions and used in initiation rituals.

In the resort's Beachfront Wing hangs a large wooden plaque, a product of the Eastern Sepik region, probably from the Sawos people. The plaque is carved in complex openwork designs that have been variously interpreted as abstractions of hornbilled birds, pigs, and patterns from cavities of the human skull. A rounded projection above the openwork design has details suggestive of human features. At the bottom, a row of hook-like projections point upward, a device typical of plaques from this region. Melanesian plaques such as this were mounted on ritual-house walls and are believed to be memorials to boys who died during the initiation rites. A related function was served by two massive ancestor tablets from the Middle Sepik region (which are displayed in the hotel's Promenade). Originally, these tablets were installed in spirit houses along with the skulls of captured enemies or, on occasion, groups of such sculptures were stood on end in the ground to define the dance area for ritual ceremonies. In both examples the human face is the dominant motif, stressed through geometricized features and heavily patterned, incised areas around the eyes and mouth. The protruding tongue seen on one tablet is an artistic convention frequently employed in Oceania to convey physical and spiritual power and protection from enemies and malevolent spirits.

Also in this group is a wooden mask from Vanuatu, a chain of islands that stretches for more than five hundred miles to the southeast of New Guinea. One of the larger islands in the group is Malekula, often described as the major source for art in the region and believed to be the provenance of this sculpture. The mask is carved of hardwood in a double-headed form characteristic of Malekula productions and totally unlike the basketry masks of New Guinea. Faces on its front and back appear below a simplified, helmet-like shape typically associated with mythic personages. The planes of the face are bold, projecting from under a wide and bony brow, and its fierce expression is more indicative of human emotion than other works in the Oceanic collection. Masks such as this were erected on ceremonial grounds in front of the men's ritual house and were carved by the sponsor of the candidate for initiation.

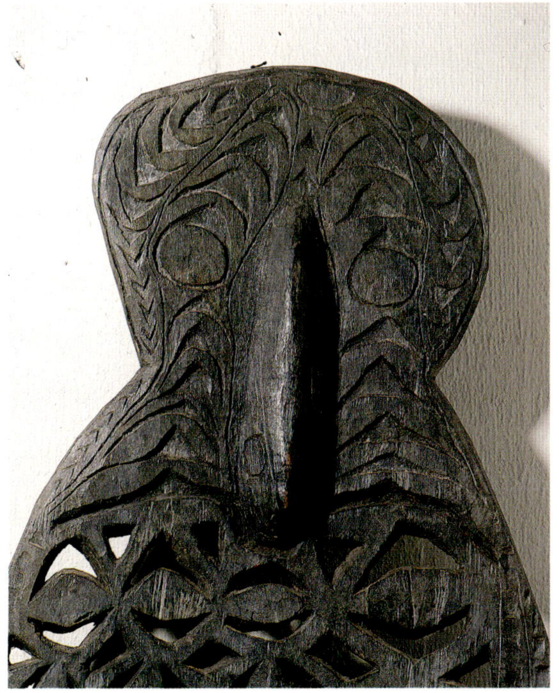

The motifs on this memorial plaque from the Eastern Sepik region are derived from a variety of animals, including birds, and from the human skull. The motifs are difficult to identify because openwork carving demands simple designs; only this spectral visage on the plaque's upper projection is clearly defined.

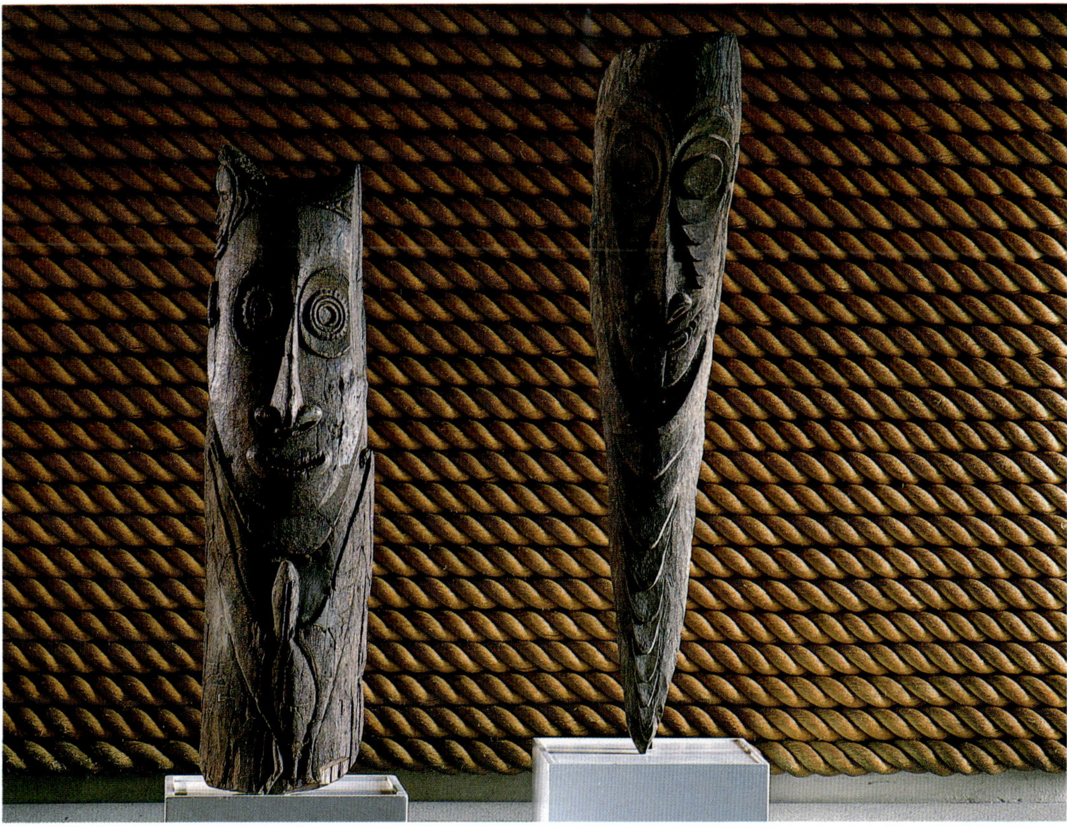

These massive ancestral tablets from New Guinea's Middle Sepik region show an exaggerated phallus and a protruding tongue.

Oceanic Shields

New Guinea, wood with raffia and feathers, heights 33 to 106 inches.

All but a few of the thirty-four carved and decorated shields in the Mauna Kea's Oceanic collection are from the Middle Sepik region, and most are creations of the Iatmul people. The shield is one of the most universal protective devices used by warring peoples. Around the globe, shields display enormous variety in shape, size, material, and color, but typically they have been made in a style that identifies a particular group. Historically, shield bearers often believed a shield could provide not only a physical barrier against attack but also a magical one. Christian shields were decorated with a cross or patterned with monograms derived from the name of Christ—especially for wars with nonbelievers. In Islam, shields often bore Arabic inscriptions from the Qur'an invoking the name of Allah or professing the Muslim confession of faith. Neither Christians nor Muslims could read their enemies' signs or inscriptions when in battle, but each group recognized the shield as a threat and symbol of enemy power.

These Oceanic shields served the same purpose. Many of these works can be described as colorfully painted low-relief sculptures. Some are extraordinarily abstract, others recognizably figurative; all carry signs of a particular clan or of a warrior's rank within the clan, and all were understood to have magical properties as well as practical utility.

Oceanic shield decoration is complex: the sides and fronts of many shields are adorned with plant tassels, and most bear a vertical, totem-like series of carved and painted heads with fiercely expressive eyes and mouths and the familiar protruding tongues. These depictions of spirits may have provided power to ward off the enemy. The shield's totemic design connected the faces to each other through spiral and saw-tooth patterns probably derived from scarification marks. A peg protruding from the top of most of these shields served to suspend decorative and symbolic appendages. Pegs on many shields in the collection still carry feathers or raffia clumps. In some cases, the peg has been carved into a small human face, perhaps to represent the head-hunting skills of the warrior.

In some New Guinea tribes, shields were awarded to initiates by their elder sponsors in recognition of having attained a certain grade or rank. The shield provided not only protection but also prestige, individually as well as communally. Not all were intended for use in battle, as some were created for ceremonial dances while others were installed on doors and elsewhere within the men's ritual house to affirm the powers of the tribe's living warriors. Less frequently, such shields were attached to the ridges below the roof of the men's house, their decorated sides pointing downward.

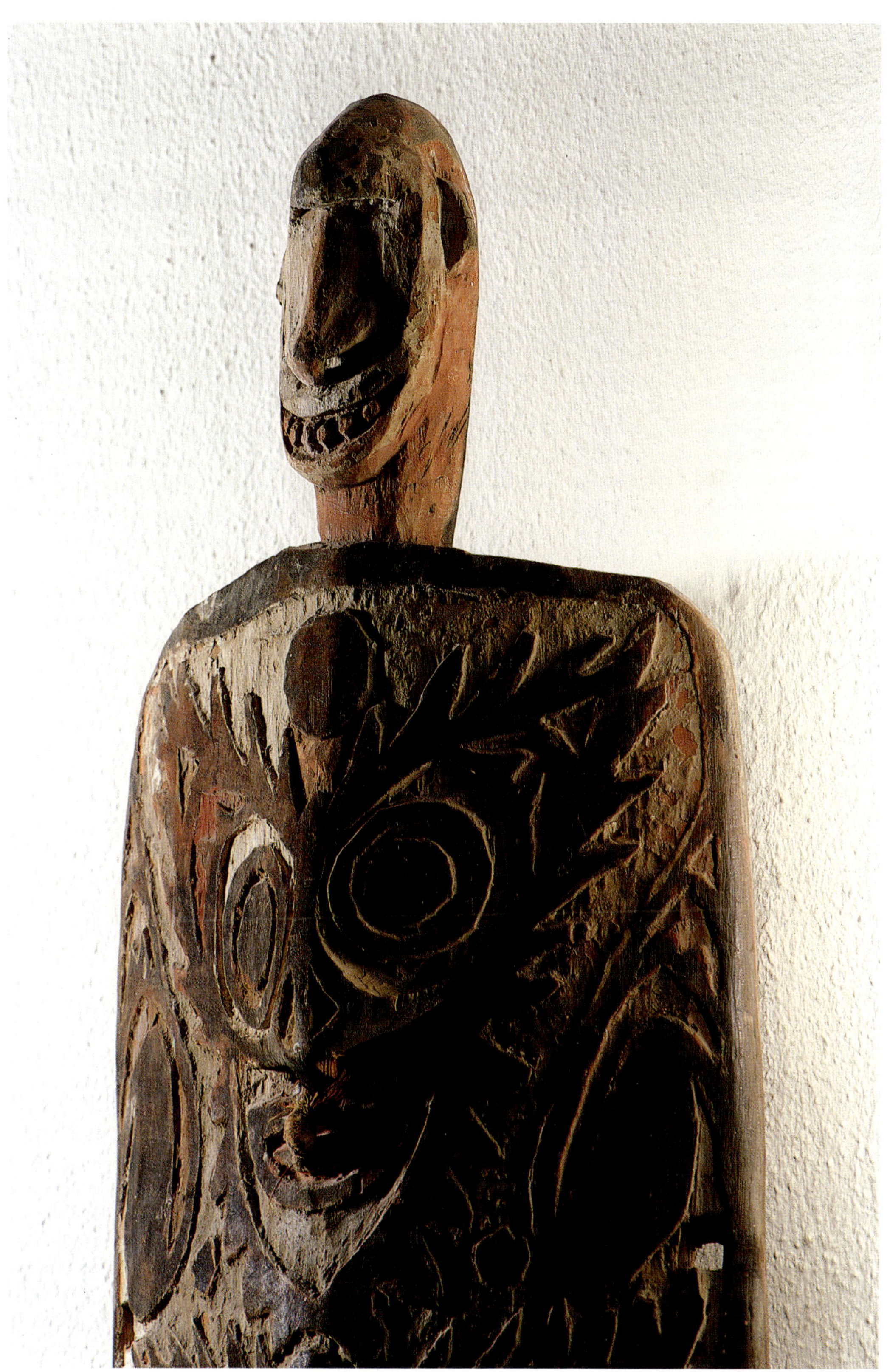

When carving shields, the Iatmul people often shaped a peg at the top, as this detail photograph shows. The pegs were ancestral as well as headhunting emblems and were often carved to depict a human face. They were also thought to symbolize the shield's phallus—the source of its spiritual power against an enemy.

Food Containers and Utensils

New Guinea, Solomon Islands, and other regions, wood and coconut-shell implements, lengths 7 to 41½ inches; carved ceremonial platter, length 69 inches.

A NUMBER of objects used in the preparation and serving of food are displayed in the resort's Garden restaurant. Rockefeller chose these works from New Guinea peoples and many other Melanesian cultures because their symbolic ornamentation reflects the unity of spirituality and everyday life. Fashioned from a wide variety of natural materials and in some cases richly decorated, these utensils also reflect the resourcefulness of the Melanesian peoples and their ability to transform the simplest materials into art.

The problems of attribution are especially rife for tools because, unlike ritual sculpture, they were not intended for permanent installation in the village and were sometimes sought after and collected by peoples far away (just as the eighteenth century Burmese bronze drums in the collection were created for export to hill tribes in Southeast Asia but also appealed to Thai royalty). Such "dislocations" occurred not only through trade but also through looting of a vanquished enemy.

Melanesian peoples delighted in colossal food containers and serving platters, as did the peoples of Polynesia. Each vessel's dimensions were determined by its intended ritual use, whether for ceremonies within the ritual house or outside, for entertaining one's own clan and village, or for impressing visitors from neighboring regions.

The Mauna Kea's grandest example of a Melanesian food container is a six-foot-long platter from the eastern Solomon Islands, an archipelago close to one thousand miles long, lying east of New Guinea. A platter of this size was suited for use by the regional leader (or "big-man," in Melanesian pidgin English) when entertaining many important guests, the exuberance of its artistry a sign of the leader's prestige. The most important works of the Solomon Islands region (including shields, sculptures, and voyaging canoes) share the distinctive type of inlaid decoration that characterizes the Mauna Kea's platter.

The huge vessel is carved in the form of a dugout canoe, the wood blackened to set off a mosaic inlay of iridescent shell that depicts shark heads on both ends of the platter. Sharks were traditional emblems; their potent spirits were thought to safeguard ocean voyages by placating storms and strong currents. The finely cut, carefully shaped shell pieces are set into the wood and affixed with a black resinous substance. The inlay was planned to create a glittering, symmetrical design that conforms to and accentuates the sculptural shape of the platter.

Additional bowls and implements from the Solomon Islands, the Manus (Admiralties), the Trobriand Islands, the Huon Gulf region, the Siassi Islands, and the island of New Guinea itself are also displayed in the Garden restaurant. The implements include

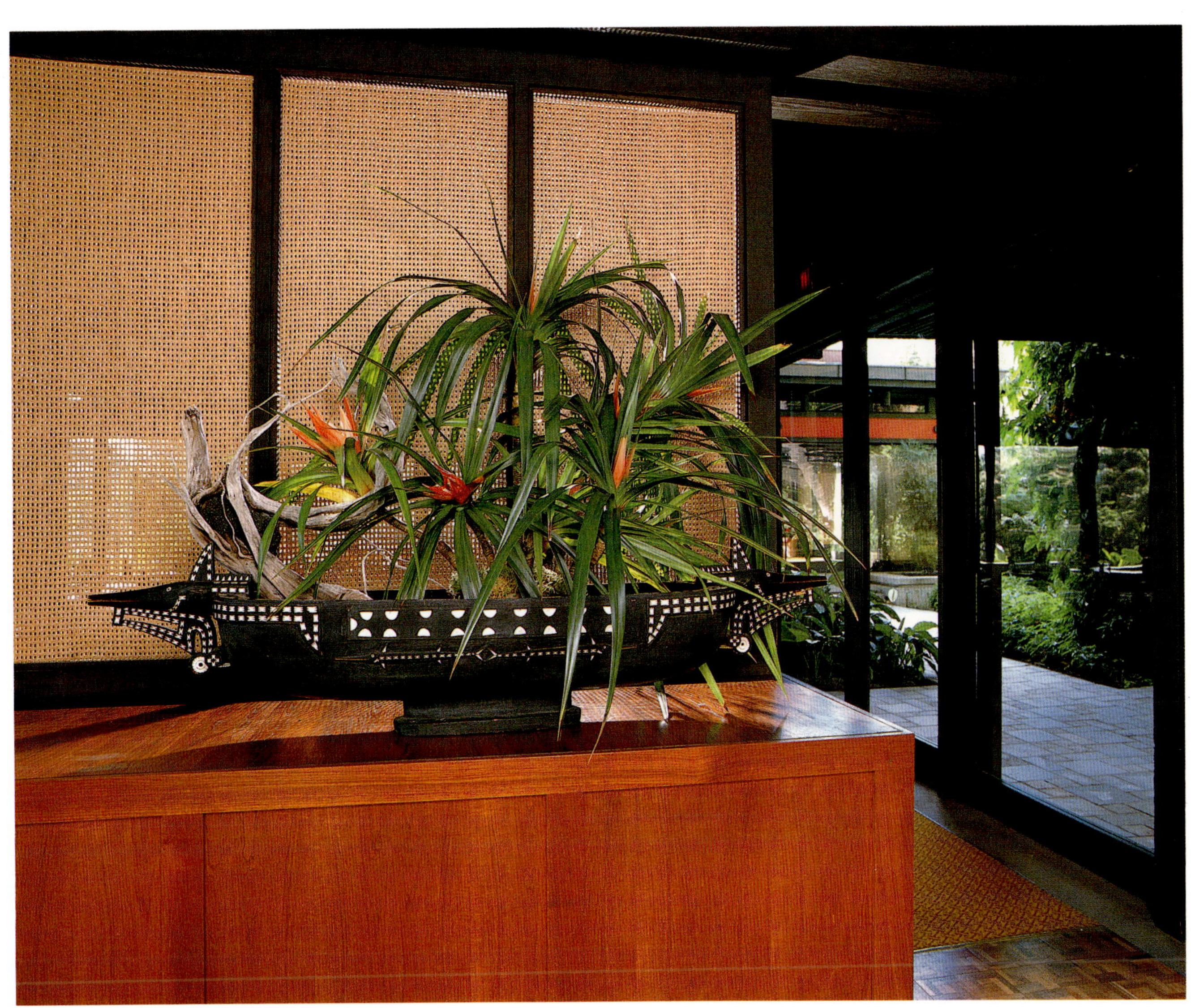

coconut-shell dippers and wood forks, and wood scoops and pounders for sago, taro, and breadfruit. Here, too, as in parts of Southeast Asia, are implements associated with the consumption of betel nut, including elegantly shaped, carved wood spatulas, and mortars and pestles for grinding the nuts. Many of these works employ the image of the frigatebird, a guardian symbol venerated throughout much of Oceania.

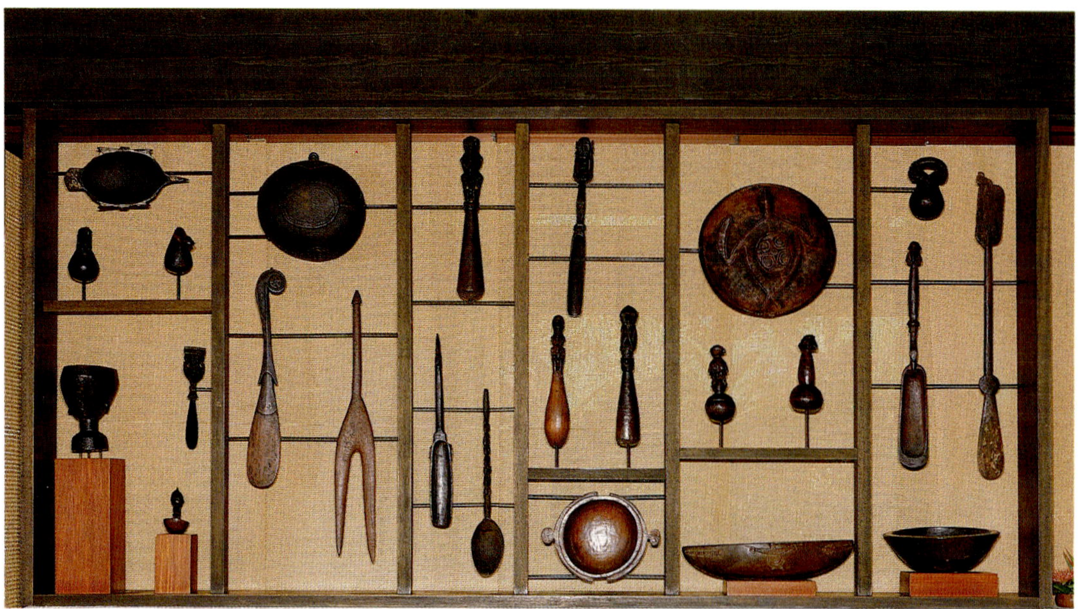

This intriguing assortment of decorated Melanesian food containers and utensils is displayed in the Garden restaurant. Many Oceanic peoples decorated food-related implements for use in festivals; some utensils acquired the status of ritual sculpture because of the symbolic importance of their decorations. (Display panel by sculptor Edward Brownlee.)

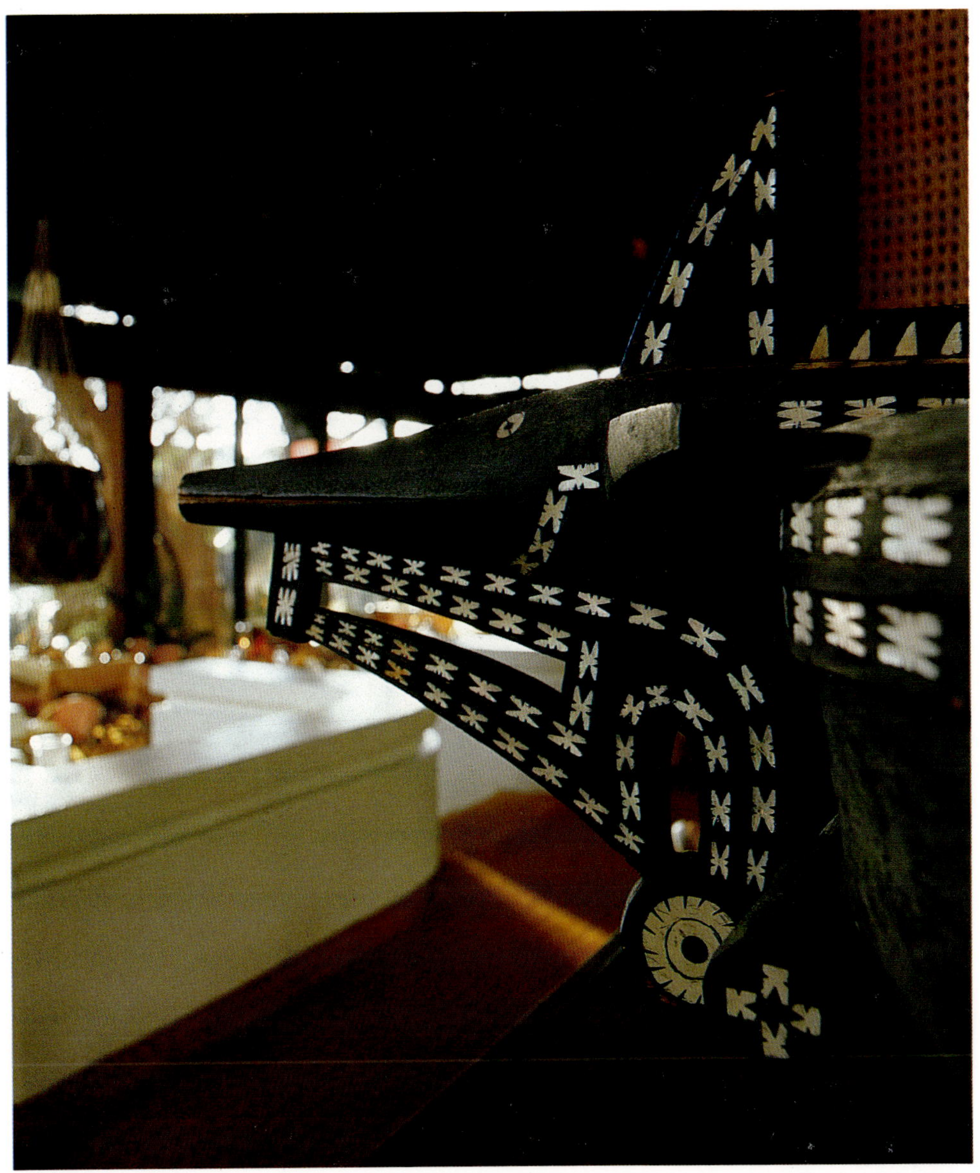

The prow of this Solomon Islands ceremonial platter was shaped to resemble the head and dorsal fin of a shark, an animal these people associated with warriors of great prowess. The irregular pattern of decorative shell may represent rows of shark teeth. The use of shell conveyed wealth, protection, and magical powers.

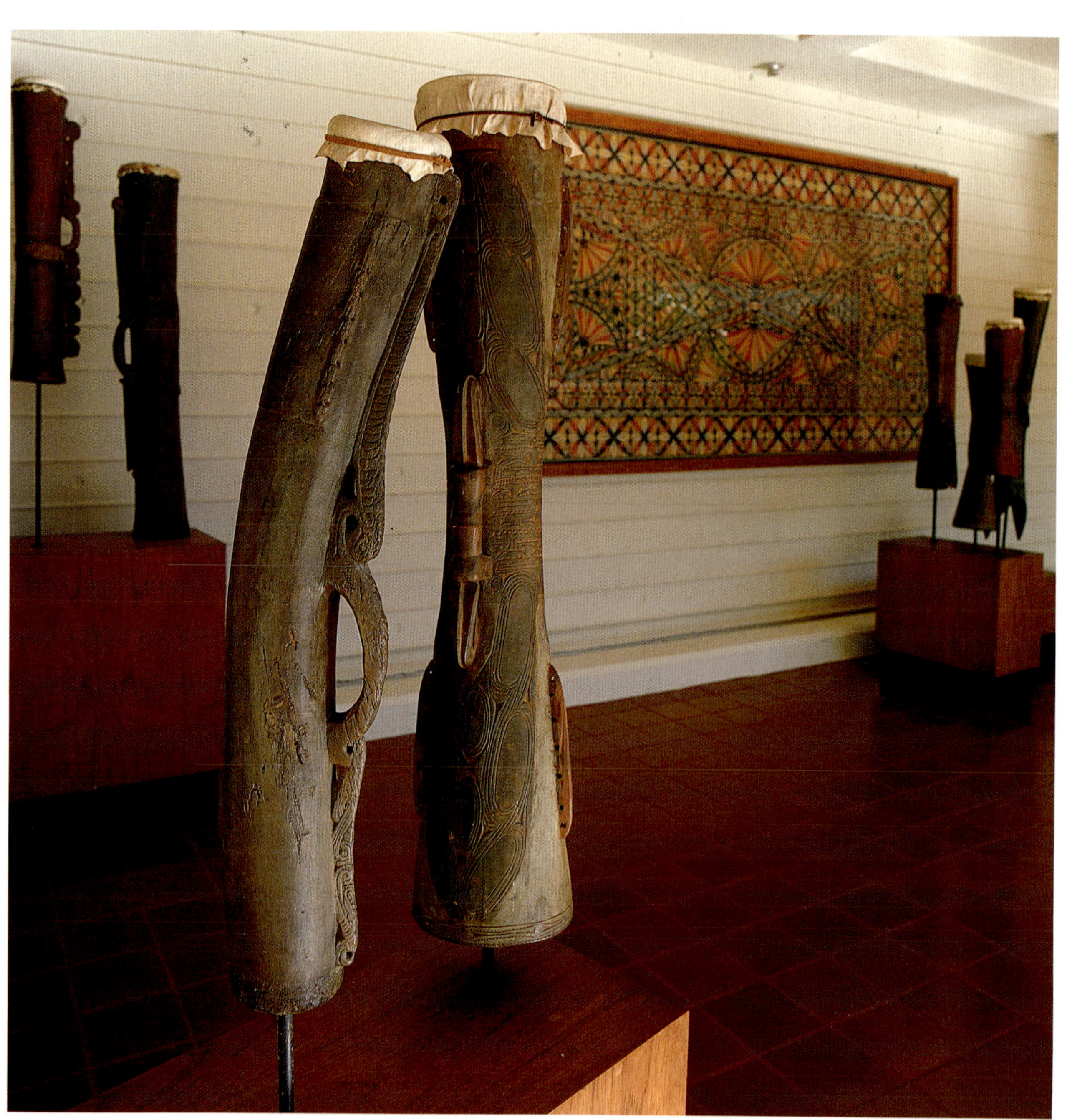

Drums and Dance Wands

New Guinea and Solomon Islands, wood, lengths 58 inches (slit-gong drum) and 43 to 63 inches (dance wands), heights 21 to 40½ inches (hourglass drums).

A LARGE group of Melanesian drums at the Mauna Kea conveys the often elusive distinctions between religious and secular celebrations. Drums had important ritual uses but also functioned as a means of communication with clan members away from the village. Each male clan member had an identifying three-part drumbeat pattern. One type of drum roll was derived from identifying patterns of beat from the father's village, and another pattern of beat was from the mother's village; the third sequence of drumbeats designated the current grade or rank of the individual within the clan.

The Melanesians have employed a variety of drum types, and examples of the two most typical forms, slit-gong and hourglass, are included in the collection. From the Middle Sepik region of New Guinea comes a large slit-gong made by hollowing out a section of tree trunk through a large opening carved along its length. The finished work carries human and animal decorative images: a male figure drapes across the back of a crocodile, while the crocodile itself is carved with swirls of a pattern that might be interpreted as spines but may also denote scarification designs. Some researchers suggest these drums derive from mythic lore and seek to reproduce the sound of a man-eating primeval crocodile; others interpret the body of the drum as human, the large slit as an open mouth, and the drum chamber itself as a voice for ancestral spirits. This type of slit-gong was set horizontally on the ground, resting on the crocodile's legs, and was beaten on its top.

A group of elegantly formed drums in the collection comes mostly from the eastern New Guinea region—from the Trobriand Islands (Massim region) and the Huon Gulf. All are variations on the hourglass shape and bear bands of finely carved curvilinear decoration typical of the region. The drum tops are reptile skins, and almost all have a single handle on the body. These drums were stood upright and beaten on the side of the sound chamber.

Throughout New Guinea, the sound of drums was equated with spirit voices and, to awaken its latent spirituality, each new drum was "initiated" through elaborate ritual. Clan ceremonies to initiate drums (and masks) typically involved reenactment of myths and included dances often performed with ceremonial weapons or dance wands—slender, decorative staffs.

Often a specific number of wands with distinctive attributes were associated with particular categories of mask, headdress, and dance. Wands were an important part of public ceremonies presented for the uninitiated in the village, primarily women and children. They were a principal accompaniment to dances that acted out clan myths and were frequently used in burial rites and in ceremonies intended to placate ancestral spirits.

One of the two Solomon Island dance wands in the Mauna Kea collection displays the same carefully controlled sense of form and decoration evident on the large Solomon Island platter. Like the food vessel, it is stained black with a pigment and burnished to a soft lustre; its handle bears understated, low-relief carved decorations. This wand shows the elegant design typical of this category of ceremonial dance implement: the flared head of the wand is carved into a flat and extremely graceful arc, perhaps an abstract representation of a fish leaping out of water, a motif sometimes seen in arts of the Solomon Islands.

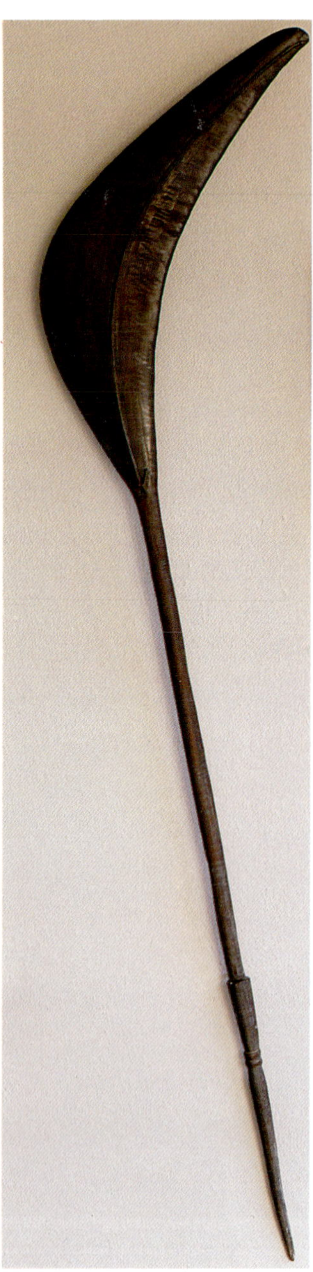

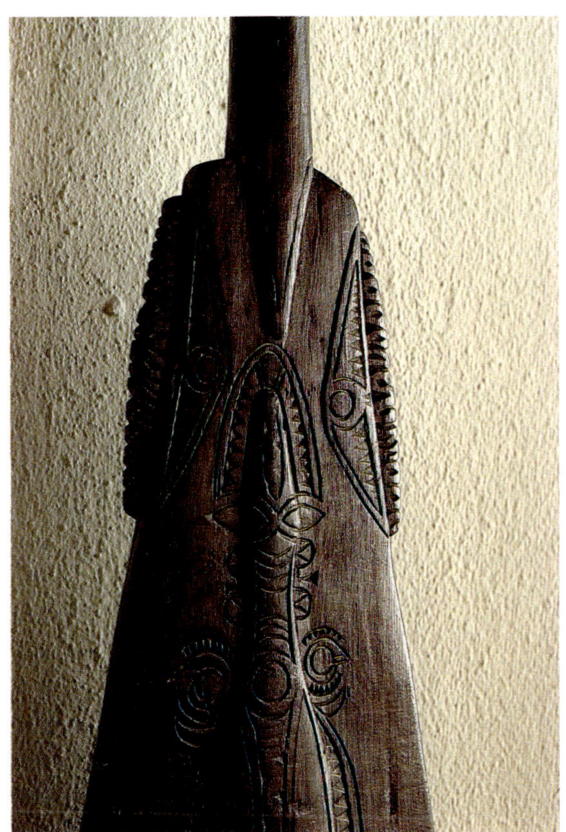

The image of a crocodile appears on this canoe paddle from the Siassi Islands to procure magical protection for maritime voyagers. The creature is seen from above, in a bird's eye view; swirling patterns around its forelegs suggest movement through water.

Implements for Maritime Voyages

New Guinea (Trobriand and Siassi Islands, Massim region), wood, heights 27 and 17¼ inches (canoe splashboards), lengths 43 to 82 inches (canoe paddles) and 88 inches (canoe).

WORKS of the Massim region, which comprises the southeastern tip of New Guinea and nearby island groups, are characterized by a fairly distinct artistic style. In this region, unlike other parts of Melanesia, sculpture in the round and religious arts are rare. Most artistic productions take the form of low-relief wood sculpture decoratively carved in linear designs. This relative homogeneity of artistic style is thought to result from inter-island travel by dugout and sometimes sail-equipped outrigger canoes. Islanders often communicated through ceremonial exchange of ritual objects, especially objects related to sea travel, such as the canoe splashboards and paddles in the resort's collection.

The Trobriand Islands, an important archipelago within the Massim region, have given rise to perhaps the most excellent art of the Massim area, the result of a rather formal apprenticeship system. In general, the Trobriand people produced few figural images, such as masks or ancestral sculptures, and are famous especially for two-dimensional, low-relief carved works. Men's societies and ceremonial houses are absent from the Trobriands, although magical rituals to control the spirit world were conducted. This absence of ritual architecture may be responsible for the emphasis on arts of a practical nature.

Trobriand canoes bear ornamented splashboards inset at prow and stern, two of which grace the Mauna Kea collection. Designs on both are curvilinear, abstract, and intricate, as is typical of Trobriand art. One is painted bright red; on the other, a pigment derived from lime was pressed into the incised design to heighten its visual impact. The carved designs likely issue from images of snakes and birds, in particular the frigatebird, whose ability to soar great distances inspired its presence on canoes in the hope that it would magically guide voyagers. Trobriand canoe paddles in the collection have similarly delicate, rhythmic curved patterns, as do the tribe's shields, where sometimes the entire surface is carved in a network of interlocking spiral shapes.

Between the Huon Gulf and New Britain are the Siassi Islands, whose artifacts, in contrast to those of the Trobriands, reflect New Guinea figural traditions. Carved images appear on two paddles from the Siassis, one a human figure, the other a crocodile as seen in a bird's-eye view. The crocodile is a frequent motif in these islands, appearing not only on marine implements but also on village houseposts. A serpentine figure decorates the outside of a small ceremonial canoe from the Siassis; figures carved within the stern and prow represent a full-bellied woman in a birthing posture.

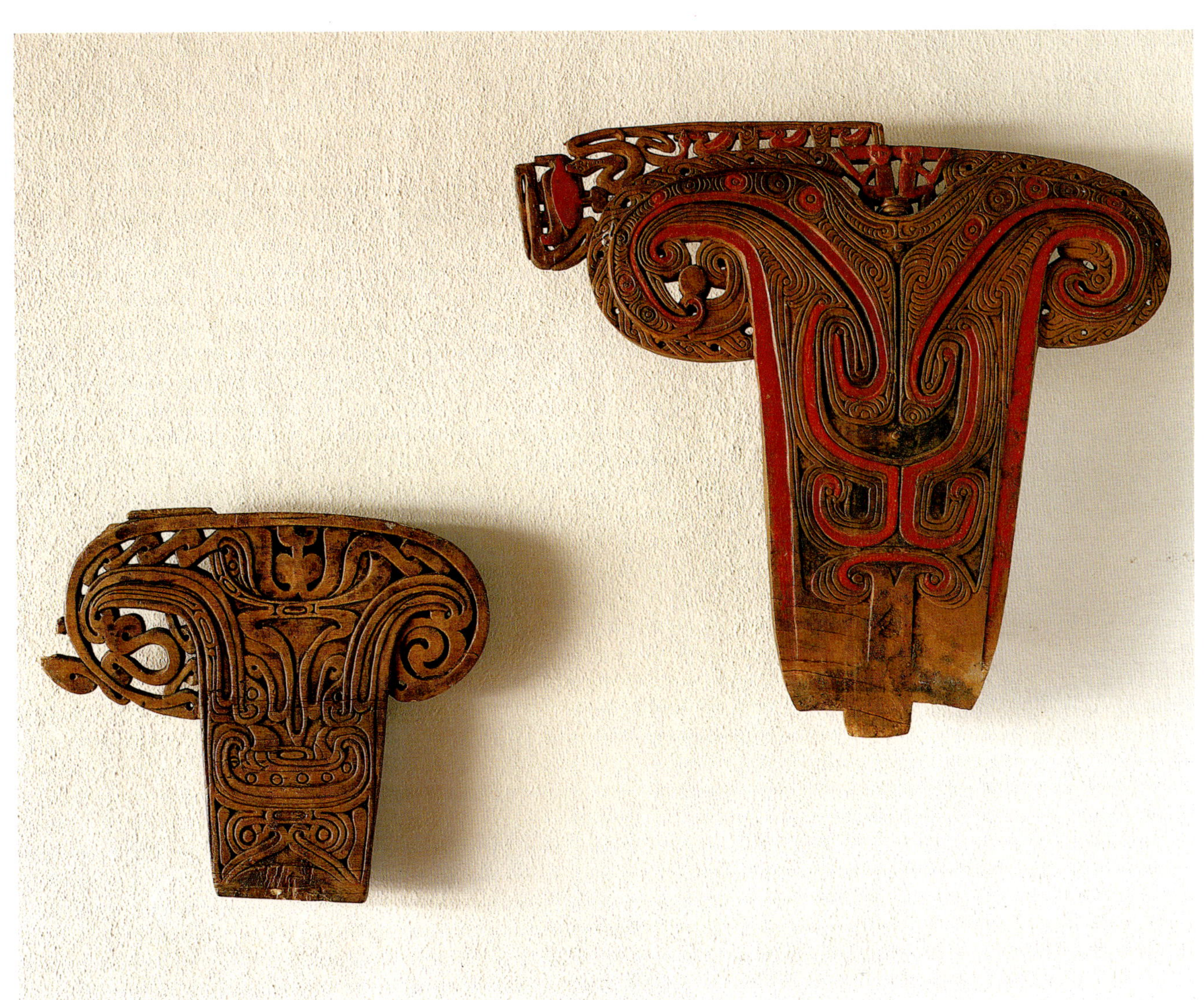

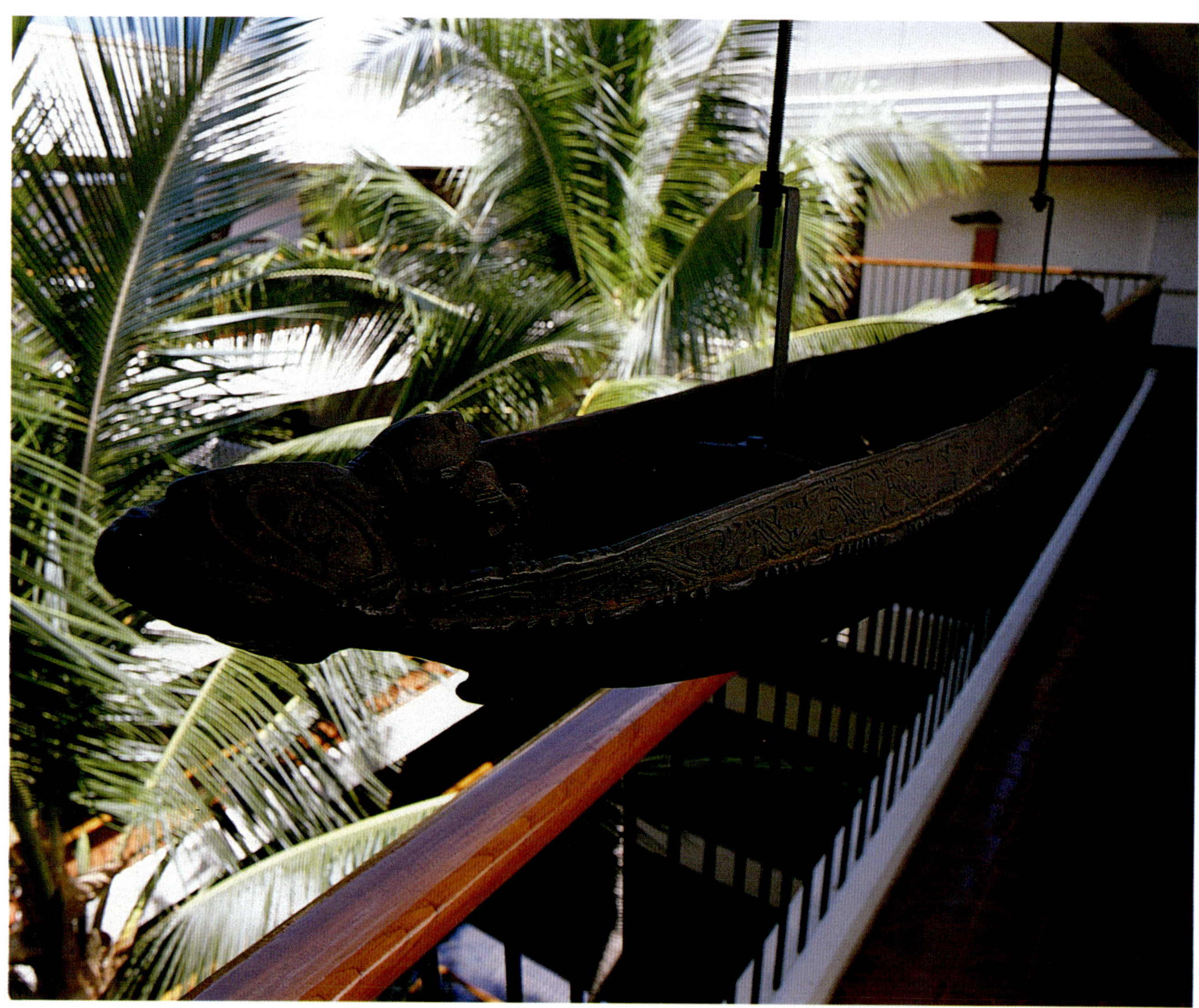

This highly decorated canoe was created in the Siassi Islands for ceremonial purposes. Crocodile and human forms and a serpentine design are carved on the outside; inside, female figures squat in birthing positions at both ends of the canoe. The full-bellied females may represent clan ancestors or may relate more generally to islanders' creation myths.

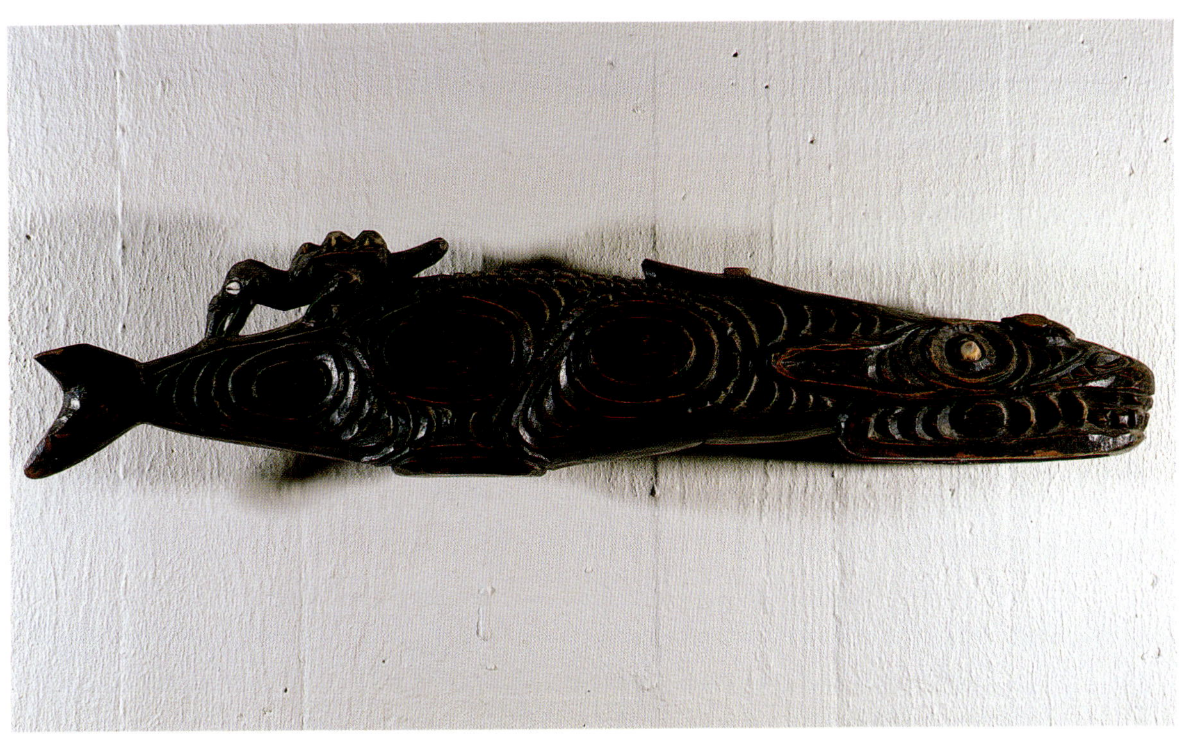

Ceremonial canoes of the Asmat people of New Guinea's southwest coast (an area now known as Irian Jaya, a part of Indonesia) often bear prow sculpture such as this fish. The bird riding on the back of the fish is likely a heron, a bird whose renowned hunting skill was perhaps intended to set an example for initiates. The bulging eye of the fish is an operculum, the inner valve of a sea snail; elsewhere, cowrie shell is inlaid in the wood.

POLYNESIA

POLYNESIA is a triangular region extending from Hawai'i in the north to New Zealand in the southwest and Easter Island in the southeast. Within this area are five major island groups: the Society Islands, Tahiti, the Marquesas, the Cook Islands, and the islands of Western Polynesia. These archipelagos are separated by the vast Pacific, often by thousands of miles.

Polynesia was the last part of the earth to be settled, the culmination of a long series of migrations that began in the second millennium B.C.; Hawai'i was first populated in the early centuries of the Christian era and New Zealand in A.D. 750–1000. Migration to and across Polynesia demanded extraordinary skill in canoemaking and navigation, and the Polynesians preserved the history and genealogies of their remarkable voyages in epic chants. So important was this oral history and literature that each island group maintained schools to teach it to succeeding generations. The Maoris of New Zealand especially named and remembered the great canoes of their migration—in considerably more detail than American schoolchildren learn the names of Christopher Columbus's ships and those of the Pilgrims.

Though the islands are widely dispersed and varied in climate and geography, the Polynesian peoples share similar cultures. Unlike Melanesia, Polynesia developed relatively complex belief systems and aristocratic rather than egalitarian social organizations. Polynesian theology was based on reverence for rulers and their ancestors; noble families were understood to be descendants of the gods, who represented natural forces. These beliefs parallel Shinto views of the imperial family as being descended from the Sun Goddess, as well as the cult of the *devaraja* seen in Cambodia. Polynesians' respect for people of noble birth and for the priesthood also seems kindred to the Hebraic esteem for the hereditary monarchy and priesthood recounted in the Old Testament. In Hawai'i, an aristocratic hierarchy determined by descent produced a stratified society wherein there was little chance of mobility in social rank. An important exception was the Maoris of Aotearoa (modern-day New Zealand), whose social structure was based on kinship more than class hierarchy, with chieftains rather than kings.

Polynesians were guided in daily life by the concept of *mana*, a spiritual and creative power that resided in the gods and, to a greater or lesser degree, in people, places, and objects. Polynesian works of art were often intended as emblems of rank but also signified the *mana* of a person, place, or thing. *Mana* was established through noble lineage and could be acquired as well through development of skills, in a cumulative effect, though even the greatest of accomplishments would not raise a human's *mana* above that of a god.

Mana could be lost through violating the system of taboo (also tabu; *kapu* in Hawai'i) whether inadvertently or intentionally. Transgressors of a taboo not only lost *mana* but were punished according to societal law. The taboo system also acknowledged psychically negative powers that could threaten an individual's *mana*. (These are generalized interpretations of the power and sources of *mana*; other views of its complexity and significance exist.)

Throughout Oceania and Asia, religion has been the principal transmitter of artistic style. In Buddhism, artists followed a strict canon of proportions in creating Buddha images; in Melanesia, the potency of each religious image was bound to an unalterable style of artistic rendering. Although Polynesians originally shared in this attitude of artistic constancy, recent history has interfered with the continuing transmission of styles. By comparison to New Guinea and related island groups, where traditional patterns of tribal life and art survive today, most of Polynesia has undergone severe cultural disruption over the last two hundred years as a result of European contact. The introduction of European diseases, metal technology, weapons, and Christianity has had a much more destructive impact on these small, relatively accessible cultures than on Melanesian societies.

In the Mauna Kea's collection, Polynesia is represented mainly by selections from New Zealand and Hawai'i. The creativity of the Maori people is illustrated by maritime and architectural arts commissioned by Rockefeller from the New Zealand government–sponsored Maori Arts and Crafts Institute in Rotorua. Like other Polynesian peoples, the Maoris experienced armed conflict with Western colonists, particularly in the first half of the nineteenth century when there was a sudden massive influx of Britons seeking escape from the overpopulated industrial cities of England and Scotland. These wars reduced the indigenous population and threatened the continuity of Maori art and culture. Later in the nineteenth century, a Maori resurgence of interest in traditional arts and culture produced a renaissance of Polynesian skills that continues into this century.

Many of the Maori pieces bear designs resembling those worn by the people in the form of tattoos. In centuries past, the arts of tattooing were highly developed in New Zealand, in a variation of scarification as it was practiced elsewhere. Pigments were rubbed into cuts on the body, commonly on the lips of women and on the entire face and often the thighs of men. Tattoos were associated with warfare, and war between tribes was frequent prior to European contact. So important were tattoos that practitioners were regarded as artists, their typically curvilinear designs an important part of cultural traditions.

The acquisition of works of art to represent Hawai'i at the Mauna Kea presented a variety of problems, particularly because few works of pre-nineteenth-century Hawaiian culture still exist. The scarcity of these older arts is in part due to their construction from relatively fragile materials subject to decay. Most of these works, however, were destroyed—by Hawaiians, when the *kapu* system was overturned in 1819 after the death of

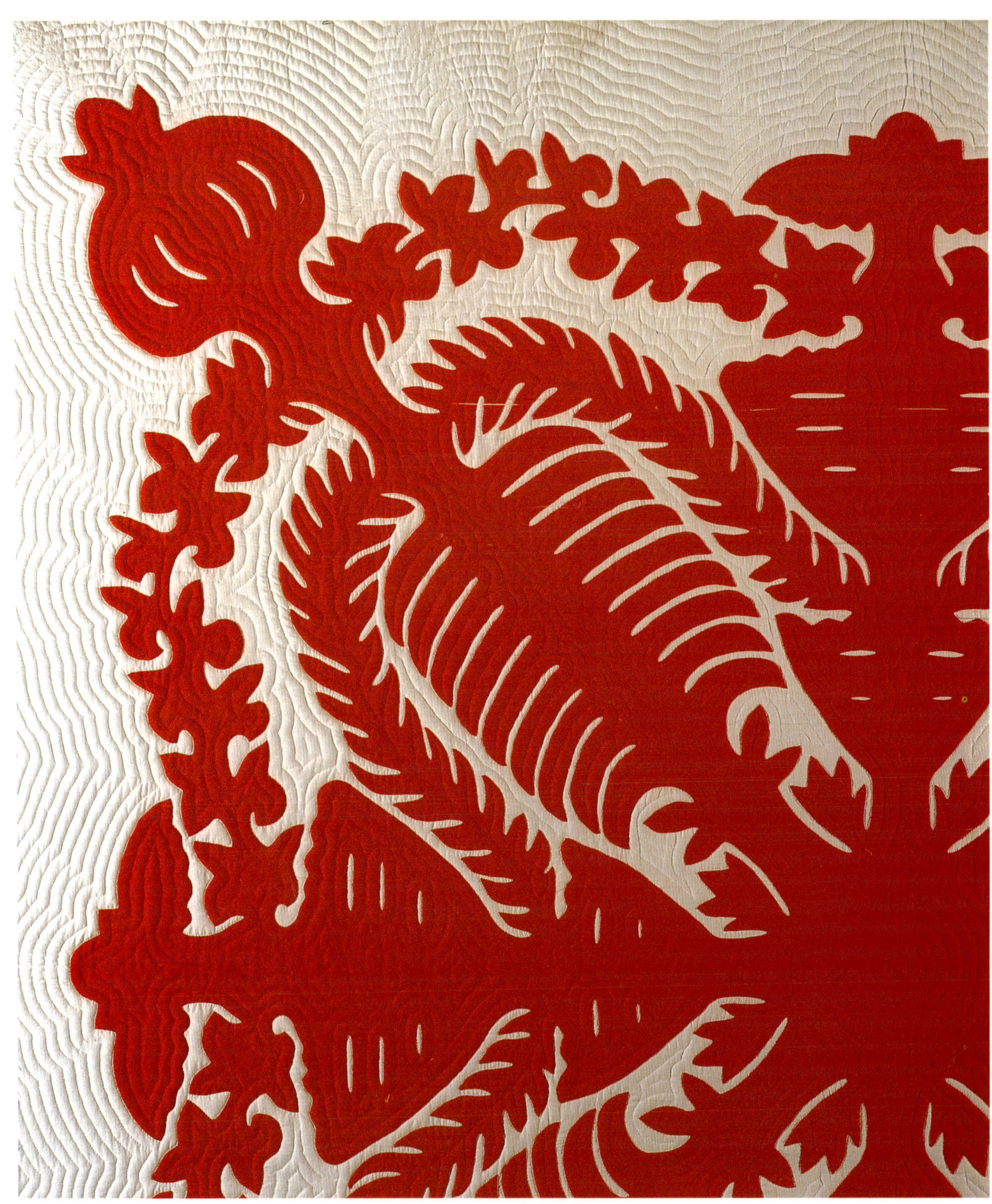

The Hawaiian quilt shown here in detail features the *kāhili* and the *maile lei*. *Kāhili* are emblematic standards constructed of feathers and were traditional symbols of Hawaiian chiefs. *Maile* is a highly revered, sweet-smelling, glossy leafed vine that grows in the mountains. The use of *maile* held great significance in ancient Hawaiian rituals.

King Kamehameha I, and by Christian missionaries, who began arriving in the islands the following year. The missionaries also retrieved some artifacts and sent them to America and Europe as symbols of their victory over Polynesian "heathenism." The traditional forms of Hawaiian art, often heavily associated with the system of *kapu*, were eventually destroyed in the last stages of missionary conquest, a time during which the Hawaiians were also forced to give up their land and way of life. Rockefeller felt that commissioning imitations of these older art forms might offend Hawaiians, and he therefore acquired for the hotel works in forms that remain alive in Hawai'i—tapa, quilts, and modern paintings and sculpture. The spiritual and artistic traditions of Hawai'i represented in these works demonstrate the contributions of enduring Polynesian culture to the enrichment of the fiftieth state.

Canoe Decorations

Maori, wood with shell inlay, heights 46 inches (canoe prow), 78 and 94 inches (canoe sterns), and 24 inches (bailer).

THESE large prow and stern decorations are among the best examples of Polynesian arts in the Mauna Kea's collection. The Maori great canoes, eighty-foot-long dugout vessels propelled by paddlers seated two abreast, traveled the rivers as well as coastal waters. New Zealand, home of the Maori, has temperate climates and abundant natural resources, including the indigenous pines that furnished the raw material for these huge canoes and most other sculptural forms. Known as the *totara* (*Podocarpus totara*) and *kauri* (*Agathis australis*), these pines had light, soft woods that were durable and suitable for fine carving.

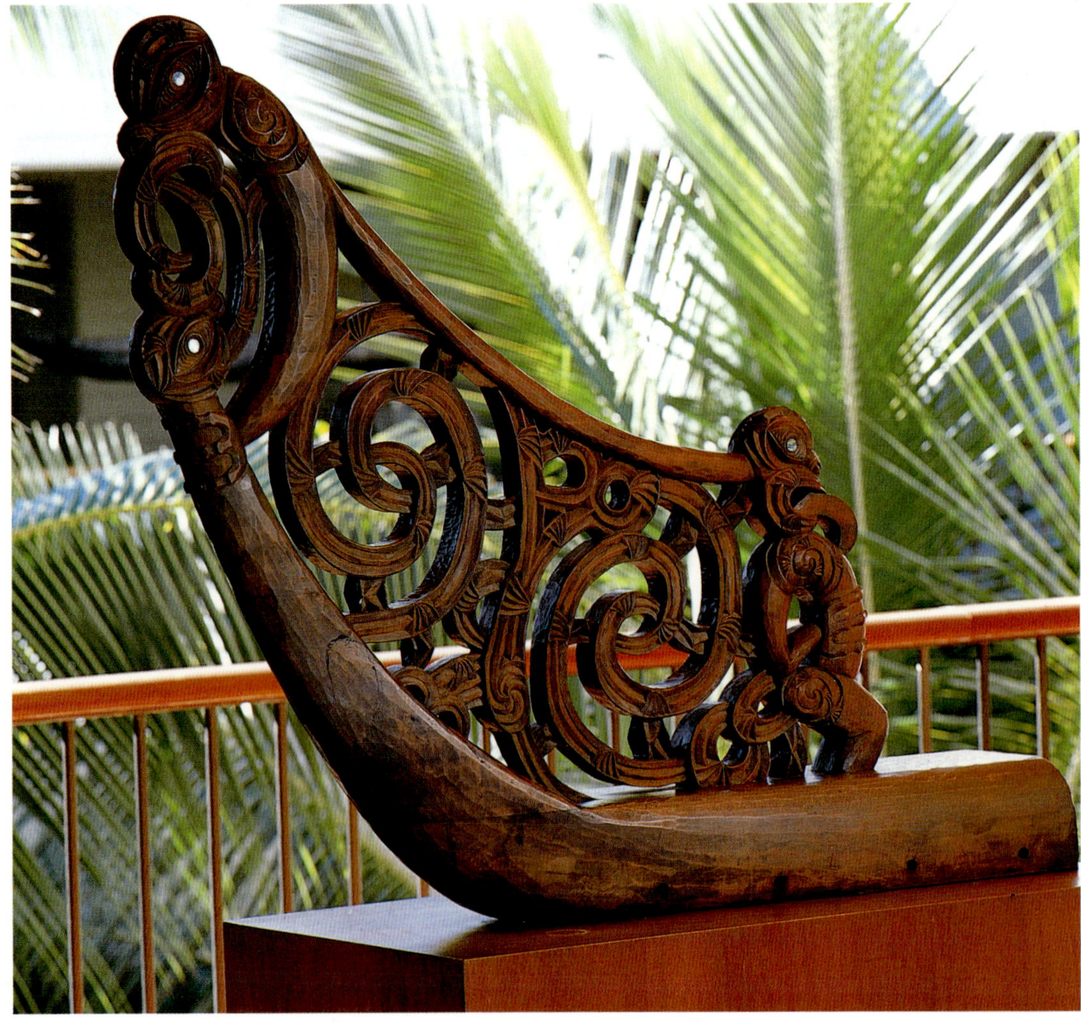

Double-spiral openwork carving along the length of this canoe prow connects a protective figure at the bottom to a *manaia* figure at the top. The half-bird, half-man *manaia* probably symbolized the destructive powers of the clan's naval warriors.

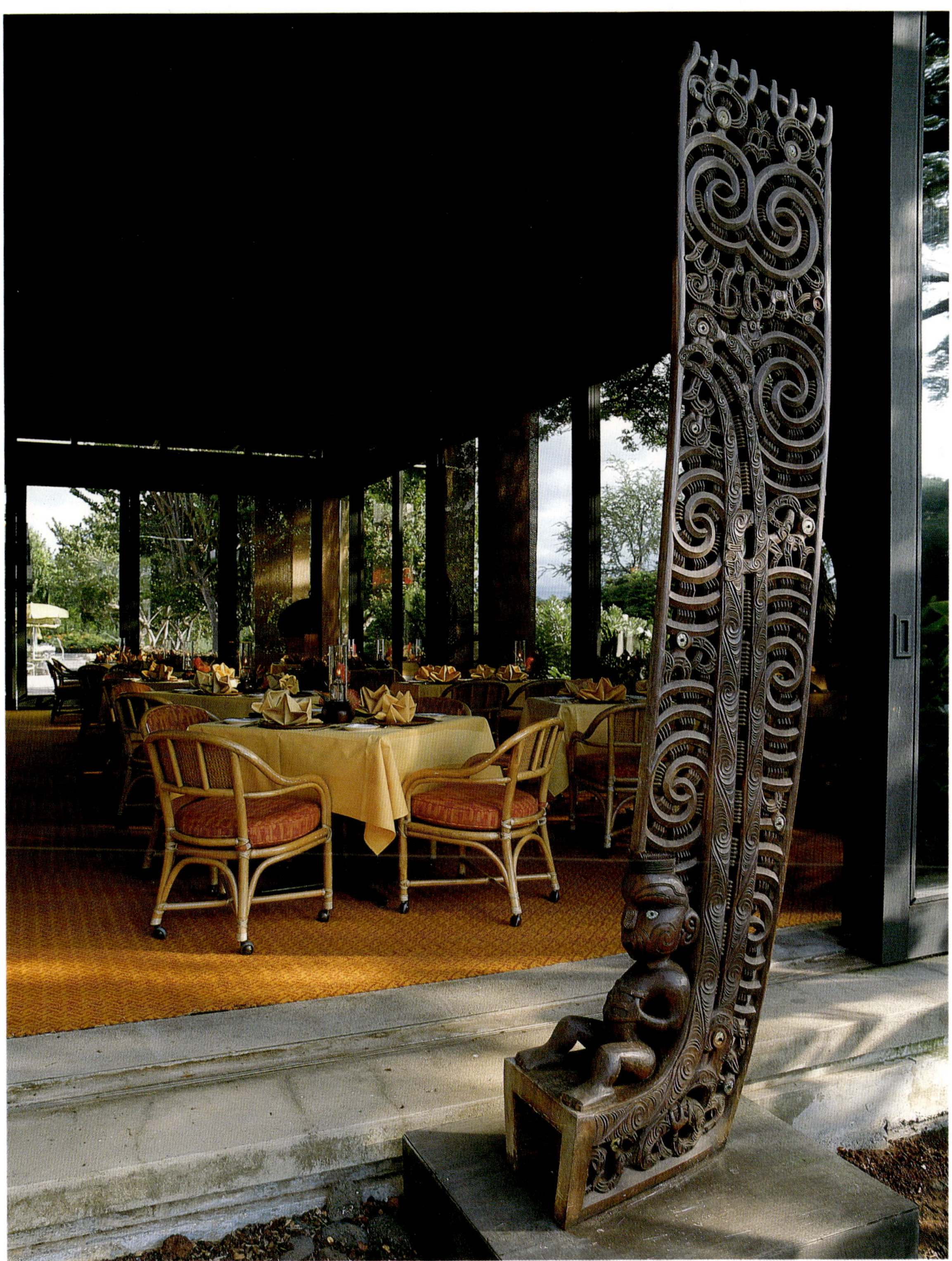

The pierced openwork carving of complex spirals on this Maori war canoe stern is reminiscent of the intricate curvilinear patterns tattooed on the warriors themselves. The human figure at the base of the stern, a protective ancestral spirit, was situated to watch over the paddlers.

The Mauna Kea's canoe prow is carved in openwork. Traditional in both subject and style, the double-spiral decorative pattern within its frame echoes the gently arched form of the prow. This web of swirls follows down the frame to terminate at the arched back of a human figure carved at the base of the prow. This figure, poised tense and flexed, would have originally looked into the canoe toward the Maori paddlers.

In the uppermost area of the prow is a figurehead that bears some anthropomorphized features but is much more abstract and complex in subject than the figure at the base. This upper figure is a *manaia* or "bird man," a ubiquitous form in Maori arts, which is variously interpreted. The essential visual feature of the *manaia* is a head in profile; sometimes the body is also in profile. The face often seems to have a beak, as here, which accounts for the bird association. The lower body is often lizard-like, a tradition that may have originated in myths that equated lizard forms with death. The *manaia* and related motifs of other spirit creatures are believed to lure crews of enemy canoes to their death by drowning, and this belief in the *manaia*'s protective value ensures its frequent appearance in Maori art—a potent spirit challenge to enemies of the clan.

Some art historians note similarities between the *manaia* in Maori art and the ferocious masks of ancient Chinese bronzes. These masks often combined two profiles to be read as a frontal view, a convention also seen in the tattoo designs of Maori warriors. Because of the seemingly perpetual connection between Maori curvilinear designs and the tattooed patterns on warriors, scholars believe that the repertoire of motifs in this Polynesian culture was derived from such body decorations. Tattoo designs are extremely conservative among peoples practicing this form of body decoration in order to preserve ancient patterns. Indeed, the tradition of tattooing may have been the way artistic forms were transmitted from China to Indonesia and Oceania and the areas between.

The eight-foot-tall, dramatically vertical stern decoration at the Mauna Kea represents another traditional Maori format for canoe decoration. Similar to the prow ornament, its curved base is adorned with a semi-realistic human figure, which also would have watched over the warrior paddlers (page 19). Issuing upward from this figure are swirling patterns that eventually fuse with the *manaia* at the top. Similar patterns, related to tattoos, are seen on a Maori canoe bailer and on a large ceremonial wooden bowl elsewhere in the collection. Interestingly, these swirls are also kindred to those found on Ainu garments from Japan in the collection.

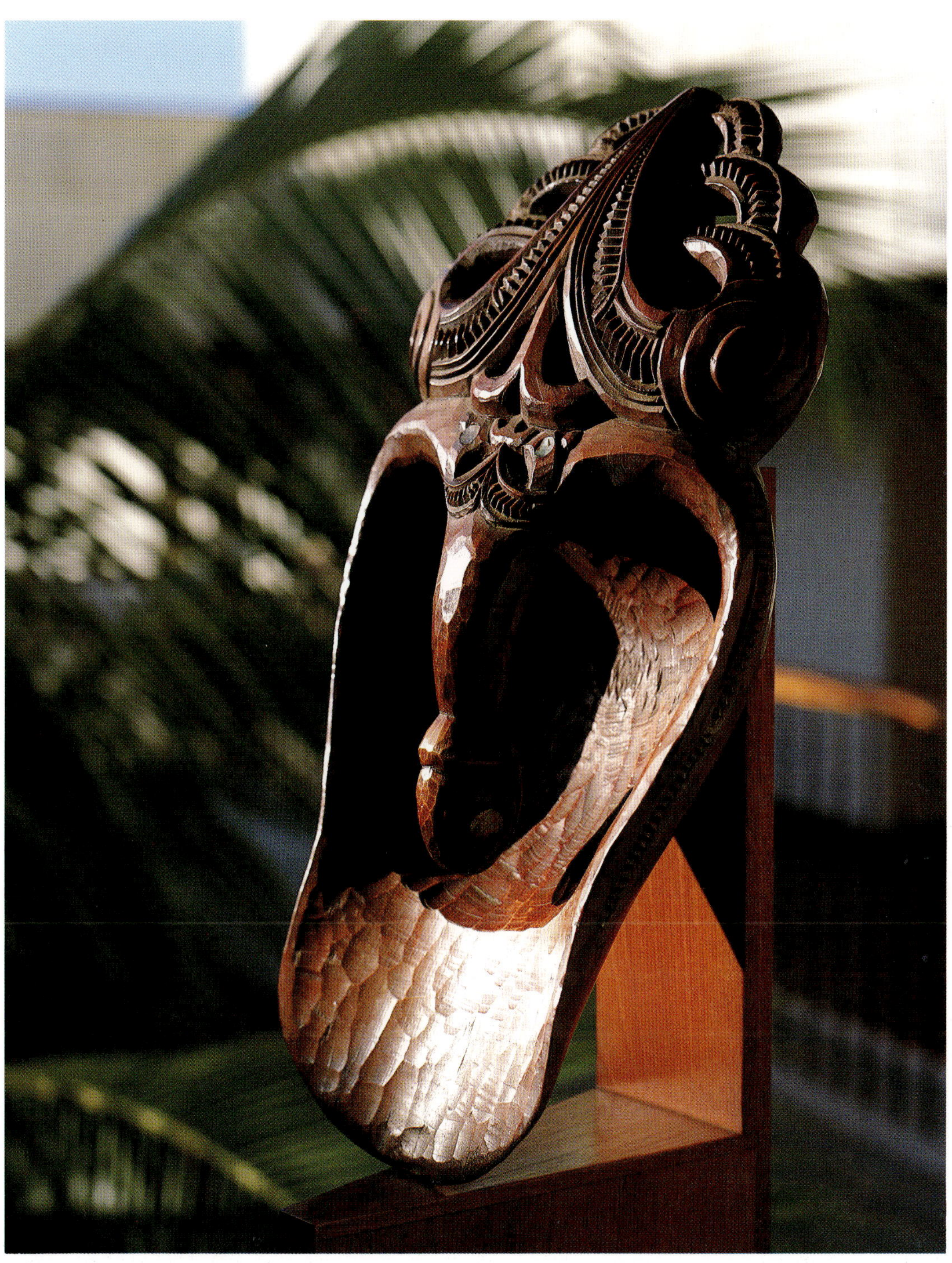

This traditionally shaped Maori canoe bailer is decorated with swirling patterns kindred to those tattooed on warriors and carved on ancestral sculptures. The bailer's elongated handle is highly phallic, perhaps to generate protective powers.

Architectural Ornaments (lintels)

Maori, wood with shell inlay, heights 22 inches and 23 inches.

THIS pair of carved lintel boards, which would have been placed over a door or window in a Maori ceremonial house, attest to the traditional importance of architectural decoration. Cultural preservation efforts in New Zealand over the past century have often focused on the great ceremonial houses, the traditional center of village life. All parts of these structures were ornamented: outer bargeboards, lintels, interior posts, rafters, ridge beams, and walls. Decorations were either painted or carved, and the figural motifs were highly conventionalized; anthropologists report that innovation was prohibited, and punishment as severe as execution was meted out to carvers who deviated from the norm. Walls were joined by sculpturally carved wooden posts that stood between rigid lattice-work mats (*tukutuku*) painted in bold and colorful designs.

Since communal houses also functioned as storehouses, frequently lintel decorations featured overtly sexual fertility symbols. (In nineteenth century American and European institutions that occasionally displayed such works in their collections, the sexual organs on these sculptures were usually effaced in deference to the mores of non-Polynesians.) A *tiki* form provides the focal point on each of the pair of lintel sculptures at the resort. In both cases, the figure is an anthropomorphized deity represented as a female, her genitalia exposed and exaggerated, flanked by *manaia* forms similar to those on the canoe decorations. The goddesses' violent grimaces, tongues protruding from their wide-stretched mouths, are a defiant expression of psychic power and protection commonly seen in Maori and Melanesian arts. Heavy patterning on the lips is a representation of tattoos.

Females were believed to have powerful compensatory energies that could counter the negative powers that might drain *mana* from the ceremonial communal house. Accordingly, female images decorated lintels to magically control everyone who entered, dispelling any negative forces they might bear. In function, these lintels are therefore not very different from the Thai folk-art goat sculpture that served to magically preserve the ritual purity of the Buddhist assembly hall.

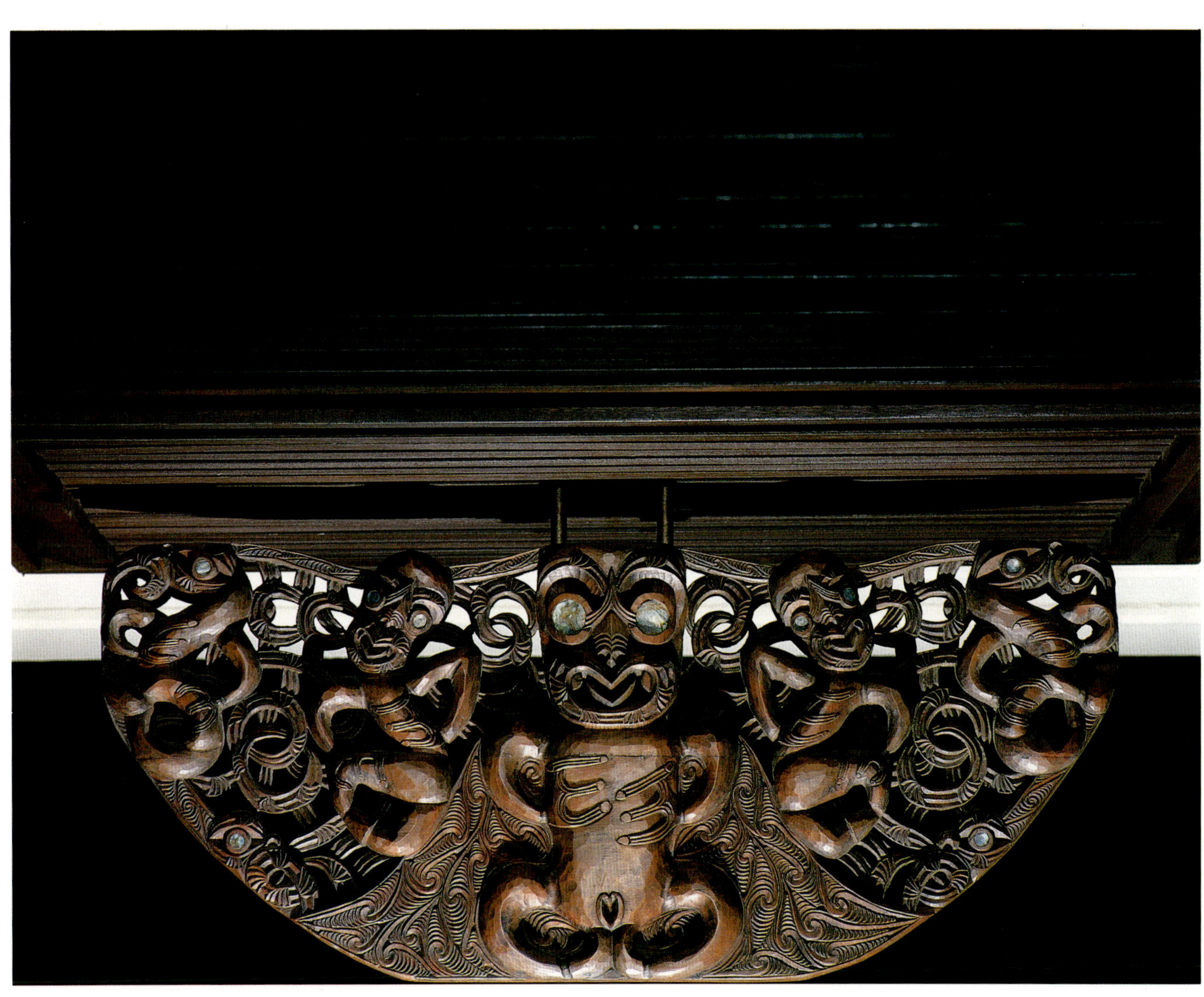

Tukutuku Panels

Maori, woven and painted reed, heights 48 inches, lengths 86 inches.

THIS group of lattice-work panels, *tukutuku*, represents the artistic style of Maori women and their contribution to traditional arts. All of the Maori arts previously discussed are associated with Maori men in their function, style, and execution in wood with curvilinear decoration. The women's style was quite different: angular, geometric, and nonfigural designs incorporated into woven basketry, mats, garments, and *tukutuku*.

Tukutuku panels fit between the wooden posts and rafters in village ceremonial houses, forming highly decorative walls that epitomized the wealth, prestige, and communal *mana* of the tribe. The panels are composed of thick reeds that are first painted and then woven together to create brightly colored patterns. The geometric motifs vary from panel to panel and include rectangular, herringbone, chevron, diamond, and other shapes. In these houses, each *tukutuku* was different from the others, resulting in a display that sometimes seems a celebration of optical patterns, quite opposite the regularized motifs in the men's style. Since these panels are not totally flat, having a depth and a sense of movement due to the rounded reeds, their designs often change with the viewer's angle of vision.

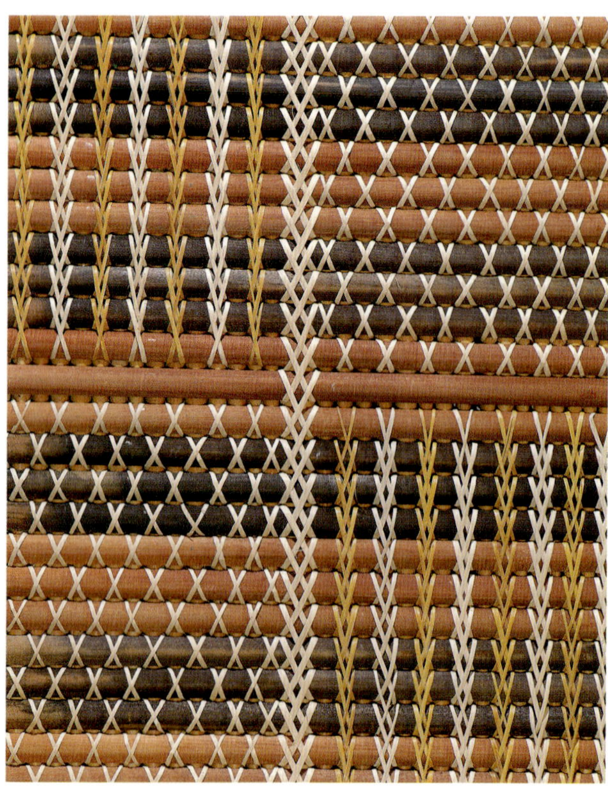

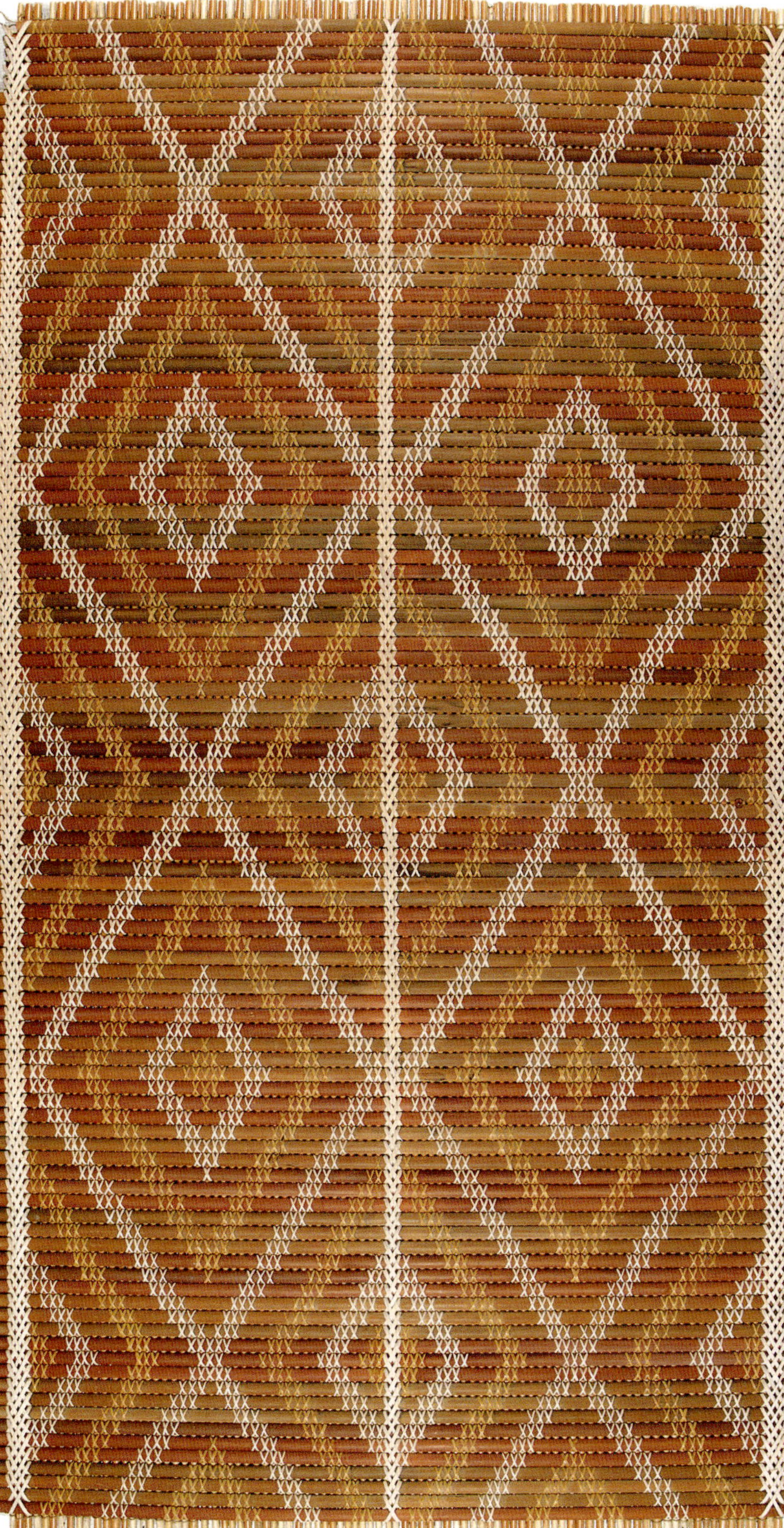

Tapa Collection (bark cloth)

Hawai'i, 19th century cloth with decorations added by Malia Solomon in 1965, lengths 90 inches.

THE MAUNA KEA'S collection of bark cloth, or tapa (*kapa* in Hawaiian), was commissioned by Rockefeller to honor the highly refined, ancient skills of Hawaiian tapa makers. All the Mauna Kea's tapas were decorated by Malia Solomon, a Hawaiian and an acknowledged authority in the field. Although tapa fell into disuse in Hawai'i shortly after cotton cloth became available through European contacts (in the first half of the nineteenth century), Solomon was able to acquire undyed tapas almost one hundred years old to carry out the commission. These she painted and printed with traditional vegetal dyes and tools.

Hawaiian tapas are the most distinctive of Polynesian bark cloth creations, and this is evident in the Mauna Kea's collection, which also includes tapas from Tonga, Samoa, and Fiji. While other island groups preferred highly repetitive designs produced by stenciling or rubbing the cloth with a carved tablet, Hawaiian tapa makers combined painted, printed, and "watermark" impressions to compose seemingly random designs that, with careful inspection, reveal quite sophisticated artistic intentions. For example, in one of the tapas painted by Malia Solomon, a single diamond-shaped stamp is printed regularly in vertical rows down the length of the tapa, the upper tip of each diamond touching the lower tip of its neighbor. Since the diamond shapes are actually formed by slightly curving lines, a sharply contrasting secondary pattern occurs, an optical after-image in which the "negative" space becomes extremely active with undulating serpentine forms.

Throughout Polynesia, tapa was associated with ritual as well as utilitarian functions. Secular uses included bed covers, clothing, sandals, hair ornaments, door and window coverings, and room partitions; white strips of tapa were often used as a warning of taboo. In New Zealand, where the paper mulberry tree could be grown only in small quantities in certain regions of the North Island, enough tapa was produced to create the ritual cloth needed to wrap representations of the deities, but the Maoris had to forego other uses. In Hawai'i, certain healing rituals involved wrapping or covering the patient with tapa. The cloth and the chants of the healer were thought to draw the illness or disease from the afflicted person. Hawaiian tapas were also frequently perfumed with the fragrances of flowers, ferns, and other plants.

Throughout Polynesia, tapa was created from the bark of many types of trees, but the preferred source was the paper mulberry tree, the *wauke*, which was the only tree expressly cultivated for this purpose. With sharp shells, trunks of trees seldom more than two years of age were stripped of their outer bark, and then further stripped to release the soft inner bark. This bark was rolled into bundles and soaked in water to soften it prior to a lengthy beating process.

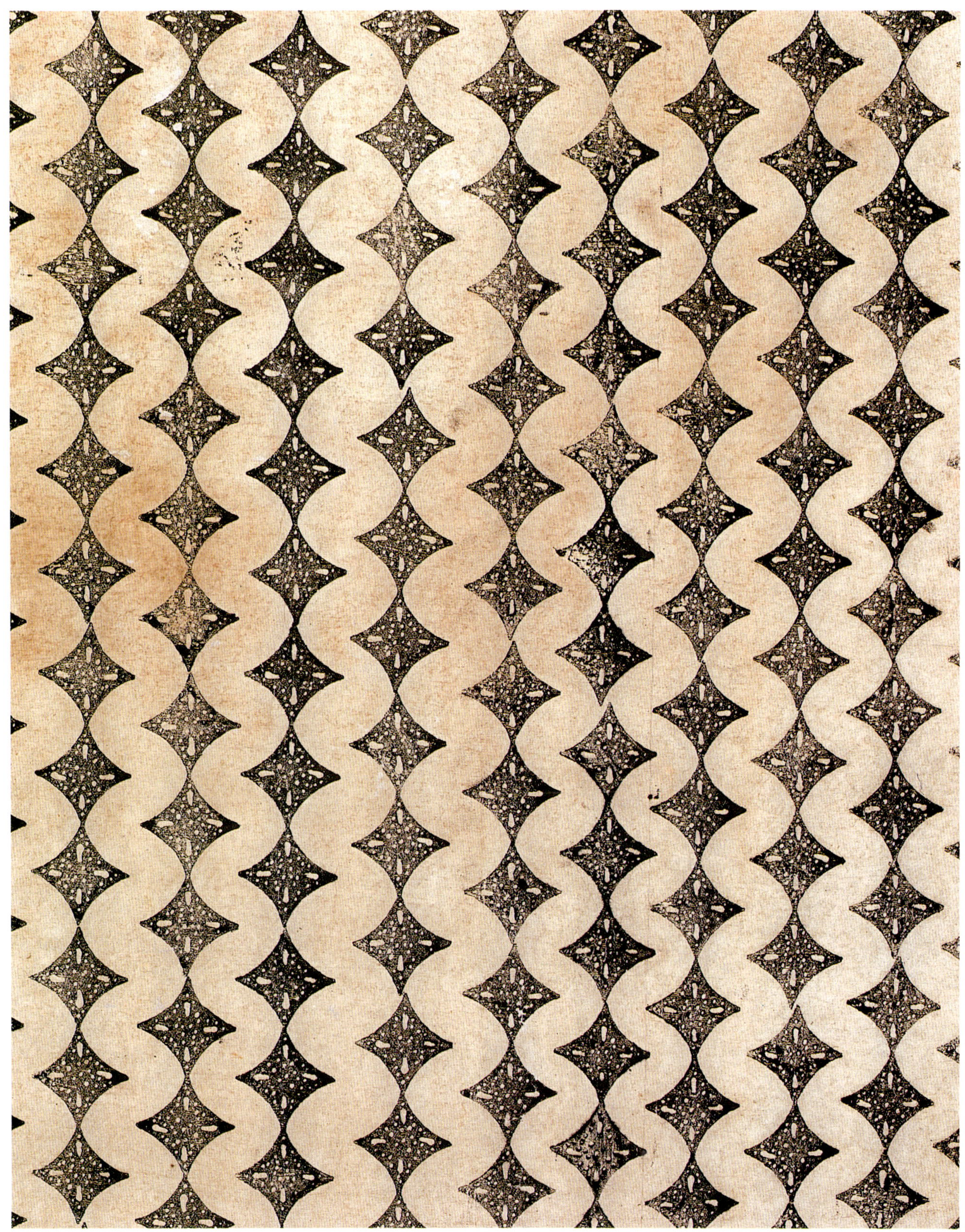

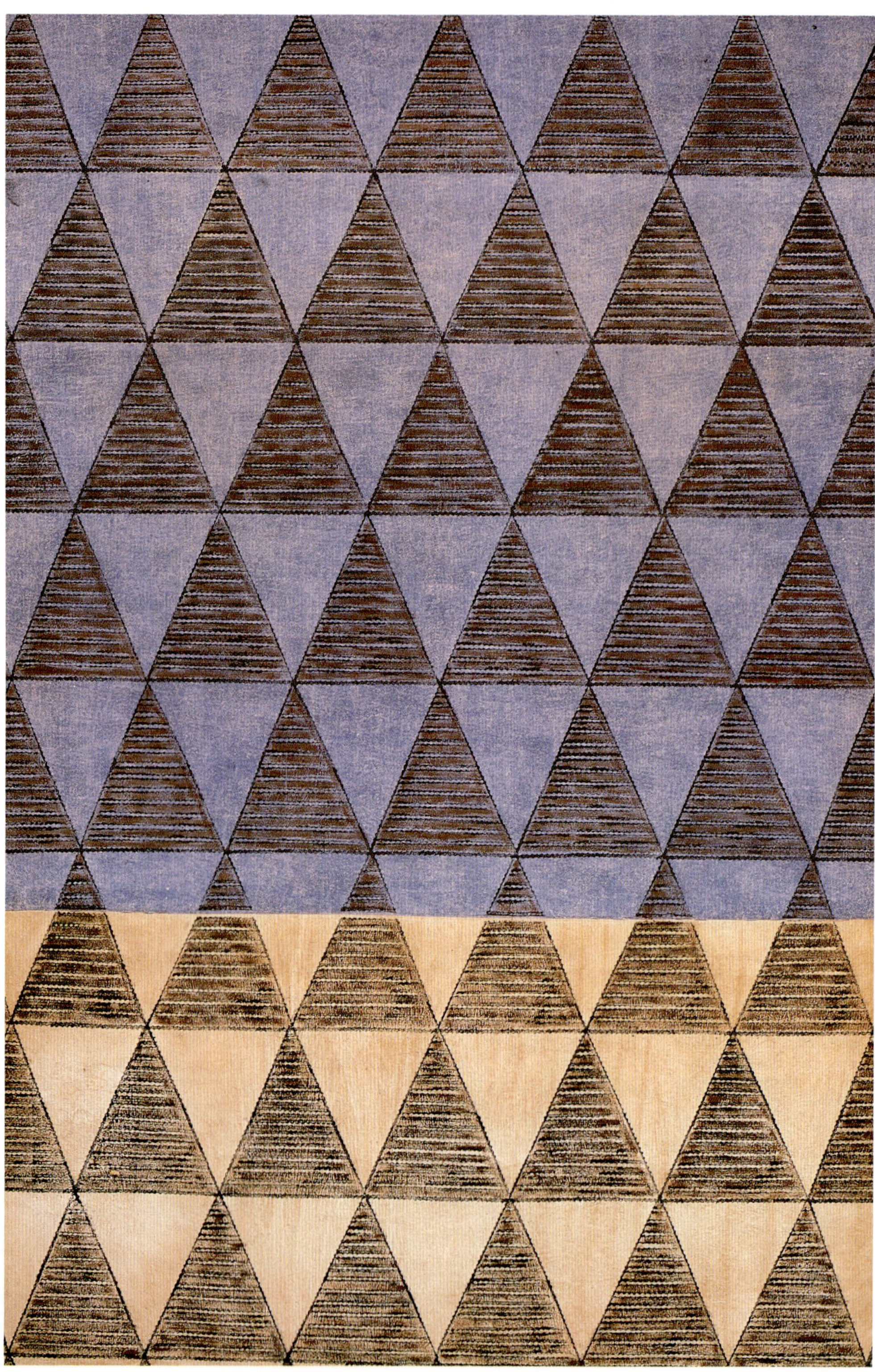

The triangle motif of this Hawaiian tapa is associated with individuals of high social rank. In traditional Hawaiian culture, geometric patterns were usually reserved for royalty or for venerated deities and appeared only on feather capes, helmets, and other ceremonial clothing. This tapa was decorated for the resort by Hawaiian artist Malia Solomon.

The unfinished bark was beaten first on stone anvils and then on wooden anvils. Each wooden anvil, a log planed to a smooth surface, inevitably had its own sound, and since these anvils were individually owned, each woman tapa maker had her distinct sound—a unique combination of the anvil's tone and her beating pattern. Occasionally, women were called upon to use their tapa beaters to signal messages.

The wooden tapa beaters had round handles and rectangular faces grooved with different patterns. Beating began with the side that had large, wide grooves; as the tapa became softer and finer, the tapa maker used other faces of the beater, until in the third stage she was working the tapa with the side that had the greatest number of grooves and the smallest spaces between them. The fourth side was smooth, producing the desired flat cloth surface.

By this stage, the bark would have spread to at least twice its original width as a result of repeated cycles of beating and soaking. After a sufficient number of such strips were produced, the pieces were joined; sometimes they were sewn, but more frequently their edges were moistened with vegetable glues and then beaten or "felted" together. Cloth of uniform thickness was achieved only through experience and skill. In Hawai'i, once such finely textured tapa was achieved, it was again beaten, this time with instruments that left patterned "watermark" type impressions. As a result of these refinements, Hawaiian tapa is recognized as the softest and most supple in Polynesia.

After the tapa had been given its final shape it was dried in the sun and taken in at night to avoid dew and rain. Stones were used to weight the tapa down during the drying, a process that required intuition and dexterity as the stones had to be shifted frequently to prevent uneven drying and shrinking that might make the fabric susceptible to tearing.

Decorating tapa was equally complex. Paint pigments were derived from roots, seeds, nuts, charcoal, ash, sea shells, and other forms of sea life. The pigments were highly prized and were sometimes exchanged between islands within different archipelagos. The coloring was applied with brushes made by chewing and fraying twigs and branches of plants. In Hawai'i, particularly, printmaking techniques were also used by tapa makers who created stamps by cutting patterns into bamboo. These bamboo stamps facilitated repetitive designs, often a pattern of alternating plain and stamped bands. The printed areas were also embellished by brush strokes.

Quilt Collection

Hawai'i, 1965, designed by Meali'i Kalama, cotton, lengths 96 inches.

LAURANCE ROCKEFELLER commissioned the thirty Hawaiian quilts displayed at the Mauna Kea, the largest standing exhibit of this medium in the state of Hawai'i. The commission was conceived through Rockefeller's communications with the Reverend Abraham Akaka of Honolulu's Kawaiaha'o Church, the site of marriages and funerals for Hawaiian royalty since the 1840s. Meali'i Kalama, a member of the Kawaiaha'o congregation and the quilt artist who designed the quilts and supervised their assemblage, received a National Heritage award in 1985 for her achievements in Hawaiian quiltmaking. The quilts were displayed at Kawaiaha'o Church before installation at the Mauna Kea.

The Hawaiian quilt is rich in affective and spiritual associations. Its designs are poetic and abstract, with complex emotional associations, yet the imagery is simple enough to be universally accessible and appealing. While seldom overtly religious, these designs convey a spiritual belief that God is revealed in and through nature, the prime subject of the Hawaiian quilt.

Quilting techniques were introduced to Polynesia during the first visit of New England missionaries to the island of Hawai'i in 1820. On a ship anchored off Kawaihae on the Kohala Coast (close to the site of the Mauna Kea resort), missionary women taught basic sewing techniques to a group of high-born Hawaiian women in an extended workshop. Bound up with Hawaiian history ever since, the quilt represents a fusion of Eastern and Western traditions and artistic techniques.

The precedent and inspiration for the unique style of Hawaiian quilt decoration was Hawaiian tapa, the quilt melding tapa design with cotton cloth media and needlework technique. Hawaiians continue to refer to the quilt as *kapa*. As in the tapa, negative and positive shapes are important in design, and a "double aesthetic" is produced through use of dominant and secondary patterns. In the tapa, the dominant pattern was painted or printed on the surface and subtly enhanced with "watermark" patterns. In the Hawaiian quilt, the primary design is silhouetted in monochrome on light-toned cloth; needlework in the surrounding "negative" space produces a secondary pattern that relates to the colored motif but is independent of it. This is accomplished through the "echo" or "contour" stitch, which does not repeat or follow the outlines of the main design but rather displays its own highly rhythmic pattern, evoking a feeling of continuous movement. The emblematic and formal design is thus enlivened, and all of the natural forms represented become infused with a fundamentally spiritual intent and a cosmic symbolism of light and dark, static and dynamic.

The quilt's central medallion is called *piko*, a word with many meanings in Hawaiian, including umbilicus. The word also may refer to the summit of a mountain, the very basis

Most traditional Hawaiian quilt designs reflect the history and natural scenery of Hawai'i. The plumeria blossom inspired the undulating patterns in this quilt; the highly fragrant, five-petal flower is also the symbol of the resort. Meali'i Kalama and her assistants created thirty quilts for the Mauna Kea in 1965; their commission was tithed to the historic Kawaiaha'o Church in Honolulu.

of the islands in the Hawaiian archipelago, or the borders of a land, which for islands would mean their shores. The echo stitches are intended to represent surging ocean waves carrying tidal energies full of love—aloha—to the farthest shores of the Pacific. The rippling contours of the echo stitches imply paths of movement, as parallel "peaks" of their wave-like forms move together towards the quilt's borders. The borders are referred to as *ho'opaepae*, an expression derived from the Hawaiian term *ho'opae*, "to go ashore." Quilts are therefore understood as expressive emblems of Hawai'i.

The *piko* on most quilts is an abstract representation of a fruit, flower, garland (*lei*), beautiful place or vista, or spiritual reminiscence. Hawaiian royalty and its symbols became frequent subjects after the American overthrow of the monarchy in 1893. In 1898, U.S. annexation of the kingdom made flying the Hawaiian flag a sign of rebellion (the monarchy's flag was adapted from the British Union Jack given to Kamehameha I by Captain Vancouver in 1794). In the form of a quilt, the flag could be covertly displayed for private viewing or occasional secret gatherings that venerated the ancient traditions of Hawai'i. Upon statehood in 1959, the emblem was revived and became the state's official flag.

Royal emblems appear throughout the Mauna Kea's quilt collection: the *kāhili*, or royal standard; the fans of Queen Ka'ahumanu, Kamehameha's favorite wife; the gardens of Queen Lili'uokalani, the last Hawaiian monarch to reign; and the lamps of Lono, benevolent Hawaiian god of rain and harvest, a design dedicated to Prince Kūhiō. Brilliant reds and yellows appear in most of these quilts, hues associated with Hawaiian gods and the aristocracy. The finest quilt in the collection is a clever interpretation of the Hawaiian flag; its design repeats a unit of eight red, white, and blue stripes that represent the eight major islands in the Hawaiian chain and includes the official state motto: "*ua mau ke ea o ka 'āina i ka pono*," or "the life of the land is perpetuated in righteousness." This motto was first spoken by Kamehameha III in 1843, when the independence of Hawai'i was reaffirmed by Great Britain's Queen Victoria. On completion of the thirty commissioned quilts, Meali'i Kalama presented this uncommissioned work to Rockefeller to express her gratitude for the opportunity to help preserve and revitalize an artistic tradition of Hawai'i.

Hawaiian quilts are believed imbued with *mana* and, as with all such objects containing spiritual power, they are treated with respect. Historic *kapu* allowed display in the home and on beds but only for viewing, not for sitting upon. Similarly, when a quilt shows the effects of long use, it is not cast away; Kalama's procedure was first to create a replacement, with occasional modifications of the color but not of the traditional design, and then ceremonially to burn the old quilt so as not to risk abuse of its *mana*.

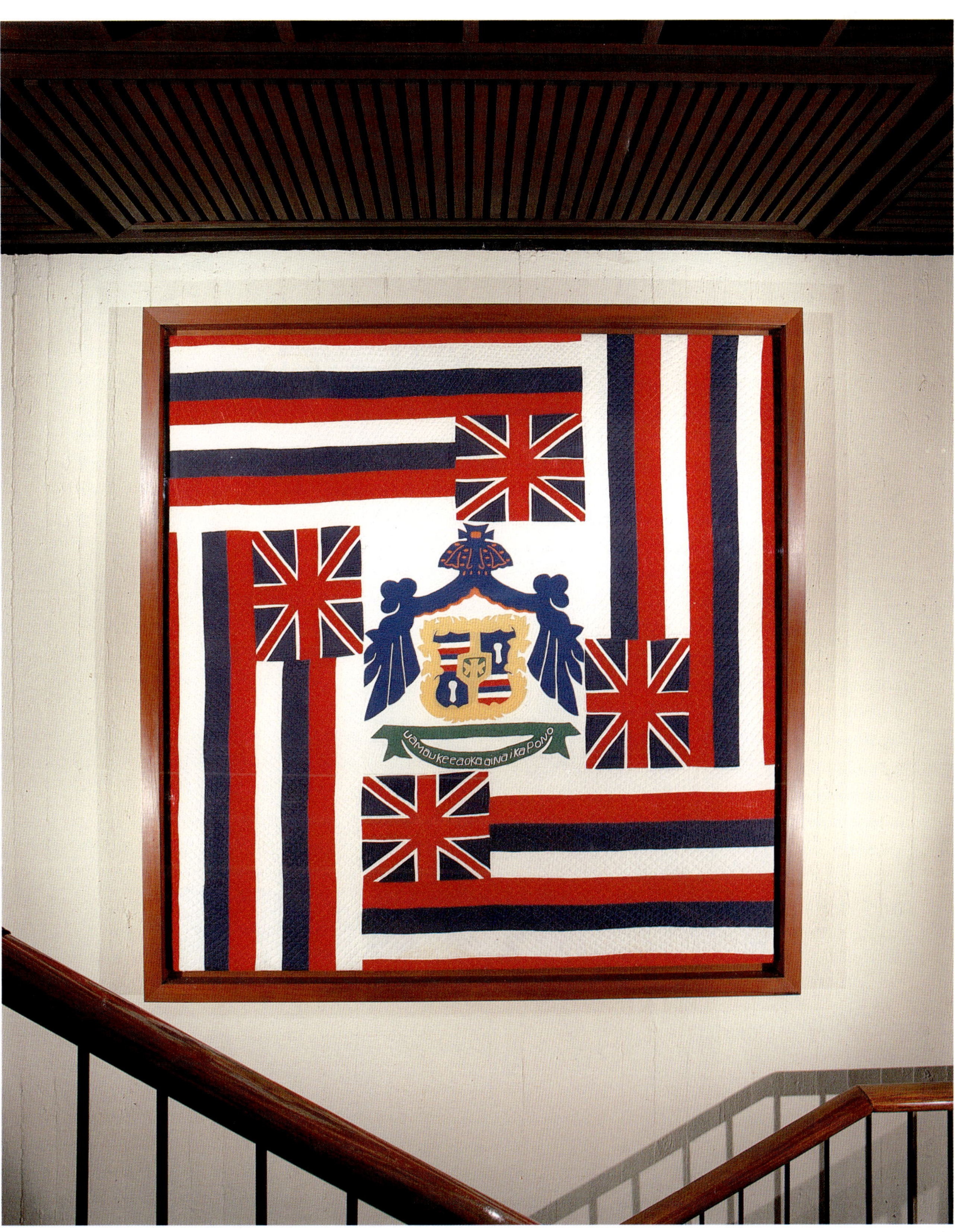

The design for this quilt, the most impressive in the collection, was based on the Hawaiian flag. The quilt display's creator, Meali'i Kalama, was declared a "living treasure" in 1985 through a Heritage Award from the National Endowment for the Arts. This particular quilt was a gift from Kalama to Rockefeller upon completion of the display project.

Kahi Ho'ākoakoa Hau'oli (Happy Gathering Place)

Hawai'i, Bumpei Akaji, 1965, bronze sculpture, height 96 inches.

THIS openwork bronze sculpture by Bumpei Akaji was commissioned by a group of Hawai'i residents as a gift to Laurance Rockefeller for display at the Mauna Kea in acknowledgment of Rockefeller's commitment to the contemporary artists of the state. In this work, Akaji depicted a series of bird forms alighting on the resort's namesake, Mauna Kea volcano. The bird shapes are simple and angular, as if they were origami (the Japanese art of folding paper), giving the substantial bronze sculpture an overall delicate and weightless appearance.

Akaji is one of the most popular contemporary artists in Hawai'i; his sculptures enhance libraries and schools as well as the Honolulu War Memorial and the Neal Blaisdell Concert Hall. Akaji's formal studies included Asian mysticism and symbolism as well as art history. Born in Hawai'i, he studied in Italy before receiving his M.A. from the University of Hawaii, and he returned to Europe to study in the early 1950s after receiving a Fulbright Fellowship. In 1961, Akaji began to experiment with bronze and copper in styles influenced by Eastern and Western art history.

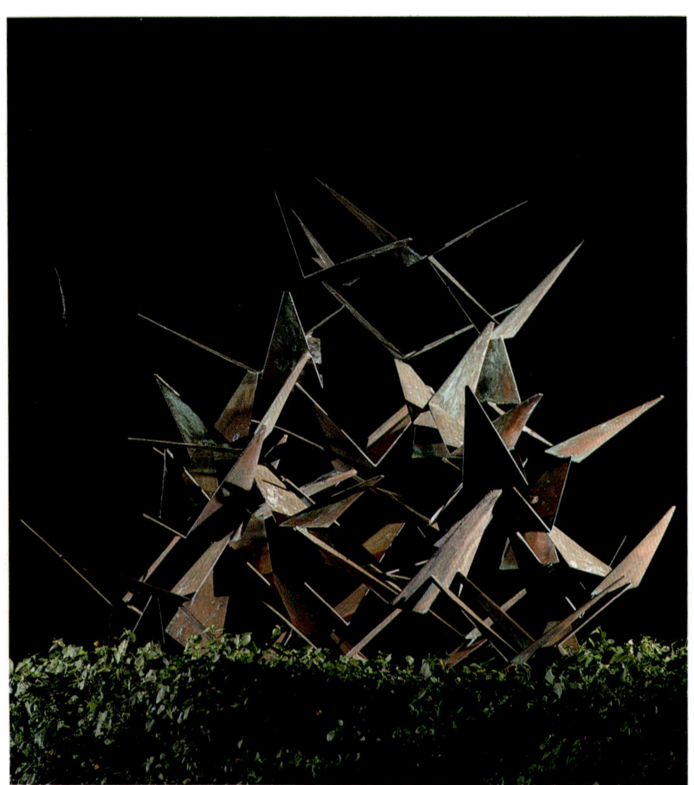

'Iwa (Frigatebird)

Hawai'i, Edward Brownlee, 1973, bronze sculpture, height 50 inches.

EDWARD BROWNLEE'S longstanding fascination with bird forms provided the inspiration for his monumental bronze sculpture at the resort, an abstract representation of the huge frigatebird (*'iwa* in Hawaiian) that is a frequent motif in the arts of Oceanic peoples. The sculpture is massive, but its impact is softened by delicate, rhythmic swirls of curvilinear pattern that resemble the Oceanic designs Brownlee came to admire through formal study of art history.

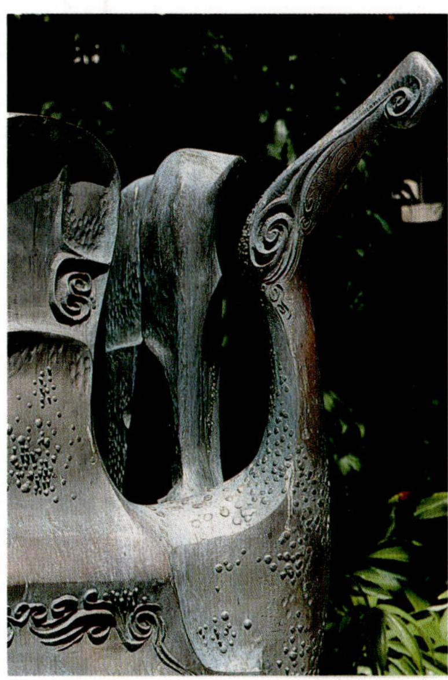

Brownlee left his native Oregon to join the army at the age of eighteen. He spent three years in Japan after World War II and settled in Hawai'i in the 1950s. He was soon awarded an M.F.A. at the University of Hawaii, having studied with Jean Charlot, one of the state's most renowned artists, and Gustav Ecke, a noted scholar of Chinese art. Along with these influences on his artistic development, Brownlee acknowledges the importance of "construction trades" on his sculptures, and his education in the trades under carpenters and metalworkers. Brownlee's skills at casting and carving, along with his sense of art history, are apparent in the subject and style of the bronze sculpture, and in the elegant teak display vehicles he created for the Mauna Kea, including the Japanese-inspired "gateway" form for the Pacifica Collection in the Beachfront Wing, and the Garden restaurant room partition that holds Oceanic food implements. The Hawaii State Foundation on Culture and the Arts has commissioned many of Brownlee's sculptures for public display throughout the state, and he is represented in the collections of the Honolulu Academy of Arts.

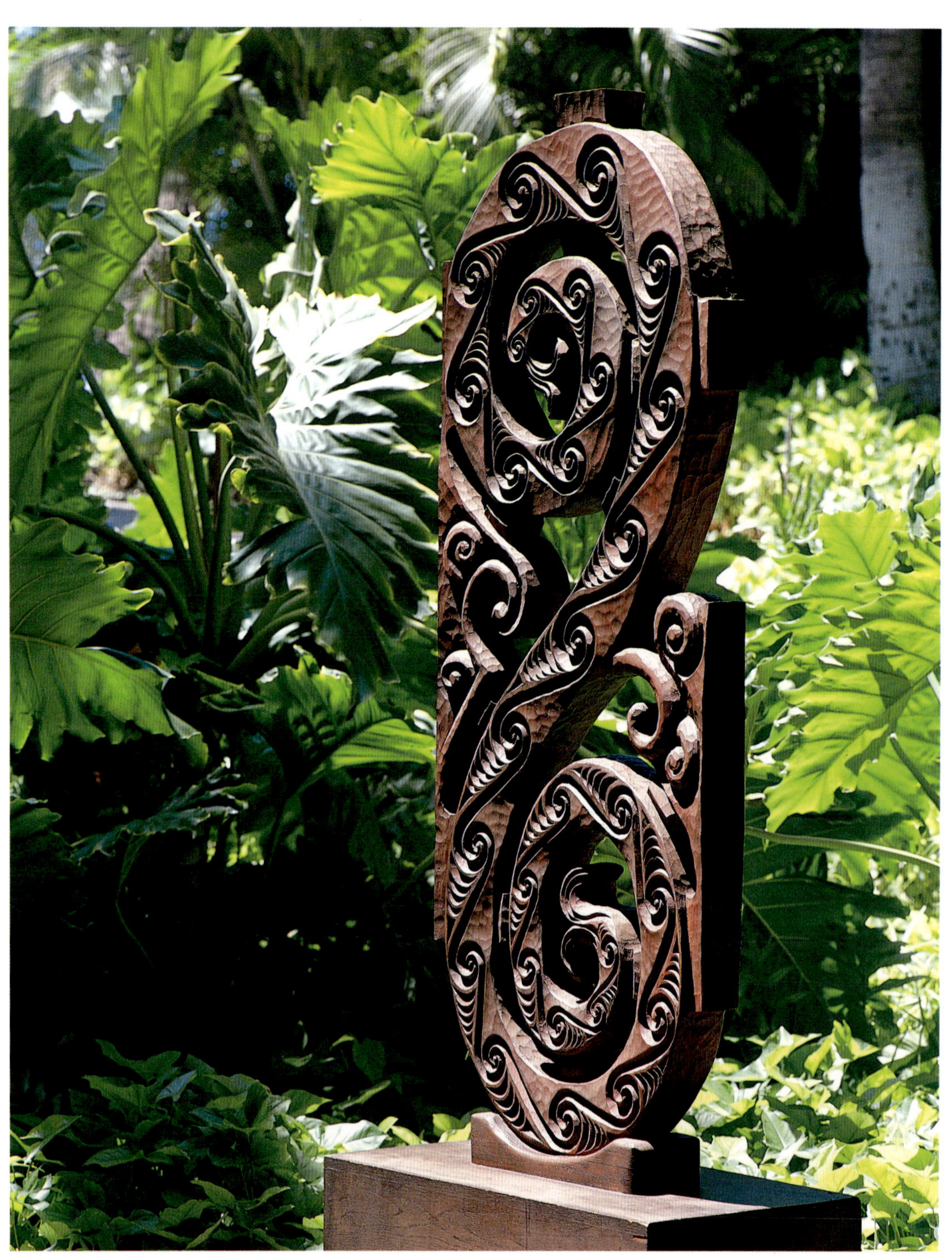

Abstraction/Mythic Sources

Hawai'i, Sam Ka'ai, 1973, wood sculpture, height 62 inches.

SAM KA'AI of Maui is one of the most important and influential of the state's Hawaiian artists and is well known for his dedication to preservation of traditional culture. Rockefeller commissioned Ka'ai to create a large wood sculpture for the Mauna Kea. The abstract sculpture incorporates a number of mythic symbols and spiritual concepts from traditional Polynesian societies. Its balanced design of opposing spiral forms represents dualistic aspects of ancient beliefs: human mortality in opposition to the eternal spirit world of deities.

Through history and philosophy as well as technical skills, in this work and others, Ka'ai seeks to instill a new generation of Hawaiians with pride in their Polynesian heritage. His authoritative command of the methods and materials used in ancient crafts has earned him the honored title of *kahuna*. As a respected teacher of tradition, from 1974 through 1987 Ka'ai participated in the Polynesian Voyaging Society's project to reconstruct an ancient voyaging canoe and explore and demonstrate ancient Polynesian mastery of navigational skills. The resulting craft, the *Hōkūle'a*, was fitted with a traditional altar with attendant deities that were carved by Ka'ai, who was also a member of the crew that accomplished an extremely trying series of maritime voyages throughout the Pacific in the thirteen-year period. The crew of the *Hōkūle'a* included sailors and navigators from major Polynesian island groups and also from Micronesia, in a demonstration of Oceanic unity.

Hawaiian Flora

Hawai'i, Lloyd Sexton, 1964 and 1984, oil on canvas, heights 41 inches.

OIL PAINTINGS and prints by Honolulu artist Lloyd Sexton grace the walls of many meeting and guest rooms at the Mauna Kea. Born Leo Lloyd Sexton, Jr., in Hilo in 1912, he is the great-grandson of Boston missionaries to Hawai'i who arrived in 1840. Sexton's artistic style seems related to that of nineteenth century European and American artists who sought to depict the visual stimuli of the islands. The early works were mostly botanical prints; the artists, inspired by Darwin's theory of evolution, took delight in analyzing the unusual flora that had adapted to the tropical environment. Sexton's many charming depictions of flowers and foliage are both meticulous botanical records and artistic responses to the lushness of the Hawaiian flora.

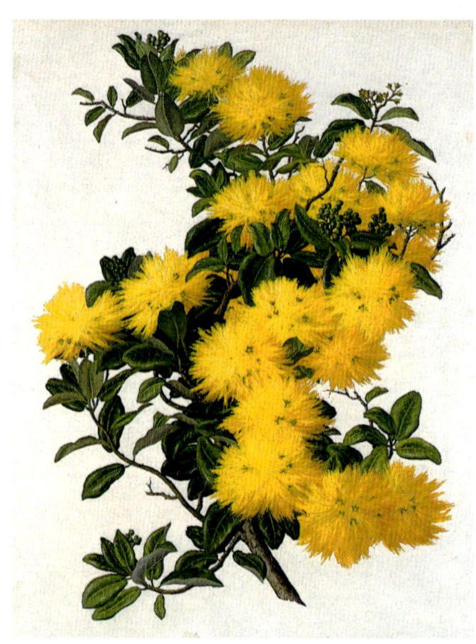

The *'ōhi'a lehua* is a favorite native Hawaiian tree. The common red *lehua* is the flower of the island of Hawai'i; the yellow variety, shown here, is rare.

Nine large works in oil are displayed in the resort's Sexton Gallery, which was named for the artist. These canvases provide a wealth of detail on the brilliant foliage and flowers of many island plants, including the yellow *hau*, yellow *lehua*, red *kou*, lavender jacaranda, pink plumeria, pink hibiscus, royal poinciana, blue morning glory, and red poinsettia. Some of these plants are native to Hawai'i, while others were brought to the islands in the nineteenth century.

Sexton's works are included in many distinguished public and private collections. He studied at the Boston Museum School of Fine Arts and at the Slade School of Art at London University in England. His paintings have been exhibited at the British Royal Academy and in one-man shows at the Honolulu Academy of Arts and Honolulu's Contemporary Art Center (now called "The Contemporary Museum").

Birds, Horses, Abstract Landscape, Abstraction

Hawai'i, John Young, 1977 and 1985, oil on canvas, lengths 41 to 92 inches.

JOHN YOUNG'S paintings are also displayed throughout the Mauna Kea—watercolors in guest rooms and four oil paintings in resort meeting rooms. His subjects include figurative motifs of bird, horse, and human forms, as well as abstract images of landscape and still life.

Born in Honolulu and of Chinese extraction, Young has been represented in shows at the Metropolitan Museum, the Smithsonian Institution, San Francisco's de Young Museum, and other important national and international institutions, including the Honolulu Academy of Arts, where he was also an art instructor. Privately, he collects works of Oceanic cultures, as well as Chinese Shang bronzes and Japanese *haniwa*, all of which have influenced his own art. Although he spent many years in Paris studying painting and graphic arts, Young's art shows a consciousness of his Chinese origins. Most of his paintings reflect a calligraphic sensitivity, the result of years of training in brushwork techniques. His works tend toward the experimental, displaying multicultural sources in a broad range of styles and media that include oil, watercolor, casein, lithography, and woodcut.

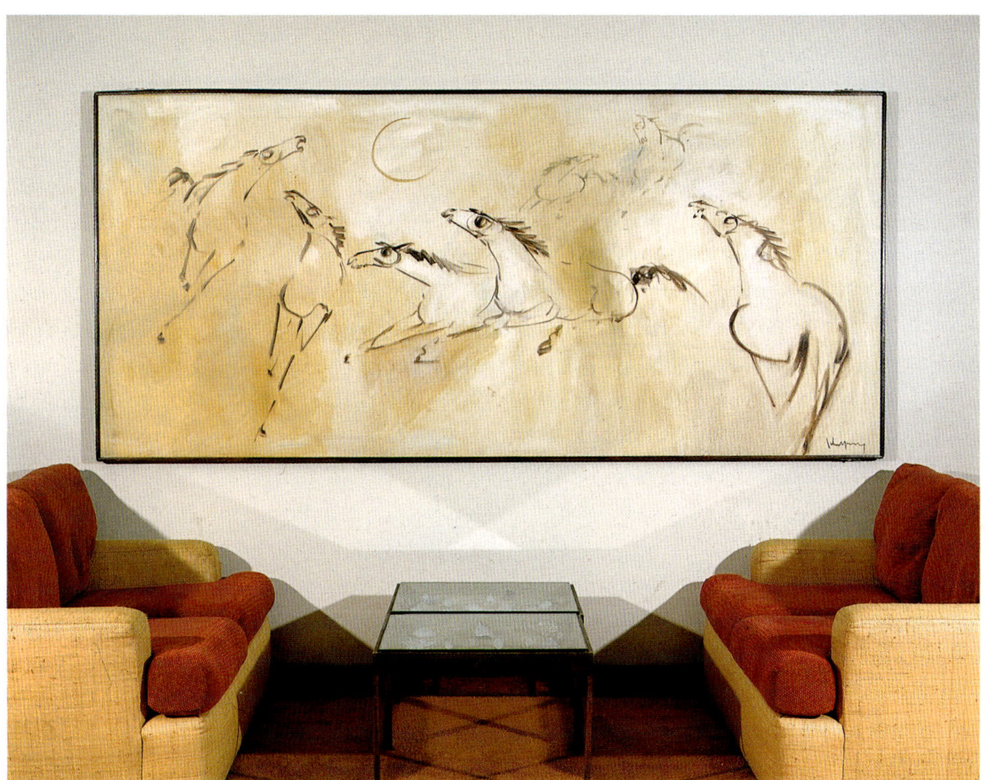

LIST OF WORKS IN THE COLLECTION

ASIAN

India

Seated Buddha, 7th century, granite, height 63 inches. (Aesthetic restoration work on the head performed in 1987 by the Pacific Regional Conservation Center, Bishop Museum, Honolulu.)
LOCATION: North Garden. (frontispiece, pp. 39, 40, 41)*

Eight Chests, 18th century, wood and metal, lengths 47 to 56 inches.
LOCATION: Fifth, sixth, and seventh floors.

Collection of Twenty-Six Votive Sculptures, 18th and 19th centuries, bronze and brass, heights 8½ to 23 inches.
LOCATION: Fifth floor. (pp. 36, 43, 44)

Eight Brass Storage Vessels (Chamlas), 19th century, brass, heights 37 to 44 inches.
LOCATION: Lobby, Promenade, atrium lounges. (pp. 46, 47)

Pair of Chests, 19th century, brass, heights 13 and 16 inches.
LOCATION: Executive offices and hotel lobby.

Six Candelabra, 19th century, brass, height 66½ inches.
LOCATION: Pavilion restaurant.

Cambodia

Khmer Head of a Deified Ancestor, circa 1300, sandstone, height 21 inches.
LOCATION: Fourth floor lounge. (p. 51)

Khmer Head of a Deified Ancestor, 15th century, sandstone, height 24 inches.
LOCATION: Second floor lounge. (p. 52)

Burma

Seventeen Bronze Drums, 18th century, bronze, heights 16½ to 21½ inches.
LOCATIONS: Lobby and lounges throughout the resort. (pp. 53, 54)

Thailand

Head of a Buddha, 13th century, stucco, height 19 inches.
LOCATION: Sixth floor. (p. 57)

Standing Divinity on a Fabulous Bird, 18th century, wood and polychromed mirrored glass mosaic, height 93 inches.
LOCATION: Lobby. (p. 59)

Temple Sculpture—Fabulous Bird, 18th century, wood with polychromed mirrored glass, height 56 inches.
LOCATION: Third floor lounge. (p. 67)

Buddhist Wheel of the Law, 18th century, stone, height 23 inches.
LOCATION: Second floor lounge.

*Page numbers are given for works illustrated in this book.

Pair of Buddhist Disciples, late 18th century, gilt bronze with mirrored glass, height 40 inches.
LOCATION: Lobby. (pp. 14, 31, 61)

Pair of Buddhist Votive Tablets, 18/19th century, gilt and painted wood, height 22 inches.
LOCATION: Fifth floor. (pp. 62, 63)

Buddhist Altar, 18/19th century, wood, height 66 inches.
LOCATION: Pavilion restaurant. (p. 64)

Buddhist Sutra Chest, 18/19th century, wood with gold and black lacquer, height 41 inches.
LOCATION: Fifth floor. (p. 65)

Temple Sculpture—Dragon, 19th century, wood, mirrored glass, and gilt, length 92 inches.
LOCATION: Fourth floor lounge. (p. 68)

Temple Sculpture—Fish, 19th century, wood, mirrored glass, and gilt, length 108 inches.
LOCATION: Sixth floor. (p. 69)

Temple Sculpture—Fabulous Bird, 19th century, wood with polychromed mirrored glass, height 72 inches.
LOCATION: Second floor lounge.

Betel Nut Containers, 19th century, lacquered wood, height 46 inches.
LOCATION: Fourth floor lounge. (p. 70)

Pedestal Bowl, 19th century, dry lacquer, height 24 inches.
LOCATION: Fourth floor lounge. (pp. 70, 71)

Crouching Goat, late 19th century, painted and lacquered wood and metal, height 15 inches.
LOCATION: Second floor lounge. (p. 72)

Pair of Guardians, 19th/20th century, bronze with mirrored glass, height 62 inches.
LOCATION: Beachfront Wing entry. (pp. 74, 75)

China

Altar/Scholar's Table, 18/19th century, wood, height 44 inches, length 168 inches.
LOCATION: Fifth floor. (pp. 78, 81)

Altar Table, 19th century, lacquered wood with metal, height 52 inches, length 110 inches.
LOCATION: Fifth floor.

Japan

Buddhist Sculpture, circa 1300, wood, height 25 inches.
LOCATION: Lobby. (pp. 79, 82)

Pair of Guardians, circa 1500, wood, height 19½ inches.
LOCATION: Pavilion restaurant. (pp. 85, 86)

Pair of Votive Horse Figures, 18th century, wood and mixed media, heights 50 inches and 54 inches.
LOCATION: Promenade. (p. 87)

Nine Japanese Chests (Tansu), 18th and 19th centuries, wood with lacquer, heights 31 to 59 inches.
LOCATION: Lounges throughout the resort. (pp. 63, 90, 91)

Monumental Bowl, 18th century, wood with copper liner, length 38 inches.
LOCATION: Sixth floor.

Head of a Rakan, early 19th century, wood, height 15 inches.
LOCATION: Third floor lounge. (p. 93)

Monumental Bronze Pedestal Bowl/Pool, early 19th century, bronze, height 32 inches, diameter 9 feet.
LOCATION: Pavilion Terrace.

Pair of Bronze Koi, mid-19th century, bronze, length 72 inches.
LOCATION: Pavilion Terrace. (p. 99)

Collection of Eleven Gongs/Knockers in the Form of Fish, 19th century, wood, heights 9 to 14 inches.
LOCATION: Fourth and sixth floor lounges. (pp. 94, 95, 98)

Drum, 19th century, wood with lacquer, height 24 inches.
LOCATION: Second floor lounge. (p. 97)

Six Jizai *(hanger-hooks)*, 19th century, wood, heights 17 to 23 inches.
LOCATION: Lounges throughout the resort. (p. 101)

Four Jizai *(iron pots)*, 19th century, iron, wood, and bamboo, heights 46½ to 61 inches.
LOCATION: Promenade. (p. 102)

Carved Mortar, 19th century, wood with copper liner, height 24½ inches.
LOCATION: Pavilion restaurant.

Carved Mortar, 19th century, wood with copper liner, height 20 inches.
LOCATION: Pavilion restaurant.

Five Bowls, late 19th century, bronze, diameters 18 to 26½ inches.
LOCATION: Lobby and restaurants throughout the resort.

Collection of Five Ainu Garments, late 19th century, cotton with applique and embroidery, lengths 43½ to 52½ inches.
LOCATION: Sixth and seventh floors. (pp. 103, 105)

Shiryu Morita, *Four-Panel Screen*, *circa* 1965, gold on black lacquer, length 124 inches.
LOCATION: Lobby (elevator foyer). (p. 107)

OCEANIC

All undated Oceanic works of art in the collection were created during the twentieth century.

Melanesia

Seventeen Abelam Ritual Masks (New Guinea), woven rattan, heights 17 to 33 inches.
LOCATION: Lounges throughout the resort. (pp. 115, 116)

Ritual-House Mask (New Guinea), woven rattan and clay, height 58 inches.
LOCATION: Seventh floor. (p. 119)

Carved Ritual Mask (Vanuatu/New Hebrides), wood, height 18½ inches.
LOCATION: Eighth floor.

Ancestral Figure (New Guinea, Karawari River region), wood, height 73 inches.
LOCATION: Lobby. (pp. 110, 121)

Ancestor Tablet (New Guinea, Middle Sepik region), wood, height 64 inches.
LOCATION: Promenade. (p. 125)

Ancestor Tablet (New Guinea, Middle Sepik region), wood, height 55 inches.
LOCATION: Promenade. (p. 125)

Men's House Sculpture (New Guinea, Eastern Sepik region), wood, height 50 inches.
LOCATION: Terrace restaurant. (p. 18)

Memorial Tablet (New Guinea, Eastern Sepik region), wood, height 66 inches.
LOCATION: Second floor. (p. 125)

Ritual House Cult Figure (New Guinea, Karawari River region), wood, height 66 inches.
LOCATION: Fifth floor. (p. 123)

Frigatebird Sculpture (New Guinea, Eastern Sepik region), wood, height 37 inches.
LOCATION: Garden restaurant. (p. 122)

Thirty-Four Oceanic Shields (New Guinea), wood with raffia and feathers, heights 33 to 127 inches.
LOCATION: Lounges throughout the resort. (p. 127)

Twenty-Four Food Preparation Implements (New Guinea and other areas), wood and coconut shell, lengths 7 to 41½ inches.
LOCATION: Garden restaurant. (p. 130)

Carved Ceremonial Platter (Solomon Islands), wood with shell inlay, length 69 inches.
LOCATION: Garden restaurant. (pp. 129)

Collection of Eight Hourglass Drums (New Guinea), wood, heights 21 to 40½ inches.
LOCATION: Eighth floor. (p. 132)

Slit-Gong Drum (New Guinea), wood, length 58 inches.
LOCATION: Garden restaurant.

Dance Wand (Solomon Islands), wood, length 63 inches.
LOCATION: Eighth floor. (p. 134)

Dance Wand (Solomon Islands), wood, length 43 inches.
LOCATION: Eighth floor.

Pair of War Clubs (New Guinea), wood, lengths 31 and 30 inches.
LOCATION: Eighth floor.

Canoe (New Guinea, Siassi Islands), wood, length 88 inches.
LOCATION: Eighth floor. (p. 138)

Three Canoe Prows (New Guinea, Middle Sepik region), wood, lengths 26 to 33 inches.
LOCATION: Second and eighth floors. (p. 139)

Canoe Splashboard (New Guinea, Trobriand region), wood, height 27 inches.
LOCATION: Eighth floor. (p. 137)

Canoe Splashboard (New Guinea, Trobriand region), wood, height 17¼ inches.
LOCATION: Eighth floor. (p. 137)

Collection of Eight Canoe Paddles (New Guinea, Trobriand and Siassi Islands, Massim region), wood, length 43 to 82 inches.
LOCATION: Eighth floor. (p. 135)

Canoe Shield-Mask (New Guinea, Middle Sepik region), wood, height 30 inches.
LOCATION: Second floor.

Three Ancestral Figures (New Guinea, Middle Sepik region), wood, heights 46 to 103 inches.
LOCATION: Eighth floor and Terrace restaurant.

Carved Bowl (Solomon Islands), wood, diameter 33 inches.
LOCATION: Garden restaurant.

Carved Bowl (Manus/Admiralty Islands), wood, diameter 29½ inches.
LOCATION: Garden restaurant.

Group of Five Carved Bowls (New Guinea and other regions), wood, diameters 10 to 49 inches.
LOCATION: Garden restaurant. (p. 113)

Bowl (New Guinea), clay, height 14 inches.
LOCATION: Garden restaurant.

Pedestal Bowl (New Guinea), clay, height 14 inches.
LOCATION: Garden restaurant.

Food Hook (New Guinea), wood, length 27 inches.
LOCATION: Third floor.

Food Hook (New Guinea) wood, length 20½ inches.
LOCATION: First floor.

Polynesia

New Zealand (Maori)

Canoe Stern, wood with shell inlay, height 94 inches.
LOCATION: Garden restaurant. (p. 19, 145)

Canoe Stern, wood with shell inlay, height 78 inches.
LOCATION: First floor.

Canoe Prow, wood with shell inlay, height 46 inches.
LOCATION: Eighth floor. (p. 144)

Canoe Bailer, wood with shell inlay, height 24 inches.
LOCATION: Eighth floor. (p. 147)

Architectural Decoration (lintel), wood with shell inlay, height 22 inches.
LOCATION: Beachfront Wing, lobby-level elevator foyer. (p. 149)

Architectural Decoration (lintel), wood with shell inlay, height 23 inches.
LOCATION: Third floor.

Five Tukutuku *Panels*, woven and painted reed, heights 48 inches, lengths 86 inches.
LOCATION: Second and third floors. (pp. 150, 151)

Carved Bowl, wood, length 24 inches.
LOCATION: Garden restaurant.

Tonga

Carved War Club, wood, length 45½ inches.
LOCATION: Eighth floor.

Carved Tapa Beater, wood, length 16 inches.
LOCATION: Eighth floor.

Carved Tapa Beater, wood, length 18 inches.
LOCATION: Eighth floor.

Collection of Eight Tapas (bark cloth), tree bark, heights 50 to 85 inches.
LOCATION: Second, fourth, and eighth floors.

Cook Islands

Carved Canoe Paddle, wood, length 37 inches.
LOCATION: Eighth floor.

Fiji

Carved Kava Bowl, wood, diameter 32 inches.
LOCATION: Garden restaurant.

Collection of Ten Tapas (bark cloth), tree bark, heights 72 to 98 inches.
LOCATION: First, second, fourth, and eighth floors.

Samoa

Collection of Six Tapas (bark cloth), tree bark, lengths 35 to 96 inches.
LOCATION: First, second, third, and eighth floors.

Hawai'i

Carved Calabash, 19th century, wood, diameter 24½ inches.
LOCATION: Garden restaurant. (p. 111)

Collection of Eleven Tapas (bark cloth), 19th century cloth with decorations added by Malia Solomon in 1965, lengths 90 inches.
LOCATION: Seventh floor. (pp. 153, 154)

Collection of Thirty Quilts, 1965, cotton, designed by Meali'i Kalama, lengths 96 inches.
LOCATION: Beachfront Wing lobby-level elevator foyer, fifth and sixth floors. (pp. 142, 157, 159)

Bumpei Akaji, *Kahi Ho'ākoakoa Hau'oli (Happy Gathering Place)*, 1965, bronze sculpture, height 96 inches.
LOCATION: Garden entry to Lobby. (p. 160)

Edward Brownlee, *'Iwa (Frigatebird)* 1973, bronze sculpture, height 50 inches.
LOCATION: Garden restaurant entry. (p. 161)

Sam Ka'ai, *Abstraction/Mythic Sources*, 1973, wood sculpture, height 62 inches.
LOCATION: Second floor. (p. 162)

Lloyd Sexton, *Hawaiian Flora* (eight paintings 1964; *Poinsettias* 1984), oil on canvas, heights 41 inches.
LOCATION: Sexton Gallery. (p. 164)

John Young, *Birds*, 1977, oil on canvas, length 41 inches.
LOCATION: Executive offices.

John Young, *Horses*, 1985, oil on canvas, length 92 inches.
LOCATION: John Young Room. (p. 165)

John Young, *Abstract Landscape*, 1985, oil on canvas, length 66½ inches.
LOCATION: John Young Room.

John Young, *Abstraction*, 1985, oil on canvas, height 41 inches.
LOCATION: John Young Room.

Miscellany

Ena De Silva, *Collection of Seven Batiks* (Sri Lanka), 1965, cotton, heights 50 to 85½ inches.
LOCATION: Batik Room.

Pacifica Collection—Forty-seven Drums, Gongs, Bells, and Chimes (India, China, Japan), 19th/20th century, wood and metal, heights 2 to 14 inches.
LOCATION: Third floor. (p. 98)

GLOSSARY

Ainu	Tribal people of early Caucasic stock, thought to be the first inhabitants of Japan and often regarded as descendants of the early neolithic Jomon culture. The Ainu today inhabit only the northern Japanese island of Hokkaido, although archaeological evidence suggests they once lived throughout the archipelago. The Ainu are shamanistic in their religious orientation.
Ancestor tablets	Flat, board-like wooden tablets depicting mythic spirits and ancestors and usually installed in men's ceremonial houses in Melanesian cultures; also referred to as spirit boards.
Animism	From the Latin word *anima,* or soul, the understanding that all things of nature have souls or spirits. These spirits are sometimes thought to separate from their physical abodes during illness or dreams and at death. Shintoism, popular Taoism, and some forms of Buddhism subscribe to animism. Animatism, the understanding that inanimate phenomena also have spiritual consciousness and personality, is found among both Oceanic and Asian cultures.
Arabori	A Japanese word meaning "rough-hewn," used to describe wood sculpture with a purposely cultivated unfinished or crude appearance. This appearance is in part achieved by allowing chisel marks to remain in the wood.
Betel nut	The fruit of the *Areca catechu* palm, mixed with tobacco, lime, and cloves and wrapped in the leaves of the betel pepper (*Piper betle*). Betel is chewed as a stimulant by Indian, Southeast Asian, and Oceanic peoples.
Bodhisattva	The Sanskrit name for one who postpones nirvana out of compassion for others. The goal of a Bodhisattva is to bring all of humankind to salvation. Bodhisattvas are depicted in princely garb so that they resemble Prince Siddhartha Gautama before he became the Buddha.
Bodhi tree	The sacred fig tree (*Ficus religiosa*) under which Siddhartha Gautama achieved enlightenment and became the historical Buddha. "Bodhi" is Sanskrit for "enlightenment."
Buddha	Sanskrit for the "Awakened or Enlightened One," a title given to the founder of Buddhism, Indian Prince Siddhartha Gautama (*circa* 563–483 B.C.), after his enlightenment. Other honorific names include Shakyamuni, the "Sage of the Shakyas," the clan into which the prince was born, and Shakyasimha, the "Lion of the Shakyas." The title "Buddha" is also used to refer to other great Buddhist teachers or archetypal figures.
Cire perdue	The lost-wax method of casting metal. In this method, a hollow clay core is covered with wax into which decorative designs are subsequently cut or pressed. Handles and other separate decora-

tive pieces are affixed to the surface after being formed in molds or freely shaped. An outer mold of clay is then applied, aligned with the inner mold, and openings are provided for wax to flow out during kiln firing, which also hardens the clay mold. Next, a molten metal alloy is poured into the mold through these same openings and the entire form is buried to cool and harden. Eventually, the mold is broken open to remove the bronze form for smoothing and finishing by hand. Monumental works using this technique often retain the clay core as structural reinforcement; smaller works are usually solid metal.

Dance wand — A wooden staff, paddle-like in form, often finely carved, and used by many tribal cultures in Melanesia in ritual dance ceremonies.

Devaraja — From *deva*, a heavenly being or god, and *raja*, a king, chief, or ruler. In Khmer culture, rulers were worshipped as *devaraja*s or "god kings" in a belief that the divine was incarnate in royalty. The *devaraja* is usually depicted with religious symbolism derived from images of the Buddha.

Dry lacquer — An originally Chinese technique of creating a lightweight form. The Thai adaptation uses a lacquer adhesive to laminate layers of cloth or paper over a wood, clay, or basketry core; the final surface is coated with a dry lacquer paste.

Garuda — A mythic creature, part human and part bird, derived from Indian Hindu symbolism and frequently depicted as the vehicle for the god Vishnu.

Hinayana — "The Lesser Vehicle," one of the two major divisions in Buddhism, also known as Theravada, "Teaching of the Elders." Hinayana is the earlier school of Buddhism and emphasizes doctrinal teaching rather than worship of the Buddha (see also Mahayana).

'Iwa — The Hawaiian name for the Great Frigatebird (*Fregata minor*) found in tropical areas of the Pacific Ocean. The *'iwa* is a large seabird whose identifying characteristics include long, slender wings, a deeply forked tail, and a beak sharply curved at the tip. The *'iwa* has a reputation for robbing other birds of their prey and its image is frequently carved on utensils and ceremonial vessels in Oceanic cultures.

Kapu/Tabu (Taboo) — The Polynesian concept of impersonal, supernatural powers in people, things, or places as negative forces. Belief in these forces creates a system of prohibitions ranging from abstinence to avoidance, violation of which could produce various catastrophic misfortunes including illness and death.

Lakshana — Symbolic body marks used in artistic depictions of the Buddha to convey his superhuman powers. Although thirty-two such marks are conventionally used, the most noticeable are the three that characterize the Buddha's head: elongated earlobes, the sign of the Buddha's royalty; a mole-like mark on the forehead, the "third eye" or *urna* that conveys the belief that he had superhuman perception and insight; a cranial protuberance, the *ushnisha*, that is an emblem of the Buddha's "superhuman" consciousness and knowledge.

Mahayana — "The Greater Vehicle," one of the two major divisions in Buddhism (see also Hinayana). Mahayana is the later school and is more theistic, emphasizing a divine pantheon of Buddhas and Bodhisattvas.

Mana — The Polynesian concept of impersonal, supernatural powers in people, things, or places as positive forces. Such powers could be controlled to facilitate achievements, good fortune, and magical powers; they could also be dissipated by breaking *kapu*.

Manaia — A Maori art motif of varying interpretations. The motif represents a powerful, supernatural spirit in a fusion of human, bird, and lizard forms. (Bird/human forms are frequently depicted subjects in both Polynesian and Melanesian arts.)

Melanesian — From the Greek words *melas* ("black") and *nesos* ("island"), a term derived from the skin color of this region's native peoples and used to identify them. Melanesia, Polynesia, and Micronesia make up the three major island groups in the Pacific.

Mudra — Buddhist ritual hand and finger gestures used in art to convey virtues and characteristics of deities. Four *mudra*s are frequently used in depictions of the Buddha:

> *Abhaya*, "fear not," a *mudra* of reassurance where the right hand is raised palm out, fingers vertically extended. *Bhumisparsa*, "earth touching" gesture, in which one hand reaches to the ground. *Dharmacakra*, "turning the Wheel of the Law" gesture, where the hands are held chest high and the thumb and index finger of the right hand join and touch one of the left hand's fingers. *Dhyana*, "meditation" gesture, in which the hands rest on the lap, right hand on left, with fingers horizontally extended.

Another frequently seen gesture, the *Anjali mudra*, is used for both greeting and reverence and is typically associated with depictions of attendants to the Buddha. In this *mudra*, hands are held together, palms touching and fingers vertically extended.

Body poses for the Buddha, Buddhist deities, patriarchs, and priests are also formalized; the most frequent pose is *padmasana*, the lotus posture. In this case, the Buddha is seated on a lotus "throne," legs crossed, feet placed soles upwards, usually with each foot on the opposite thigh.

Polynesian — From the Greek words *polys* ("full" or "many") and *nesos* ("island"), a term used for the light-skinned people of Hawai'i, Samoa, Tahiti, New Zealand (Maori), and other island groups, all of which are linguistically related. Polynesia, Melanesia, and Micronesia make up the three major Pacific Island groups.

Rakan — (Sanskrit: Arhat; Chinese: Lohan) A Buddhist patriarch honored for achieving enlightenment through meditation, and often depicted as an ascetic recluse. The term is sometimes used to refer to an original disciple of the Buddha.

Scarification — Incisions and punctures of the skin made by skilled craftsmen to create permanent marks and designs on the body; irritants introduced into these cuts helped create the desired abundance of scar tissue.

Shaman
In the beliefs of some northeastern Asian peoples, the shaman is a priest who has the ability to contact and control both good and evil spirits.

Sosho
The Japanese term for free-style, cursive calligraphy; often an intensely personal style of writing that is difficult to decipher.

Stupa
A form of Buddhist shrine; a relic mound symbolic of the universe. *Stupa*s originated in India and eventually became common throughout Southeast Asia. The first *stupa*s were built over ashes of the Buddha. Later, the remains of locally revered ascetics and monks were venerated.

Sutras
The sacred texts of Buddhism, usually attributed to Shakyamuni, the historic Buddha.

Tapa/*Kapa*
Unwoven bark cloth of a papery texture, usually made from the mulberry tree and sometimes decorated with intricate designs. In creating tapa, strips of mulberry bark are pounded with elaborately carved utensils to achieve a smooth, flat, and soft cloth. Tapa is used in both ritual and everyday aspects of life in many Oceanic cultures. In Hawai'i, the word *kapa* is also used to refer to Hawaiian quilts.

Tattoo
As with scarification, deliberate punctures and incisions of the skin; indelible colors pressed into these cuts create permanent decorative patterns.

Tukutuku
Lattice-work panels constructed of vertical reeds and horizontal laths and used on interior walls in Maori ceremonial architecture. *Tukutuku* bear abstract and geometricized patterns in bright colors and are solely the work of Maori women.

Wheel of the Law
(Sanskrit: *dharmacakra*) A term and symbol for the Buddhist *dharma*, or law. The Buddha's first sermon is traditionally called the "Wheel of the Law" sermon.

Zen
"Meditation," referring to the meditative sect of Buddhism. Zen is the Japanese pronunciation of the Chinese word Ch'an, which is the Chinese pronunciation of the Sanskrit word Dhyana, or "meditation."

SELECTED BIBLIOGRAPHY

ASIAN ARTS

Barnard, N., and D. Fraser, eds. *Early Chinese Art and Its Possible Influence in the Pacific Basin*. New York: International Cultural Arts Press, 1972.

Basham, A.L. *The Wonder That Was India*. London: Sidgwick and Jackson, 1954.

Bowie, T., ed. *The Arts of Thailand*. Bloomington: Indiana University, 1960.

Bowie, T., ed. *The Sculpture of Thailand*. New York: Asia Society, 1972.

Commission for Protection of Cultural Properties. *Art Treasures from Japan*. Tokyo, 1965.

Ecke, G. *Chinese Domestic Furniture*. Tokyo: C. E. Tuttle, 1963.

Ecke, T.Y. *Chinese Folk Art in American Collections: Early 15th through Early 20th Centuries*. New York: China Institute in America, 1976.

Fairservis, W., Jr. *Costumes of the East*. Riverside, Connecticut: American Museum of Natural History, 1971.

Fontein, J., and M.L. Hickman. *Zen Painting and Calligraphy*. Greenwich, Connecticut: Boston Museum of Fine Arts, 1970.

Fraser-Lu, S. "Frog Drums and their Importance in Karen Culture," *Arts of Asia*, vol. 13, no. 5 (1983).

Giteau, M. *Khmer Sculpture and the Angkor Civilization*. New York: H. N. Abrams, 1966.

Harle, J.C. *The Art and Architecture of the Indian Subcontinent*. Harmondsworth: Penguin, 1986.

Hauge, V., and T. Hauge. *Folk Traditions in Japanese Arts*. Tokyo: Kodansha International Exhibitions Foundation and the Japan Foundation, 1978.

Kung, D. *The Contemporary Artist in Japan*. Honolulu: East-West Center, 1966.

Mori, H. *Sculpture of the Kamakura Period*. Translated by K. Eichmann. New York: Weatherhill, 1974.

Paine, R.T., and A.C. Soper. *The Art and Architecture of Japan*. New York: Penguin, 1974.

Pal, P. *Ideal Image: The Gupta Sculptural Tradition and its Influence*. New York: Asia Society, 1978.

Rowland, B. *The Art and Architecture of India*. Harmondsworth: Penguin, 1970.

Rowland, B. *Art in East and West*. Cambridge, Massachusetts: Harvard University Press, 1954.

Rowland B. *Evolution of the Buddha Image*. New York: Asia Society, 1976.

Sethi, R., ed. *Aditi: The Living Arts of India*. Washington, D.C.: Smithsonian Institution, 1985.

OCEANIC ARTS

Anderson, R.L. *Art in Primitive Societies*. Englewood Cliffs, New Jersey: Prentice-Hall, 1979.

Barrow, T. *Maori Art of New Zealand*. Wellington: A. H. & A. W. Reed and the UNESCO Press, 1978.

Buehler, A., T. Barrow, and C.P. Mountford. *The Art of the South Sea Islands*. New York: Greystone Press, 1962.

Corbin, G.A. *Native Arts of North America, Africa, and the South Pacific*. New York: Harper and Row, 1988.

Force, R. *The Fuller Collection of Pacific Artifacts*. New York: Praeger, 1971.

Fraser, D. *Primitive Art*. New York: Doubleday, 1962.

Gathercole, P., A.L. Kaeppler, and D. Newton. *The Art of the Pacific Islands*. Washington, D.C.: National Gallery of Art, 1979.

Guiart, J. *The Arts of the South Pacific*. New York: Golden Press, 1963.

Haar, F., and P. Neogy. *Artists of Hawaii*, vol. 1. Honolulu: University of Hawaii Press, 1974.

Hammond, J.D. *Tifaifai and Quilts of Polynesia*. Honolulu: University of Hawaii Press, 1986.

Jones, S.M. *Hawaiian Quilts*. Honolulu: Honolulu Academy of Arts, 1973.

Kaeppler, A.L. *"Artificial Curiosities": An Exposition of Native Manufacturers Collected on the Three Pacific Voyages of Captain James Cook, R.N.* Special Publication no. 65. Honolulu: Bishop Museum Press, 1978.

Koojiman, S. "Tapa in Polynesia," *Bernice P. Bishop Museum Bulletin* no. 234. Honolulu, 1972.

Kuykendall, R.S. *Hawaii: A History, From Polynesian Kingdom to American State*. Englewood Cliffs, New Jersey: Prentice-Hall, 1961.

Mead, S.M., ed. *Te Maori: Maori Art from New Zealand*. New York: Abrams, Inc., 1984.

Newton, D. *Art of Oceania, Africa and the Americas from the Museum of Primitive Art*. Greenwich, Connecticut: Metropolitan Museum of Art, 1969.

Newton, D. *Masterpieces of Primitive Art*. New York: Knopf, 1978.

Schleck, R.J. *The Wilcox Quilts in Hawaii*. Kauai: Grove Farm Homestead and Waioli Mission House, 1966.

Wingert, P.S. *Primitive Art: Its Traditions and Styles*. New York: New American Library, 1962.

ABOUT THE AUTHOR

DON AANAVI received his doctorate in art history from Columbia University in 1969. He has held undergraduate and graduate teaching positions at Hunter and Lehman colleges of the City University of New York, and at the University of Hawaii, where he currently teaches art history at the Hilo campus and is an affiliate faculty in religious studies and Japanese studies. Professor Aanavi has organized exhibitions at the Metropolitan Museum of Art, where he was an assistant curator and a Clawson Mills research fellow, and at the Honolulu Academy of Arts. He has written numerous exhibition catalogs and articles, and he was a consultant to the college teachers program in art history for the National Endowment for the Humanities. A recipient of many honors and awards, he has traveled widely and is fluent in a number of European and Asian languages. He was an East-West Center fellow and is an honorary Woodrow Wilson fellow. Professor Aanavi has been the consultative curator for the art collection at Mauna Kea Beach Hotel since 1986. He lives in Nīnole on the island of Hawai'i.